ARCHAEOLOGY

A BRIEF INTRODUCTION

FOURTH EDITION

Brian M. Fagan

University of California, Santa Barbara

 HarperCollins*Publishers*

TO

Lucia, Karen, and other friends at Whittier
College who gave me the idea for this book.

And, as usual, to my cats, who were as subversive
as ever. They did everything they could to
prevent me from revising the manuscript by
stepping on it with muddy paws. As you can see,
they failed!

Sponsoring Editor: Alan McClare
Project Editor: Karen Trost
Design and Cover Coordinator: Mary Archondes
Cover Design: Wanda Lubelska Design
Cover Illustration: Aztec Rain God, Library of Congress
Production: Willie Lane/Sunaina Sehwani
Compositor: David E. Seham Associates, Inc.
Printer and Binder: R. R. Donnelley & Sons Company
Cover Printer: New England Book Components, Inc.

Archaeology: A Brief Introduction, Fourth Edition

Library of Congress Cataloging-in-Publication Data

Fagan, Brian M.
    Archaeology : a brief introduction / Brian M. Fagan.—4th ed.
      p. cm.
    Includes bibliographical references and index.
    ISBN 0-673-52135-4
    1. Archaeology. I. Title.
  CC165.F28 1991
  930.1—dc20   90-40766
                                                        CIP

92   93   9 8 7 6 5 4 3

CONTENTS

TO THE READER

Archaeology always seems an exciting and romantic subject, especially when you read about the magnificent tomb of the golden pharaoh Tutankhamun or the imposing Maya temples of the Peten. Most archaeological sites are less spectacular and are excavated on a far smaller scale. But that does not make them any less fascinating for archaeologist and nonarchaeologist alike. This book is designed to give you some idea of how archaeologists go about studying human behavior of the past. We cover the basic concepts and methods of archaeological research—excavation, survey, analysis of artifacts and food remains, and such topics as dating and the dimensions of time and space. *Archaeology: A Brief Introduction* ends with a look at career prospects in archaeology and at ways in which individuals—like you—can help save the past for future generations. References for more detailed readings are given at the end of the book.

I hope that this text will give you new insights into the fascinating world of the past. Good luck with your adventures in archaeology!

Brian M. Fagan

TO THE INSTRUCTOR

This book is designed as a brief introduction to the fundamental principles of method and theory in archaeology, beginning with the goals of archaeology, going on to consider the basic concepts of culture, time, and space, and discussing the finding and excavation of archaeological sites. The last four chapters summarize some of the ways in which archaeologists order and study their finds. Throughout the book, I emphasize the ethics behind archaeology and end with a discussion of how nonarchaeologists should relate to the finite resources that form the archaeological record. In my experience this subject is often neglected in introductory anthropology courses.

Our assumption is that this small book will act as supplementary reading for a general course on anthropology, and that your students will spend two or three weeks on the subject matter. Every attempt has been made to keep technical jargon to a minimum. Inevitably, a book of this length and scope glosses over many complex problems or smoldering controversies. I have proceeded on the assumption that at this stage of learning, a positive overstatement is better than a complex piece of inconclusive reasoning. Errors of overstatement can always be corrected in class or at a more advanced stage.

If there is a theme to this volume, it is that the patterning of archaeological artifacts we find in the ground can provide valuable insights into human behavior in the past. In pursuing this theme, I have attempted to focus on the basic concepts of archaeology and leave you to impose your own theoretical viewpoints on the various chapters that follow. My assumption is, too, that you will fill in such additional details as you feel your students need. For this reason, I have drawn again and again on a few well-known sites from New World and Old World archaeology, such as Olduvai Gorge and Teotihuacán, rather than distracting the reader with a multitude of site names. At the suggestion of several users, I have added brief descriptions of these major sites in a special "Sites and Cultures" information section at the back of the book.

The fourth edition of *Archaeology* has undergone major revision, both to include suggestions by dozens of instructors and students and to reflect the increasing complexity of modern archaeology. This edition begins with a chapter on the beginnings of archaeology, designed to give the reader a sense of the excitement of archaeological research. It also introduces some basic ideas about archaeology that are amplified in later chapters. The book has been updated throughout, and two new chapters added—one on the development of archaeological thinking and the other on the study of culture change. The sections on preservation, site formation processes, and research design have been rewritten and some illustrations changed, but in general the book remains much the same. This is because the fundamental principles of archaeology remain the same through the years, whatever new and sophisticated theoretical models or scientific methods are brought to bear. These principles provide the foundation for all the multifarious research projects that archaeologists carry out, whether near to home or far afield.

I am grateful to all those who have criticized previous editions of this book, especially to the students who took the trouble to write while they were using the book, making their comments even more useful and immediate. Many colleagues have sent me information or read portions of the revised manuscript. In this connection, I am especially grateful to George Michaels, who guided me through the minefields of quantitative archaeology. My grateful thanks also to Stephen A. Mrozowski, University of Massachusetts; Arthur J. Jelinek, University of Arizona; Thomas P. Volman, Cornell University; Malcolm C. Webb, University of New Orleans; and Gary C. Wright, State University of New York—Albany.

As always, I would much appreciate hearing from readers with suggestions for improving future editions of this book.

Brian M. Fagan

1

ARCHAEOLOGISTS LEARN TO STUDY PAST CULTURES

The advance of science is not comparable to the changes of a city, where old edifices are pitilessly torn down to give place to new, but to the continuous evolution of zoologic types which develop ceaselessly and end by becoming unrecognizable to the common sight, but where an expert eye finds always traces of the prior work of the past centuries.

Jules Poincaré, 1904

"I contrived to sit; but when my weight bore on the body of an Egyptian, it crushed like a bandbox . . . I sank altogether among the broken mummies, with a crash of bones, rags, and wooden cases, which raised such a dust as kept me motionless for a quarter of an hour, waiting until it subsided again." Giovanni Battista Belzoni, circus strongman turned tomb robber, explored and ravaged Ancient Egyptian sepulchers in 1817. Belzoni was adept with levers, ropes, and gunpowder, but by no stretch of the imagination could he be called an archaeologist. He was an adventurer of restless ambition, who thought the ancient Egyptians would be a way to fame and fortune.

Unsolved mysteries, lost civilizations, and great treasures—these are the stereotypes of archaeology in the popular imagination. We archaeologists are seen as eccentric, pith-helmeted professors, perpetually deciphering ancient inscriptions. This image is long gone, for late-twentieth-century archaeology is a highly sophisticated, scientific discipline. But the roots of archaeology lie in the adventures and excavations of yesteryear. In this chapter, we take a brief look at how archaeology began, at some of the exciting discoveries made by our early predecessors, and at some of the theories they developed to explain the past. This is a good starting point for this book, for every science, be it archaeology or zoology, is a creation not only of its modern-day practitioners, but of the pioneers who began research in the field.

EARLY SPECULATIONS AND EXCAVATIONS

People have speculated about human origins and the remote past for centuries. As early as the eighth century B.C. the Greek writer Hesiod wrote that humanity had passed through five great ages of history. The earliest was an Age of Gold, when "people dwelt in ease," the last an Age of War, when everyone worked terribly hard and experienced great sorrow. In the sixth century B.C. the Babylonian monarch Nabonidus dug deep into ancient city mounds near the Tigris and Euphrates rivers. His workmen uncovered the foundations of the temple of the goddess Ishtar at Agade near Babylon. The find, says an ancient tablet, "made the king's heart glad and caused his countenance to brighten." In later centuries, the Greeks and Romans were intensely curious about their primitive ancestors, about Scythian "barbarians" living on the northern plains who drank from cups made from human skulls, and the Britons far to the northwest who painted themselves blue.

The centuries of the Renaissance saw quickened intellectual curiosity, not only about the world beyond the narrow confines of Europe, but about the Classical civilizations as well. People of leisure and wealth began to follow the path of Renaissance scholars, traveling widely in Greece and Italy, studying antiquities, and collecting examples of Roman art. The same travelers were not above some illicit excavation to recover statuary from ancient temples and Roman villas. Soon the cabinets of wealthy collectors bulged with fine art objects and the study of Classical lands became a major scholarly preoccupation. In 1738, Italy's King Charles III commissioned Spanish engineer Rocque Joaquin de Alcubierre to excavate the famed Roman city of Herculaneum, buried under deep layers of volcanic ash by an eruption of Vesuvius in A.D. 79. Alcubierre blasted and tunneled his way through rock-hard ash, tunneling sideways into underground galleries where he found jewelry, statues of well known Herculaneans, and fragments of bronze horses. Visitors were lowered down narrow shafts to walk through the buried theater, marble-columned houses, and frescoed rooms. Hundreds of men, including prisoners, labored below ground, recovering bronze busts, hundreds of texts written on papyrus scrolls, and copies of now-lost Greek masterpieces. Toxic gases, slime, and collapsing tunnels brought an end to this glorified treasure hunt.

Many antiquarians were not wealthy enough to travel to Classical lands, so they stayed at home and searched for antiquities in their own backyards. Stonehenge on the uplands of southern England was the most famous curiosity, a place where "stones of wonderful size have been erected after the manner of doorways." The antiquarians indulged their insatiable curiosity by digging into burial mounds and river gravels, recovering all manner of prehistoric finds—clay vessels, stone axes and adzes, bronze implements, even occasional gold orna ments. Their digging methods were brutally crude, usually little more than a hasty pit sunk into the center of a mound to recover a skeleton and its grave goods as quickly as possible. Some expert diggers would open two or three mounds a day. The accounts of their excavations frequently include complaints that a delicate find "crumbled to dust before their eyes," a common complaint on Victorian excavations. Until well into the nineteenth century, archaeology was little more than a glorified treasure hunt, even a sport. Not only that, but the archaeological record of prehistoric times was a complete jumble. "All that has come down to us . . . is wrapped in a thick fog," complained one Danish antiquarian in 1806.

THE THREE AGES AND THE ANTIQUITY
OF HUMANKIND

While some eighteenth-century antiquarians were content to display their finds in cabinets, others puzzled over the people who had made their artifacts. Were they hunter-gatherers and farmers like the American Indians, or little more than animals? Had they developed more complex societies as time passed? What was needed was some way of classifying and dating the past.

The first breakthrough came in 1807, when Danish archaeologist Christiansen Jurgensen Thomsen opened National Museum of Antiquities in Copenhagen to the public. For years, philosophers and antiquarians had talked of three ages, a Stone Age when people had no metals, a Bronze Age, and an Iron Age. A man with a passion for order, Thomsen took the confusing jumble of artifacts in his museum and laid them out in different rooms. In one gallery he displayed implements of the Stone Age, "when little or nothing at all was known of metals." In another he showed those with stone and bronze but no iron, and in a third grave finds belonging to the Iron Age. His new scheme soon became known as the Three Age system, a system still used to this day for classifying the prehistoric past. Thomsen knew that his scheme was mere theory, but one of his assistants, Jens Jacob Worsaae, went out and excavated more burial mounds and other sites, and proved that Stone Age occupations did, in fact, underlie Bronze Age levels, and that Iron Age sites were the latest of all. Nyerup's "fog" was soon dispelled. The Three Age system was in widespread use by the 1860s.

How long had human beings lived on earth? Between Medieval times and the late eighteenth century, everyone believed in the literal historical truth of the Scriptures. Genesis 1:1 stated that God had created the world and its inhabitants in six days. The story of Adam and Eve provided an entirely consistent explanation for the creation of humankind and the world's population. In the seventeenth century,

Archbishop James Ussher used the genealogies in the Old Testament to calculate that the world was created on the night preceding October 23, 4004 B.C. These bizarre calculations soon became theological dogma and were defended with almost frenzied fanaticism by theologians in the early nineteenth century, when another group of experts showed that humans had lived on earth much longer than a mere 6000 years.

The Industrial Revolution of the late eighteenth century with its massive canal and railroad building schemes created a demand for a new breed of scientist—the field geologist. Men like Englishman William "Strata" Smith made their living surveying the earth's layers. Smith realized that the earth had been formed not by Divine creation but by natural processes such as erosion, weathering, and sedimentation. These processes had been operating for a very long period of time, far longer than 6000 years. This theory of the earth's formation became known as **uniformitarianism.** Many of Smith's geological strata contained the fossils of long extinct animals, fossils that French scientist Georges Cuvier pieced together. Cuvier reconstructed pterodactyls and mammoths, used his fossils to place geological layers in order, each with their distinctive fossil animals. But how old were these strata? Cuvier believed that God had created each successive layer of the earth, after great floods had wiped out earlier life. Humans belonged to the time of the last flood. In other words, the world was but 6000 years old.

Cuvier was wrong, for the proof that human beings had lived in far earlier times was in front of his very nose. As early as 1600, the bones of an elephant and a stone axe were found in the heart of London, but no established scientist took these, or many subsequent finds of the same type, seriously. Uniformitarian theories were well established in geology by the 1830s, when an eccentric French customs officer named Boucher de Perthes began digging for fossils in the gravels of the Somme River near Abbeville in northern France. He was surprised to find dozens of stone axes alongside the bones of extinct animals like the hippopotamus. De Perthes claimed that these tools were the work of people who had lived long before the Biblical flood, but scientists just laughed at him. It was not until stone artifacts and the bones of rhinoceroses, mammoths, and cave bears were found in the sealed layers of a cave near Brixham in southwestern England in 1858 that the scientific establishment finally sat up and took notice. There could be no doubt of the association, and a steady stream of British geologists and archaeologist crossed the Channel in 1859 to examine de Perthes's finds. "The stone hatchets of Amiens and Abbeville seem to me as clearly works of art as any Sheffield [steel] knife," wrote one excited expert.

The same year—1859—saw the publication of Charles Darwin's essay *Origin of Species,* the pivotal scientific essay of the nineteenth century. This described the theory and mechanisms of evolution and provided a theoretical framework for a human history not a more 6000 years long, but one that extended back far into the remote past. Darwin himself said little about human ancestry, but this assumption that human beings were descended from apelike ancestors horrified many devout Victorians. "My dear, let us hope it is not so," exclaimed one distraught mother. As the controversy over evolution raged, scientists began the long search for human ancestors, a search that continues to this day.

In 1857, quarrymen working in the Neanderthal cave near Dusseldorf in Germany unearthed an odd-looking skull with beetling brows quite unlike anything anatomists had seen before. Many experts dismissed the find as that of a modern hermit, or even as one of Napoleon's soldiers, but the great Victorian biologist Thomas Huxley thought otherwise. He examined the skull and compared it to those of modern humans and chimpanzees, pointing out that it had some apelike characteristics. Here, then, was the first scientific evidence that humans had some evolutionary links to the apes. In the decades that followed, the search for what was soon called "The Missing Link" between apes and humans took hold of the popular imagination. Even today, discoveries of early human fossils cause considerable excitement, and often turn their discoverers into media figures. Raymond Dart caused an international furor when he announced the discovery of a primitive ape-human, *Australopithecus* ("southern ape-men") in South Africa in 1924. Richard and Mary Leakey searched at Olduvai Gorge in Tanzania for human fossils for more than a quarter century before they unearthed a magnificent 1.75 million-year-old *Australopithecus* skull in 1959. The ferocious debates over human evolution and early human behavior rage just as stormily today as they did in Darwin's time.

THE DISCOVERY OF THE EARLY CIVILIZATIONS

The Ancient Egyptians

Ever since Greek and Roman times, archaeologists assumed that the world's earliest civilization had flourished by the banks of the Nile River in Egypt. The ancient Egyptians were considered the fountain of all wisdom and medical knowledge, of all the institutions of civilization. The achievements remained a mystery until Napoleon Bonaparte invaded Egypt in 1798. Napoleon professed an interest in science, so he took 40 scientists along with him to record all that was known of Egypt, ancient and modern. The scholars, "Napoleon's Donkeys," as the soldiers called them, were electrified by what they found. For six years they sketched and explored, collected antiquities, and compiled a magnificent record of an exotic civilization that had built temples and pyramids that were quite unlike anything in Greece or Italy. Among their finds was the famous Rosetta Stone, a trilingual inscription that allowed the young French linguistic genius Jean Francois Champollion to decipher ancient Egyptian hieroglyphs in 1822. This was the scientific breakthrough that unlocked the secrets of civilization on the Nile, but by that time the scientists' remarkable discoveries had brought another breed of visitor to Egypt—the tomb robber.

Egyptian antiquities were so exotic and valuable that they commanded enormous prices in Europe, where the newly founded British Museum and the Louvre in Paris were competing for sensational exhibits. Well organized, ruthless tomb robbers like Giovanni Belzoni descended on the Nile. For three eventful years, Belzoni blasted and tunneled his way from one end of Egypt to the other. He searched for papyrus inscriptions in mummy caves, found the (empty) royal tomb of pharaoh Seti I in the Valley of Kings near Thebes, and was the first to penetrate the mighty temple of Abu Simbel in centuries. A tall man of immense strength and considerable charm, Belzoni, as mentioned previously, was an expert with levers, weights, and gunpowder, essential qualifications for an early-nineteenth-century tomb robber. He left Egypt precipitously in 1819 after a fracas with his enemies in which shots were fired, exhibited some of his finds in London, and perished while searching for the source of the Niger in West Africa.

Tomb robbing and looting continued unchecked in Egypt until the late nineteenth century; indeed, it persists to this day. But Jean Francois Champollion's decipherment of hieroglyphs brought another new breed of visitor to the Nile—the dedicated scientist. For example, John Gardiner Wilkinson spent ten years recording inscriptions in ancient Egyptian tombs. He wrote a magnificent, detailed account of the daily life of the ancient Egyptians, which revealed a colorful, cheerful civilization, but one that was intensely conservative, deeply religious, and preoccupied with the afterlife. All modern Egyptology has built on the work of Champollion and his contemporaries, and on more scientific excavation methods introduced to the Nile in the late nineteenth century by the British archaeologist Flinders Petrie and others.

The Assyrians and Sumerians

"He will stretch out his hand and destroy Assyria," thundered the Old Testament prophet Zephaniah, "and will make Nineveh a desolation, and dry like a wilderness." To the occasional adventurous European visitor, the lands by the Tigris and Euphrates in what is now Iraq seemed like a confirmation of the prophet's fulminations. All that remained of Nineveh by the Tigris were some desolate earthen mounds covered with crumbling bricks. And all that survived of the Assyrians were some vague references in the Scriptures (Figure 1.1).

In 1840, the French government sent Paul-Émile Botta as consul to the small town of Mosul opposite the ruins of Nineveh. His real assignment was to dig into Nineveh, to make spectacular archaeological finds. Botta had no archaeological experience, and did not dig into Nineveh deep enough to find anything worthwhile. He listened with interest when one of his men described the riches that lay under his home on another mound at Khorsabad, 14 miles away. The consul sent him away with a few men to see what he could find. A week later he returned with tales of walls covered with carvings of strange animals. Botta gasped at the bas-reliefs: winged, human-headed animals, and processions of men with long beards. He put more than 300 men to work on what turned out to be the Assyrian king Sargon's palace, a vast multi-roomed structure adorned with grandiloquent reliefs that boasted of the monarch's triumphs.

Five years later, a restless young Englishman named Austen Henry Layard started digging at the city of Nimrud downstream of Nineveh. He found two Assyrian buildings the first day and was soon tunneling deep into magnificent palaces. This was the stuff of which archaeological legends were made. The visitor to Nimrud, and later Nineveh, where Layard worked with much greater success than Botta, wandered through deep earthen tunnels that followed the rooms of the palaces. Here one gazed at "the portly forms of kings . . . so lifelike that they might almost be imagined to be stepping from the walls to question the rash intruder on their privacy." Layard excavated with a

Figure 1.1 Mesopotamian archaeology, nineteenth-century style; archaeologists climb an unexcavated Sumerian temple mound.

small army of workmen, and acted like a tribal chieftain. He arranged marriages, settled quarrels, supervised the dig all day, and recorded inscriptions until late at night. The young archaeologist was a brilliant writer; his books on Nineveh are still in print. His discoveries caused a sensation in Europe. Among other things, he uncovered a bas-relief of a royal lion hunt, and a frieze that commemorates the siege of Lach-ish, a city of Judah mentioned in the Old Testament. His diggers even uncovered the limestone slabs at the entrance to King Sennacherib's palace that bore the ruts made by his army's chariot wheels.

Layard's greatest discovery came at Nineveh, where he unearthed a complete royal library, piles of clay tablets lying a foot deep on the floor of a special chamber. He shoveled them into baskets and shipped them down the river, like all his finds on a wooden raft supported by inflated goatskins. A quarter century was to pass before even a small number of the tablets were deciphered, and when they were they yielded further sensations. In 1872, a young cuneiform expert named George Smith, who had never been to Mesopotamia, discovered a tab-let that told of a prophet named Hasisadra, who survived a great flood sent by the gods to punish humankind by building a large boat. Hasisa-dra's boat went aground on a mountain, and he sent out birds to find a resting place. The entire story bore a remarkable resemblance to the Biblical story of the Great Flood. Seventeen lines of the story were missing, so Smith was sent out to Iraq to find them. Incredible though it may seem, he discovered the tablet fragments in Layard's soil heaps in a mere five days!

Those who believed in the historical truth of the Bible were, of course, electrified by the Flood tablets. But scholars were more inter-ested in the evidence they gave for far earlier civilizations, for the As-syrians had merely copied the legend from earlier accounts. In 1877, another French diplomat, Ernest de Sarzec, excavated the ancient city of Telloh in southern Mesopotamia, where he found clay tablets and the remains of a great temple far older than that of the Assyrians. What Sarzec had found was the Sumerian civilization, the earliest literate society in the world, and a civilization as old, if not older, than that of the ancient Egyptians. A whole series of long-term excavations at other Sumerian cities like Nippur and Ur-of-the-Chaldees between the 1890s and 1930s chronicled many more details of this flamboyant, war-like civilization, a patchwork of small city-states that flourished 5000 years ago between the Tigris and Euphrates rivers.

TROY, MYCENE, AND THE MINOANS

Many of the best-known nineteenth century archaeologists were either professional travelers or adventurers. A few, like German businessman Heinrich Schliemann, were obsessed with the past. Schliemann became fascinated with the Greek poet Homer at an early age. He retired from business at the age of 46 determined to prove that Homer's *Iliad* and *Odyssey* were true stories. In 1871, he started excavations at Hissarlik in northwestern Turkey, which he soon proclaimed was the site of Homeric Troy. Schliemann thought and acted on a large scale. He employed engineers who had worked on the building of the Suez Canal in Egypt to supervise his excavations and discovered seven ancient cities superimposed one on top of the other. His excavations culminated in the discovery of what Schliemann claimed to be a treasure of more than 8000 gold ornaments and artifacts. He insisted that this was the Treasure of Priam, the Homeric king of Troy. Schliemenn was no scientific saint—almost certainly his treasure was assembled from isolated gold pieces found over many months.

Schliemann's Troy discoveries caused a popular sensation, which reached a height when he moved to Mycenae in Greece in 1876. This was, he thought, the legendary burial place of King Agamemnon, leader of the Greek armies at Troy. More than 125 men tore into Mycenae and uncovered a circle of stone slabs. Schliemann found over fifteen burials at Mycenae, many of them covered in jewels, golden death masks, and adorned with fine, inlaid weapons. "I have gazed on the face of Agamemnon," cried Schliemann. He believed he had found the Homeric king, but archaeologists now date these finds to at least three or four centuries before the Trojan War, which raged in about 1190 B.C.

Heinrich Schliemann was the last of the great adventurer-archaeologists to work in Mediterranean lands, for his methods were too unscientific even for his day. By the 1870s, Austrian and German archaeologists were working on Classical sites like Olympia with a new precision that was a far cry from the methods of Belzoni, Layard, or Schliemann. A team of architects worked with the archaeologists. The Germans renounced all claims to the finds, and built a special museum for them at Olympia itself. A new era in archaeological research was beginning that put scientific recording before spectacular discovery, precise excavation before rapid shoveling.

EARLY AMERICAN ARCHAEOLOGY

From the moment that Christopher Columbus landed in the Bahamas, people speculated about the origins of the American Indians. In 1589, a Jesuit missionary named José de Acosta first proposed the general theory of their origins that provides the basis for modern thinking on the subject. He believed it was entirely possible that "small groups of savage hunters driven from their homelands by starvation or some other hardship" had taken an overland route through Asia to their present homelands with only "short stretches of navigation." He wrote this a century and a half before Vitus Bering sailed through the Bering Strait in 1728. Today, all scientists agree that this was the route taken by the first Americans, but the date of their arrival remains a highly controversial subject. While some scholars speculated about Indian origins, others marveled at the great diversity of native American populations. Some, like the Eskimo of the far north, were hunter-gatherers, others lived in large villages or, like the Aztec of Mexico and the Inca of Peru, in sophisticated civilizations. How could one account for this diversity; also, why were some societies more highly developed than others? These questions still preoccupy archaeologists today.

When land-hungry colonists moved west of the Allegheny Mountains in the late eighteenth century, they were surprised to find large earthworks and burial mounds dotting the landscape. Those who dug into them found no gold, only human skeletons, copper and mica ornaments, and stone pipe bowls. Who had built these earthworks? Many colonists and intellectuals refused to believe that the "savage" Indians could have done so. They argued they were the work of long-vanished civilizations from foreign lands. Only a few scholars disagreed, among them Thomas Jefferson. Fascinated by what were already known as the Moundbuilders, he dug into a burial mound on his Virginia estate and uncovered several layers of human skeletons. Unlike many of his contemporary treasure-hunting contemporaries, Jefferson made careful note of the strata in the mound, the first stratigraphic excavation in the Americas.

The Moundbuilder controversy continued to smolder through the nineteenth century, pitting those who believed in an exotic explanation for the earthworks against more sober scholars like Samuel Haven of the American Antiquarian Society, who argued that the artifacts in the mounds often bore a resemblance of those used by living native American groups. Writers churned out dozens of literary fantasies about the Moundbuilders, writing about "white people of great intelligence and skill," who had waged wars of conquest over the Midwest thousands of years ago. These racist theories had no founding in scientific fact, but it was not until the 1890s that Cyrus Thomas of the Bureau of American Ethnology proved beyond all reasonable doubt that the Moundbuilders were in fact native Americans.

Further south, the Spanish conquistadors had marveled at the Aztec capital Tenochtitlán. "We were amazed on account of the great tower and buildings rising from the water. And some of our soldiers even asked whether the things we saw were not a dream," wrote one soldier. After the Spanish conquest, however, the Aztec and earlier Mesoamerican civilizations sank into almost complete historical oblivion. Dense forest covered the great Maya centers in the lowlands of Mexico and Guatemala. Only a few Catholic priests recorded details of Mayan civilization before it vanished, among them Spanish Bishop Diego de Landa. He visited Mayan temples and recorded some of

their writing in 1566, while torturing and imprisoning Indians for re-
fusing to accept the Christian faith, and burning their hieroglyphic
documents as well. Only a few reports of temples and pyramids deep
in the forest kept interest in the ancient Maya alive. It was these that
excited the imaginations of two men who are among the immortals of
early archaeology—lawyer-turned-traveler John Lloyd Stephens and
artist Frederick Catherwood. Both were experienced archaeological
travelers who had visited Egypt and the Holy Land; Stephens and
Catherwood sailed for Central America in 1939, a journey that took
them on foot and by mule into the depths of the tropical lowlands.
They struggled through dense rain forest to the Mayan city of Copán,
where they found monuments "some in workmanship equal to those
of the finest monuments of the Egyptians." The jungle-covered ruins
covered miles. While Catherwood settled down to draw the intricate
carvings, Stephens tried to buy the site from the local people for $50,
so he could exhibit his finds in New York. When the deal foundered,
he contented himself with writing a famous description of Copán. "The
only sounds that disturbed the quiet of this buried city were the noise
of monkeys moving among the tops of the trees, and the cracking of
dry branches broken by their weight. They moved over our heads in
long and swift processions, forty or fifty at a time."

Stephens and Catherwood recorded as much as they could of Copán, then visited Palenque, where they searched for parallels to ancient Egypt among the human figures at the site. Back in New York,
Stephens penned one of the seminal assessments of Mayan civilization.
"The works of these peoples, as revealed by the ruins, are different
from the works of any known people," he wrote. "We have a conclu-
sion far more interesting and wonderful than that of connecting the
builders with the Egyptians or any other people. It is the spectacle of
a people . . . originating and growing up here, having a distinct, separate, indigenous existence; like the plants and fruits of the soil, indigenous." All subsequent scientific work on Mayan civilization has been
based on these famous words. Stephens and Catherwood were to journey to the Yucatán a second time, to study Uxmal, Chichén Itzá, Cozu-
mel, and other famous locations (Figure 1.2). These studies convinced
Stephens that "these cities . . . are not the works of people who have
passed away . . . but of the same great race which . . . still clings
around their ruins."

Like Austen Henry Layard, John Lloyd Stephens was a superb
popular writer, whose books about the Maya became instant best-
sellers. And Frederick Catherwood's pictures of the ruins are among
the finest of all archaeological illustrations. In writing his books, Stephens corresponded with the Boston historian William Prescott,
whose *History of the Conquest of Mexico* set the Spanish Conquest
against a background of the Aztecs' rapid rise to power. The books by
these two men, more than any others, helped readers realize that

Figure 1.2 John Lloyd Stephens and Frederick Catherwood examining a Maya temple deep in the rain forest.

there was more to America's past than merely Moundbuilders and mythical, exotic civilizations.

CUSHING, BANDELIER, AND THE DIRECT HISTORICAL METHOD

By the late 1800s, archaeologists and anthropologists were convinced that living American Indian societies were the descendants of the first Americans. So they began to work back from the present into the past. In 1879, Frank Hamilton Cushing of the Smithsonian Institution traveled to Zuñi Pueblo in New Mexico, intending to stay only three months. He ended up staying for nearly five years, observing Zuñi life in remarkable detail, even being initiated into membership of a secret society, the Priesthood of the Bow. His widely read book *My Adventures in Zuñi* described the life and customs of a Pueblo society whose roots stretched far back into the past. His contemporary, anthropologist Adolph Bandelier, spent years wandering around the Southwest on a mule, tracking down oral histories at Pecos Pueblo and other locations (Figure 1.3). These oral traditions were to become a foundation of the archaeological research conducted by Alfred Kidder of Harvard University at Pecos from 1915 to 1929.

Bandelier and Cushing were two of the pioneers who showed the close relationship between anthropology, the study of living peoples,

Figure 1.3 Pueblo Bonito, New Mexico, a southwestern Pueblo site dated to A.D. 919–1130. The round structures are kivas, subterranean ceremonial rooms.

and archaeology, the study of past societies (Chapter 2). Thus, it was logical for Kidder to excavate the intricate strata of Pecos working backward from well documented historic levels far into prehistory. All American archaeology is based on the general principles developed by these and other pioneers, who showed the close links between ancient and modern native American societies.

EARLY ARCHAEOLOGICAL THEORY

As archaeologists began to study the early prehistory of humankind and the great civilizations, anthropologists were looking at the many diverse societies that explorers and missionaries were revealing every year. These societies ranged from the simple hunter-gatherers of the Tierra del Fuego Indians and Australian aborigines to the complex and well-organized Baganda in East Africa and the Pueblo Indians of the

American Southwest. Then there were the ancient Egyptians and the Sumerians of Mesopotamia, early civilizations that could be linked to the primeval development of Western civilization. How could one explain all this diversity, and the progress of human societies from the simple to the complex, from hunting and gathering to city dwelling? (For more on this subject, see Chapter 8.)

Unilinear Evolution

The nineteenth century was a period of remarkable industrial and technological progress, to the point that notions of progress and achievement dominated popular thinking. Darwin's theories of biological evolution seemed a natural extension of the doctrines of social progress. Both archaeologists and anthropologists alike soon wrote of millennia of gradual human cultural evolution throughout early prehistory into modern times (for definitions of culture, see Chapter 3). British anthropologist Edward Tylor (1832–1917) surveyed human development in all its forms, from the crude stone axes of very early humans to Maya temples in Mexico, to Victorian civilization. He developed a three-level sequence of human development, from simple hunting *savagery*, as he called it, through a stage of simple farming, which he called *barbarism*, to *civilization*, the most complex of all human conditions. American anthropologist Lewis Henry Morgan (1818–1881) went even further and outlined no less than seven periods of human progress, starting with savagery and culminating in a "state of civilization." Such notions of *unilinear evolution*, of simple human progress, were easy to defend in a world whose frontiers were still being explored. Archaeology was still in its infancy, the remote past known mainly from Europe and the spectacular discoveries of ancient civilizations in the Near East. It was easy for late-nineteenth-century scholars, living as they did in societies where doctrines of racial superiority were unchallenged, to speculate the human societies had evolved in a linear way, from simple unsophisticated hunter-gatherer bands, ultimately to complex, literate civilizations.

Diffusionism

As more and more data accumulated from archaeological excavations all over the world, it became clear that a universal scheme of unilinear evolution was far too simplistic an explanation for the past. Could cultures have changed as a result of external influences? Did, for example, the Ancient Egyptians spread the institutions of civilization to other parts of the Near East, perhaps even further afield? Could one account for the differences between human societies as the result of the diffusion of ideas and the migrations of peoples? In its more extreme forms, diffusionism is an assumption that many major human inventions originated in one place, then diffused to other parts of the world as a result of trade, migration, cultural contact, even exploration. Diffusionist theories of prehistory were popular in the early twentieth century, when scholars like the Egyptologist Elliot Grafton Smith argued that the "Children of the Sun," ancient Egyptians, had voyaged all over the world, taking sun worship and their civilization with them.

Like unilinear evolution, extreme diffusionism did not stand up to detailed scientific scrutiny, especially when twentieth-century archaeologists realized they were dealing with very complex problems of culture change over very long periods of prehistoric time. By the 1920s, archaeologists had refocused their efforts away from grandiose theories toward collecting basic data from archaeological sites—the cultural historical approaches described later in this book (Chapter 8).

THE EMERGENCE OF MODERN SCIENTIFIC ARCHAEOLOGY

The development of scientific archaeology and the discovery of the prehistoric past ranks as one of the outstanding achievements of nine-teenth- and twentieth-century science. The process of development began with the establishment of the antiquity of humankind, and the development of the Three Age system for subdividing prehistory. The crude excavations of Layard and Schliemann are part of the story, as are the pioneer efforts of Cushing and Bandelier to work from the present back into the past. But the technologically sophisticated archaeology of today can be said to stem from four major developments: the invention of modern scientific excavation techniques, the use of multidisciplinary approaches to study relationships between people and their environments, the increasing impact of science on archaeology, and the refinement of archaeological theory since the 1960s.

Scientific excavation can be said to have begun with the work of the Germans at Olympia in Greece, and with the remarkable excavations of retired General Augustus Lane Fox Pitt-Rivers in southern Britain in the 1880s. Pitt-Rivers ran his excavations like a military operation, employing expert supervisors, who were trained surveyors. He insisted on accurate recording, built model reconstructions of his sites, and observed even the minutest details of the stratigraphy. The military discipline of his work was apparent everywhere, even in his photographs. "The figure standing *at attention* in the foreground gives the scale," reads one of his captions.

Others built on Pitt-Rivers's experience, most famous among them the redoubtable Mortimer Wheeler, who carried out a series of beautifully executed excavations on Roman and Iron Age sites in Britain and on cities of the Harappan Civilization (now Pakistan) between the 1920s and 1950s. It was no coincidence that Wheeler had a distinguished record as a military man. He insisted on precise recording, employed photographers and other experts, and pioneered the use of trained amateur diggers on his sites. Wheeler was a harsh teacher, who realized that all excavation was destruction. He also realized that scientific archaeology could be dull and did everything he could to enliven his writings about the past. "Dry archaeology is the driest dust that blows," he once remarked. How true!

Late-twentieth-century excavation still draws on the basic principles laid down by Wheeler and his contemporaries, but has added many refinements (Chapter 7). These include specialized methods for excavating waterlogged sites, minute recording methods using electronic instruments, and sophisticated ways of excavating minute discolorations, some of which even record the positions of long vanished burials in sandy soil.

The Environment and Archaeology

In the early years of the twentieth century, a Swedish scientist, Lennart van Post, invented the science of palynology, the study of minute fossil pollen grains as a means of studying ancient environments (Chapter 4). Archaeologists soon realized that this new technique offered a chance to study ancient societies in the context of their environments, but the study of cultural ecology, as it is called, did not reach a full level of sophistication until the 1950s and 1960s. Cultural ecology is the study of the ecological relationships between human cultures and their environments, a study pioneered by archaeologist Grahame Clark at the Star Carr hunter-gatherer site in northeast England in the late 1940s. Using pollen analysis, plant remains, and animal bones, he was able to show that this 10,000 year-old hunting stand once lay in a bed of reeds backed by birch forests. He was even able to show that the site was occupied in late winter by studying the red deer antler in the deposits. Clark relied heavily on botanists and zoologists in his research. Today, teams of scientists from many disciplines routinely work together in the field, reconstructing the environments of late Ice Age societies in France, examining the landscape exploited by 100,000 year-old hunters in Southern Africa, monitoring the modifications made by farmers to Midwestern landscapes 1200 years ago.

Science and Archaeology

Archaeology is often considered to be part of history or of anthropology, but the hi-tech methods of science have had an ever-increasing impact on the field. Pollen analysis was one early contributor, as was aerial photography, which gave archaeologists an overhead view of the past (Chapter 6). Perhaps the great revolution came in the 1950s, when radiocarbon dating revolutionized prehistoric chronologies, providing the first secure time scale for the last 40,000 years of prehistoric times (Chapter 4). Since then, the impact of science on archaeology has been universal, in everything from computers to sophisticated ways of searching for archaeological sites, through rain forest canopies, to methods for studying prehistoric diets through the isotope content of human bones. The marriage between archaeology and the sciences is now so close that both the methods and theoretical approaches of many disciplines have affected the ways archaeologists go about their work.

Archaeological Theory

The simplistic unilinear and diffusionist theories of yesteryear are long gone, for archaeological theory has become far more sophisticated in recent years (Chapter 8). A major theoretical furor in archaeology began during the 1960s with University of New Mexico archaeologist Lewis Binford and others arguing for more explicitly scientific approaches to the study of culture change in the past. The debate over theoretical approaches shows no signs of diminishing as we enter the 1990s, as archaeologists continue their search for a distinctive body of archaeological theory. However, one general approach is important in the field, the notion that cultural change has not proceeded in a linear fashion, but in many different ways and directions. This idea of *multilinear evolution* is the dominant feature of thinking about culture change in archaeology, an approach that assumes that human societies have always interacted closely with their ever-changing natural environments. Such approaches, and the debates about them, are a far cry from the simplistic, linear theories that governed archaeological thinking not so long ago.

This chapter has described some of the early developments in archaeology, and has tried to give you some insights into the exciting history of our discipline. The romantic days of archaeology, the days of Layard, Schliemann, and Stephens, are long gone. Today, archaeology is a serious, meticulous scientific discipline, which seems, at times, somewhat dull to pursue. But the thrill of archaeological discovery is always there, even after a long day of digging in the hot sun. Perhaps the greatest moment of archaeological discovery ever came in 1922, when Egyptologist Howard Carter pried a small hole through the sealed doorway leading to the tomb of the pharoah Tutankhamun. He shone a candle through the aperture and was struck dumb with amazement. "What do you see," his companion Lord Carnarvon asked impatiently at his side. "Wonderful things," whispered Carter, as he stepped back from the hole. Few of us will ever be so fortunate to experience such a unique thrill as Carter did, but the excitement of archaeology is just as great with smaller, less important finds. And it is well in these days of science that we never forget these thrilling moments. In the pages that follow, we describe the basic principles of archaeological research that make such moments possible.

2

ARCHAEOLOGY AS ANTHROPOLOGY

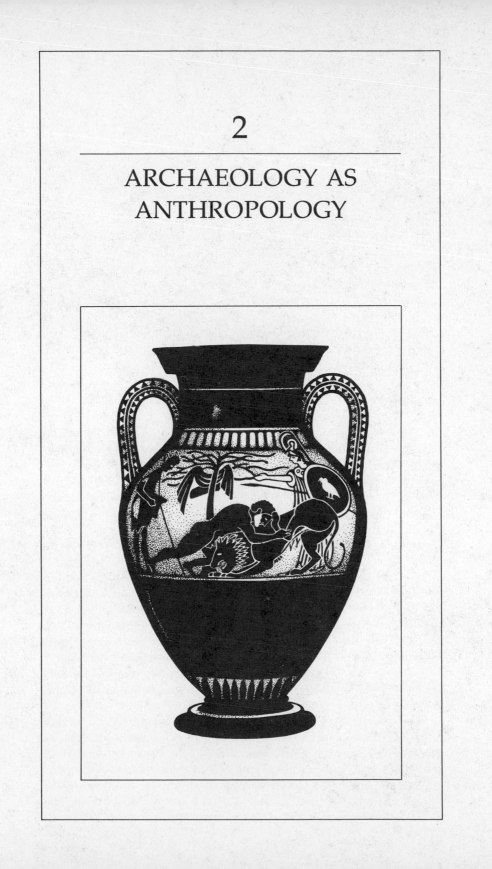

Archaeology is the special concern of a certain type of anthropologist.

James Deetz, 1967

ARCHAEOLOGY

Buried treasure, grinning skeletons, great pyramids, and golden pharoahs—these are the popular images of archaeology. And archaeologists themselves . . . well, they appear to spend their time digging for spectacular artifacts under the walls of ancient, long-abandoned cities. Everyone has seen cartoons of bearded, bespectacled archaeologists digging at the foundations of a magnificent temple and deciphering clay tablets covered by the dust of centuries. And who has not enjoyed Boris Karloff's screen portrayal of an ancient yet hyperactive Egyptian mummy in a memorable film about the curses of the pharoahs and the incredible 1980s adventures of Indiana Jones in the Temple of Doom and other exotic locales? Archaeologists have a glamorous image as bold adventurers and treasure hunters, as detectives searching for a long-lost past. But is this image accurate? What do archaeologists really do? How do they unravel the complexities of early humanity? This volume takes you not on an exotic treasure hunt, but on a fascinating journey through the world of scientific archaeology, an adventure as engaging as it is many-sided.

Our complex world is full of "unexplained" mysteries and hidden surprises, phenomena that sometimes defy obvious explanation. Many people believe that the archaeologist lives in the mysterious regions of our world, with "missing links" and long-lost civilizations. Enterprising authors and movie producers take us on fantasy rides into these strange territories of their specially selected archaeologists. From the comfort of our armchairs, via television, we can search for lost conti-

Figure 2.1 The pyramids of Giza in Egypt. "The romance of archaeology has taken people all over the world in search of the past."

nents, reconstruct Noah's Ark, and trace the landing patterns of extra-terrestrials' spaceships. Such searches are not only fantasy fun but big business as well. Millions of dollars have been made from this type of archaeology, which, unfortunately, bears little resemblance to reality.

The romance of archaeology has taken people all over the world in search of the past. Thousands of tourists visit the pyramids of *Giza** in Egypt every year (Figure 2.1). The Mexican government spent millions of pesos restoring the ancient city of *Teotihuacán* in the Valley of Mexico to promote tourism. Most popular package tours abroad now include visits to an archaeological site or two (Figure 2.2). Many sites—for example, *Stonehenge* in England and Lascaux in France—are in danger of permanent damage from the sheer volume of visiting tourists. As a result, you can no longer wander among the uprights at Stonehenge. The French government has built a magnificent replica of the Lascaux cave paintings for tourists to enjoy, but the original is closed to all but scientists. Any thinking person who visits an archaeological site faces the reality of the past, a vista of human experience that stretches far back in time. How, visitors may wonder, do archaeologists know how old a site is, and what do their finds mean? It all seems very complicated to dig for the past. And the unchanging, incredibly ancient structures that surround one add to the sense of romance and awe.

---

*Sites whose names are italicized are described in the Site Information section at the back of the book.

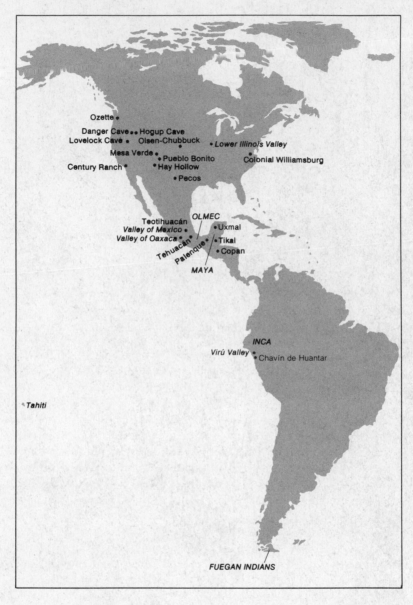

Ozette •
Danger Cave •• Hogup Cave
Lovelock Cave •   Olsen-Chubbuck
      •   • Lower Illinois Valley
   Mesa Verde •
       • Pueblo Bonito   Colonial Williamsburg
Century Ranch •   • Hay Hollow
        • Pecos

Teotihuacán   OLMEC
Valley of Mexico •   • Uxmal
Valley of Oaxaca •   • Tikal
Tehuacán   • Copan
Palenque
MAYA

INCA
Virú Valley • Chavín de Huantar

Tahiti

FUEGAN INDIANS

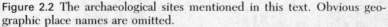

Figure 2.2 The archaeological sites mentioned in this text. Obvious geographic place names are omitted.

Most such archaeological sites now boast a museum. Eagerly, the tourist peers into the display cases and admires the glittering gold of a fine necklace or the crude stone tools made by a human hand more than a million years ago. Perhaps, at the door, the tourist pauses to buy a replica of the archaeological find in the case. It is a pleasing reminder of a fleeting visit to the past, a memento to be displayed to

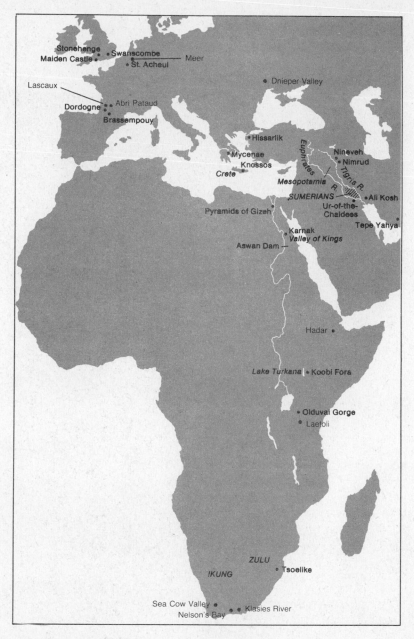

(Figure 2.2 continued)

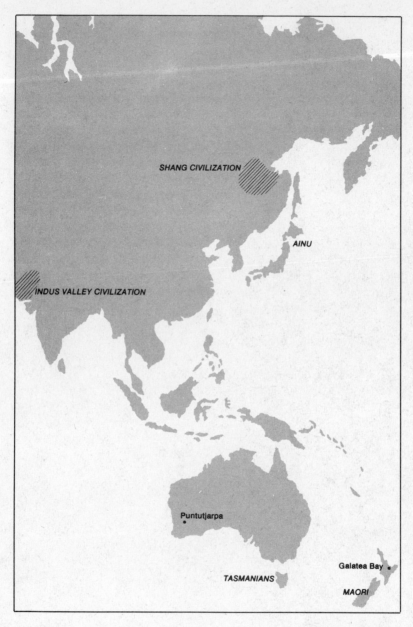

(Figure 2.2 continued)

admiring friends at home. But, unfortunately, many people are greed-ier—they covet the past and want to own a piece of the real thing.

Collectors and treasure hunters are the curse of archaeology. Many of them regard themselves as legitimate archaeologists. The van-ity of our ancestors decreed that they be buried with riches to accom-pany them in the afterlife. The greed of their descendants decrees that people today covet these riches. The antiquities dealer and the private collector pay enormous prices for pre-Columbian pots and other fine antiquities looted from otherwise undisturbed sites. Major museums compete to acquire the finest specimens of prehistoric art. The Metro-politan Museum of Art in New York has paid a cool million dollars for a Greek vase.

There seems to be some fundamental human desire to collect things and display them in the privacy of one's home. Collecting is a passion once described as "so violent that it is inferior to love or ambi-tion only in the pettiness of its aims." People collect everything from barbed wire to beer cans, and many think of archaeology as the acquisi-tion of objects. But when people collect archaeological finds, they are collecting a part of a finite resource that is rapidly vanishing, a unique archive that can never be replaced. Every object they buy or dig from a site is the product of ancient human behavior. This behavior can be partly reconstructed from objects found in the earth, but much of our insight depends on the **contexts** (positions) in time and space in which the objects occur in the ground. Removing an artifact from its context is an irreversible act that cheats us all of knowledge. Perhaps it should be mentioned that professional archaeologists also destroy sites as they excavate them, but they record the context of their finds as they go along, a critical ingredient in scientific archaeology.

Modern archaeology is not treasure hunting, nor is it a fantasy search for lost worlds; *it is the systematic study of humanity in the past.* This general definition includes not only ancient technology and human behavior, but social organization, religious beliefs, and every aspect of human culture.

TYPES OF ARCHAEOLOGY

There are, of course, many types of archaeologists. Many people asso-ciate archaeologists with Greek and Roman temples, Classical statuary and ancient art, and Egyptian pyramids and mummies. Such studies are the work of **Classical archaeologists.** Many are Classical scholars who use archaeological methods to recover data from the ground. Clas-sical archaeologists rely heavily on written sources. For the most part, they concentrate on architecture and the objects they excavate as fine examples of Classical art. Until recently, they have had relatively little interest in the minute economic and social problems that absorb prehistoric archaeologists. But this inclination is changing, as the prehistoric scholars' theories and methods influence archaeologists working on later periods.

Historical archaeologists study sites that date to recent historical times. Some excavate cities like Saxon London and Medieval Winchester, which flourished in the dim yet documented past. American historic-site archaeology focuses on pioneer settlements, such as *Colonial Williamsburg*, slave communities in the South, Spanish missions in the Southwest, or nineteenth-century frontier forts. Scholars at these sites frequently specialize in such objects as pottery imported from England, Italy, and China, Spanish-style architecture, and uniform buttons. Some archaeologists study factories or slum housing dating from the Industrial Revolution or even later.

For each of these projects, the archaeologist supplies details lacking in historical records. Contemporary historical records are usually filled with political and religious matters, with the deeds of civic leaders and statesmen. They rarely describe how people lived, the meals they ate, or where their toilets were located. Hundreds of small cottages were huddled within the walls of Medieval Winchester in England. Their owners plied their crafts, quarreled with others, even went to court to settle their differences. Court records and title deeds provide the names of the cottage owners and the details of their law cases. The archaeologist can learn more about them, tracing the long-forgotten foundations of their houses. Much of historical archaeology leads to reconstruction of ruined buildings as part of our national heritage. Colonial Williamsburg, Virginia, is the most famous of early American towns. It has been reconstructed with active help from archaeologists (Figure 2.3).

Archaeology has been used to study modern households, too. Using methods developed for studying prehistoric rubbish heaps, archaeologist William Rathje delved into thousands of Tucson, Arizona, garbage bags, studying the waste disposal of lower-, middle-, and upper-income households. He found that most people discard rubbish indiscriminately, that low-income families consume the most vitamin pills, and that the average Tucson family wastes about $100 worth of beef a year. The implications of this research for consumers and manufacturers are fascinating. The Tucson project also provided useful theoretical information for studying ancient **middens** (garbage heaps), even if Tucson itself happens to be several sizes larger than ancient Nineveh or Teotihuacán.

Underwater archaeologists study ancient wrecks in the Mediterranean, around Florida, and elsewhere. Special recording techniques have been devised to recover the smallest details of shipwrecks and the cargoes in their holds. Unfortunately, many people believe that wrecks hold rich treasure and gold doubloons. Thus, many wrecks are robbed or destroyed by inquisitive divers long before archaeologists

Figure 2.3 Excavations at Colonial Williamsburg. Historical archaeology was applied here to discover details of a colonial mental hospital.

can get to them. Although many people think of underwater archaeology as different from excavation ashore, it is not. Archaeologists working underwater have exactly the same intellectual goals as their dry-land colleagues—to recover, reconstruct, and interpret the past. Their scuba gear and recording and recovery technology for recovering finds are specialized, but they are still studying ancient cultures.

Prehistory is *that portion of human history that extends back before the time of written documents and archives.* Prehistoric archaeologists are the special breed who study human prehistory. In contrast to Classical and historical archaeologists, prehistoric archaeologists deal with an enormous time scale of human cultural evolution, which extends back at least 2.3 million years. Prehistoric archaeology is the primary source of information on 99 percent of human history. Prehistoric archaeologists investigate how early human societies all over the world came into being, how they differed from one another, and, in particular, how they changed through time.

The prehistoric archaeologist has to be a specialist in a specific area and time period. No one could possibly become an expert in every aspect of prehistoric archaeology. Some specialists deal with the earliest human beings, working closely with geologists and anthropologists who are interested in human biological evolution. Others are experts in stone toolmaking, in the early peopling of the New and Old worlds, or in the life-styles of hunter-gatherers.* Specialists in the origins of agriculture or urban civilization work closely with experts on topics ranging from architecture to cattle. All of this specialist expertise and knowledge means that most larger scale prehistoric excavations involve teams of scientists cooperating to study early human settlements in the context of their natural environments. We shall give many examples of this type of research in later chapters.

WORLD PREHISTORY

Prehistoric archaeologists study world prehistory, the prehistory of humankind on the widest possible global scale. Prehistory covers an enormous span of time, starting more than 2.3 million years ago with the emergence of the first toolmaking hominids (humanlike beings) in East Africa and extending right into modern times. A common, and conventional, distinction between "prehistory" and "history" is that of the existence of historical documentation for historic times. In these periods, archaeological finds can be amplified with documentary evidence. For example, there are inscribed clay tablets that constitute the archives of the Sumerian peoples of Mesopotamia some 5000 years ago, so we are technically in historic times.

Unlike our Victorian and early twentieth century predecessors, we are able to examine human prehistory on a truly global scale. Unfortunately, the pattern of archaeological knowledge is very uneven, so we still lack many details of the peopling of the globe. Prehistoric archaeologists are trying to document and understand the ways in which humanity adapted itself to the many and diverse environments of the globe. By studying these adaptations, we can begin to understand the astonishing diversity of human cultures that make up our own world.

---

*Some simple definitions will be helpful.

Hunter-gatherers: human societies that lived by hunting wild game, large and small, and by gathering wild vegetable foods as well as by fishing. Hunting and gathering was the only human lifeway from the earliest prehistoric times up to the development of agriculture and animal domestication in the Near East some 10,000 years ago. Only a handful of hunter-gatherer societies, such as the San of the Kalahari desert, survive to this day.

Urban: city-dwelling. Archaeologists have argued for years about how to define a city. In general, cities have more than 5000 inhabitants and are far more complex entities than villages or towns, especially in their social organization and nonagricultural activities.

City-states: cities with large, very complex social organizations that controlled specific territories. Satellite settlements throughout this territory provided food and other resources to the controlling city. City-states contrast with villages, which farmed much smaller areas of land owned by individual kin groups. Early Sumerian civilization flourished over a huge area that is now Iraq between the rivers Tigris and Euphrates. It was made up of dozens of competing city-states that controlled much smaller areas of land.

The study of prehistory is, of course, far more than just the reconstruction of an engrossing epic of human biological and cultural evolution. It is the study of a series of intricate and still little-understood
developments in our long history and of our ever-changing relationships with the world's myriad natural environments. In 1863, the great
British biologist Thomas Huxley stated: "The question of questions for
mankind, the problem which underlies all others, and is more deeply
interesting than any other—is the ascertainment of the place which
man occupies in nature and of his relations to the universe of things."
To a considerable degree, this remains one of the fundamental questions of archaeological research.

For the sake of convenience, we can divide prehistory into a series
of broad chapters, each spanning long periods of time and increasingly
complex cultural developments. In fact, it is more appropriate to refer
to these chapters as "developments," for archaeologists are concerned,
in the final analysis, with the study of evolving human cultures over
very long periods of time.

Early Prehistory

The immensely long span of prehistoric time, from the emergence of
toolmaking, upright-walking hominids in tropical Africa more than 2.3
million years ago, up to between 200,000 and 100,000 years ago, when
modern human beings first appeared, is known as early prehistory
(Figure 2.4). This was the Archaic world of early prehistoric times,
when the hominids evolved slowly into more advanced *Homo erectus*
some 1.5 million years ago. Cultural evolution was even more glacially
slow, with little fundamental change in human lifeways or technology
for nearly 2 million years. Then, about 700,000 years ago, human beings spread out of the tropics into more temperate latitudes, into Europe and Asia, adapting to far greater climatic extremes. That they
were able to do so was in part the result of the taming of fire, for heat,
perhaps cooking, and certainly for protection against predators living
in deep caves, natural shelters for human beings. For at least 600,000
years, these widely scattered *Homo erectus* populations evolved in the
general direction of anatomically modern humans, showing great genetic and anatomical variation subsumed under the general term, early
Homo sapiens. Among these populations were the beetle-browed
Neanderthals of Eurasia, who flourished from before 100,000 until
about 33,000 years ago. They lived in Eurasia during the intensely cold
climate of the early Wurm glaciation.

The Emergence of *Homo Sapiens Sapiens*

Sometime between 200,000 and 100,000 years ago, anatomically modern humans evolved in the savanna woodlands of eastern and southern
Africa. Some scientists believe, however, that *Homo sapiens sapiens*

Modern Times	A.D. 1492; Columbus lands in the New World Aztec and Inca civilizations flourish in Mexico and Peru
A.D. 1	Teotihuacán, 200 B.C. to A.D. 750 Maya civilization flourishes in Mesoamerican lowlands (before 1000 B.C. to A.D. 900 and beyond)
1200 B.C.	Olmec civilization in Mesoamerica
1600 B.C.	Cretan and Mycenaean civilizations in Mediterranean Shang civilization in China.
2700 B.C.	Harappan civilization, Indus Valley, Pakistan
3000 B.C.	Ancient Egyptian and Sumerian civilizations emerge in the Near East
4000 B.C.	Uruk in Mesopotamia, a sizable settlement, near city.
6000 B.C. or earlier	Agriculture in Mesoamerica (Tehuacán and other locations) Agriculture in China
8000 B.C.	Food production and animal domestication well established in the Near East
10,000 B.C.	Final end of the last Ice Age glaciation
15,000 B.C.	First human settlement of the Americas (?)
40,000 years ago	*Homo sapiens sapiens* begins settlement of arctic latitudes of the Old World. By this time, humans are living in Australia.
75,000 years ago	Neanderthals widespread in Europe and Eurasia, also the Near East
100,000 to 200,000 years ago	Anatomically modern humans emerge, probably in tropical Africa.
250,000 years ago	Early *Homo sapiens* evolving in many areas.
400,000 years ago	*Homo erectus* in Europe and northern China.
1 million years ago	*Homo erectus* spreads from tropical Africa into temperate Europe, and perhaps into Asia.
1.5 million years ago	Emergence of *Homo erectus* in Africa
1.75 million years ago	*Homo habilis* at Olduvai Gorge
2.3 million years ago	First toolmaking hominids in East Africa.
4 to 5 million years ago	Earliest nontoolmaking, but bipedal (standing on two feet) hominids in Africa?

Figure 2.4 Major events in prehistory referred to in the text.

emerged in many parts of the Old World. These modern people, known to us more from genetic studies than fossils, were still hunter-gatherers, but apparently more efficient in their adaptations than their predecessors. By 100,000 years ago, *Homo sapiens sapiens* had spread out of Africa into the Near East, coming into contact with other, earlier *Homo sapiens* hunter-gatherer populations.

The Peopling of the Globe by Modern Humans

In perhaps the most dramatic chapter of prehistory, *Homo sapiens sapiens* spread widely over the Old World and into the New during the closing millennia of the Ice Age. Human beings had crossed into Australia by 40,000 years ago. Less than 20,000 years later, people had developed the intricate technology needed to survive months of subzero winter cold. They flourished in a deep-frozen Ice Age Europe and on the open plains that stretched far northeast into Siberia. By 15,000 years ago, some tiny human bands had probably crossed into Alaska and the Americas. Only the far offshore islands of the Pacific remained uncolonized by humans, awaiting the development of deep-water canoes and navigational techniques.

The Origins of Food Production

The worldwide thawing at the end of the Ice Age some 15,000 years ago led to dramatic changes in global climate and geography. Human populations in the Old World and the Americas had to adapt to radically new circumstances, to highly diverse postglacial enviroments. It was about 10,000 years ago that some largely sedentary hunter-gatherer communities in the Near East started cultivating wild cereal grasses such as wheat and barley. The new adaptation was highly successful and within a few centuries, village farmers were flourishing in many parts of the Near East, and soon further afield. The herding of goats, sheep, and then cattle and pigs soon replaced hunting as a primary means of subsistence. The new economies spread like wildfire through the Nile Valley and deep into Europe. Independent centers of plant and animal domestication may have developed in India, southeast Asia, and China within a few millennia. The cultivation of indigenous plants and cereals began in the Americas at least 7000 years ago. Major debates in the field of prehistoric archaeology are waged over the reasons why humans turned from hunting and gathering to deliberate food production, a development that led to immediate, long-term changes in global enviroments resulting from overgrazing, forest clearance, and plowing.

The first scholars to speculate about early agriculture searched for the village occupied by the genius who had first planted wheat grains and watched them germinate into a new and predictable food supply.

No one has ever found this mythical genius. We now realize that farming and the domestication of animals were changes in human culture that took place over thousands of years, not only in the Near East but in other areas of the world as well. Throughout prehistory, human societies experimented with new ideas and technologies. Only a few caught on, and only a handful—among them agriculture, metalworking, writing, and wheeled transport—have radically affected culture.

The Emergence of States

Just over 5000 years ago, new highly centralized urban societies appeared in Egypt and Mesopotamia (now southern Iraq). These were state-organized societies, civilizations headed by supreme rulers and governed by bureaucracy of officials and priests. People lived in much larger communities, in cities of more than 5000 people, in societies with ranked social classes, under a social order where conformity was assured by the threat of force, and under an official religion that sanctified the deeds of the tiny minority who ruled the state.

The Sumerians of Mesopotamia, the Ancient Egyptians, the Harappans of the Indus, and other early peoples were followed by much larger empires and imperial civilizations, for example, those of the Persians, Greeks, and Romans. The process of early state formation—still only partially understood—also took hold in China, southeast Asia, and the Americas, where European explorers like Hernán Cortés came into contact with amazingly sophisticated Indian civilizations, such as the Aztec of Mexico and the Inca of Peru in the fifteenth century A.D. A continuous historical record takes us from the Sumerians of Mesopotamia through Biblical times right up to the conflicts and astonishing economic and technical achievements of Western civilization.

The Twilight of Prehistory

One of the most fascinating chapters in prehistory coincides with the expansion of Western civilization outward from its European homeland during the Age of Discovery after A.D. 1400. The five centuries that followed found Westerners coming into contact with all manner of human societies, covering the entire spectrum from simple Tasmanian hunting bands to the elaborate civilizations of the Khmer of Cambodia and the Inca. These were the centuries when the world's diverse societies were first drawn into what historians and anthropologists often refer to as the *world system*—the system of economic and political interconnectedness that is pervasive in the late-twentieth-century world.

Prehistory, then, is the compelling story of unfolding human existence, one that began at a few locations in tropical Africa and now takes us to the frontiers of outer space. The recorded archives of history take us back to but a tiny fraction of our long past, which means that the study of prehistory has much to tell us about why we are so similar and why we are so different. And, above all, it tells us that we are all part of one family, linked, whether we like it or not, by imperishable genetic ties.

3

CULTURE

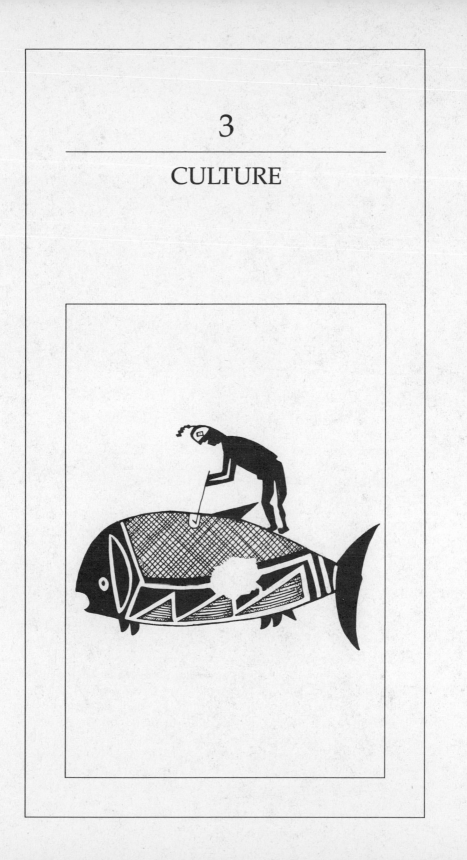

An archaeologist of 6666 A.D. *may find himself obliged to rely on the divergences between assemblages of kitchen utensils to help him recognize that by 1950, the United Kingdom and United States of America were not occupied by the same society.*

V. Gordon Childe, 1956

ANTHROPOLOGICAL ARCHAEOLOGY

Anthropology is a discipline for studying humanity in the widest possible sense, both in the past and in the present. Like archaeologists, anthropologists are often thought of as solitary fieldworkers studying primitive tribes in remote jungles or on Pacific islands. Anthropology has a long and distinguished record of such studies conducted by remarkable people—Franz Boas, who worked among the American Indians, Bronislaw Malinowski, who observed the Trobriand islanders of the western Pacific, and many others. Today, however, many types of anthropologists study all manner of specialized topics. **Social anthropologists** work primarily with social organization and the more intangible aspects of human society. Some are specialists, although they may combine their specialty with theoretical insights from social anthropology in the field. **Ethnographers** study technology and economic life, and collect data on social organization and other aspects of human culture. The **ethnologist** generalizes from the information collected by the ethnographer. The **physical anthropologist** studies human biological evolution and the biology of human beings and their closest relatives. Then there are medical, psychological, urban, and other anthropologists who study aspects of modern industrial and nonindustrial society. Archaeologists are anthropologists as well. Their goals are the same as those of their colleagues, but they concentrate on ancient societies, cultures that existed in the past and are now extinct or exist only in modified form.

The ties between archaeology and anthropology are very close in the Americas, where much of archaeology is concerned with the study of prehistoric native American societies, and where there are few historical documents to amplify the archaeological record. These ties go back to nineteenth century research among Pueblo Indians in the Southwest (Chapter 1), which established a basic principle of anthropological archaeology—the notion of working back from the present, from living societies into the past, as a means of understanding culture change over long periods of time. Under this rubric, archaeology is simply anthropology carried out not on living societies, but on ones that are no longer in existence.

Anthropology in all its forms is unified by one common thread, the concept of culture. This provides a framework that archaeology can use to both describe and explain the prehistoric past. The term has both general and specific connotations in anthropology, which we must now define.

HUMAN CULTURE

Everyone lives within a cultural context, one that is qualified by a label like "middle-class American," "Roman," or "Sioux." These labels conjure up characteristic objects or behavior patterns typical of the particular culture. We associate hamburgers with middle-class American culture and kayaks with Eskimos. Romans are thought to have spent their time conquering the world, Sioux wandering over the Great Plains. But such stereotypes are often crude, inaccurate generalizations. We think of Native Americans as legendary, feathered braves, but only a few Indian groups ever wore such headdresses. In fact, the label "American Indian" is really a biological term that includes incredibly diverse peoples, ranging from family-size hunter-gatherer bands to large, complex civilizations.

Each human society has its own recognizable cultural style, which shapes the behavior of its members, their political and judicial institutions, and their morals. Every traveler is familiar with the distinctive "flavor" of various cultures that one experiences when dining in a foreign restaurant or arriving in a new country. This distinctiveness results from a people's complex adaptation to greatly varied ecological, societal, and cultural factors.

Human culture is unique because much of its content is transmitted from generation to generation by sophisticated communication systems. Formal education, religious beliefs, and day-to-day social intercourse all transmit culture and allow societies to develop complex and continuing adaptations to aid their survival. Such communication systems also help rapid cultural change to take place, as when less advanced societies come into contact with more advanced ones. Culture is a potential guide for behavior created through generations of human experience. It provides a design for living that helps mold responses to different situations.

Human beings are the only animals to use culture as the primary means of adapting to environment. Although biological evolution has protected the polar bear from arctic winters, only human beings make thick clothes and igloos in the Arctic and live in light, thatched shelters in the tropics. Culture is an adaptive system; it is an interface between ourselves, the environment, and other human societies. Through the long millennia of prehistory, human culture became more elaborate. If this cultural buffer were now removed we would be helpless and most probably doomed to extinction. As our only means of adaptation, human culture is always adjusting to environmental, technological, and societal change.

Culture can be subdivided in many ways. Language, economics, technology, religion, and political and social organization are but a few of the interacting elements. These elements shape one another and blend to form a whole. The distribution of water and food supplies as well as flexible social organization helps determine the distribution of home bases among the San hunter-gatherers of the Kalahari Desert in southern Africa.

Culture is the dominant factor in determining social behavior; human society is the vehicle that carries our culture. Societies are groups of interacting organizers. Insects and other animals have societies but only humans have **culture** as well.

What is culture? Anthropologists have tried to define this most elusive of theoretical formulations for generations. All such definitions are concepts that are a means of explaining cultures and human behavior in terms of the shared ideas held by a group of people. One of the best definitions was that put forth by the great Victorian anthropologist Sir Edward Tylor more than a century ago. He wrote that culture is "that complex whole which includes knowledge, belief, art, morals, law, custom, and any other capabilities and habits acquired by man as a member of society." Most archaeologists prefer to define culture as the primary nonbiological means by which human societies adapt to and accommodate their environment. An archaeologist's view of culture is that it represents the cumulative intellectual resources of human societies. These resources are passed from generation to generation by the spoken word and by example. Culture is the primary means of nonbiological adaptation to the environment and regulates relationships with the environment through technology and social and belief systems.

The concept of culture provides anthropological archaeologists with a means for explaining the products of human activity. When archaeologists study **patterns of discard,** or the tangible remains of the past, they see a patterned reflection of the culture that produced them, of the shared behavior of a group of prehistoric people. This patterning of archaeological finds is critical, for it reflects patterned behavior in the past.

CULTURAL SYSTEMS

Many of the interacting components of culture are highly perishable. So far, no one has been able to dig up a religious philosophy or an unwritten language. Archaeologists have to work with the *tangible* remains of human activity that still survive in the ground. But these surviving remains of human activity are radically affected by *intangible* aspects of human culture. The *Hopewell* people of the American Midwest traded finely made ornaments fashioned of hammered copper sheet (Figure 3.1) over enormous distances 1800 years ago. These ornaments turn up in Hopewell burial mounds. The copper technology that made them was simple, but the symbolism behind the artifacts was not. They were probably exchanged between important individuals as symbolic gifts, denoting kin ties, economic obligations, and other social meanings that are beyond the archaeologist's ability to recover. Thus, the artifacts found in an excavation reflect not only ancient technology, but also the values and uses that a society placed on such objects. Ancient tools are not culture in themselves, but a patterned reflection of the culture that produced them. Archaeologists spend much time studying the linkages between past cultures and their archaeological remains.

Anthropologist Leslie White studied peoples' means of adapting to their environment. He argued that *human culture is made up of many structurally different parts which articulate with one another within a total cultural system* (Figure 3.2). This cultural system is the means whereby a human society adapts to its physical and social environment.

All cultural systems articulate with other systems, which also are made up of interacting sets of variables. One such system is the natural

Figure 3.1 Hopewell raven or crow in beaten copper.

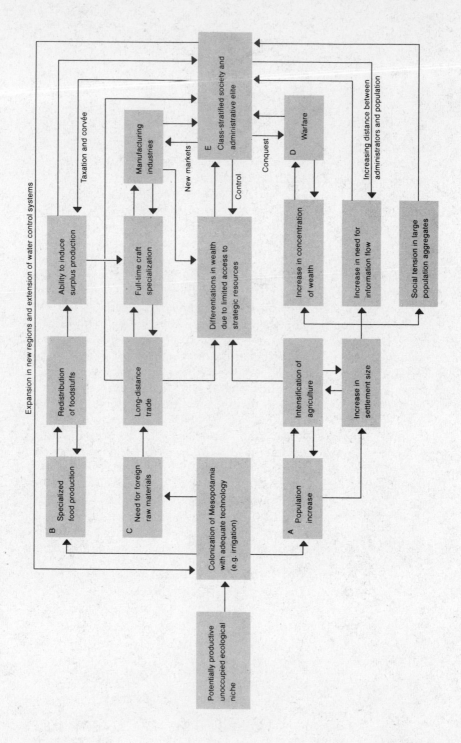

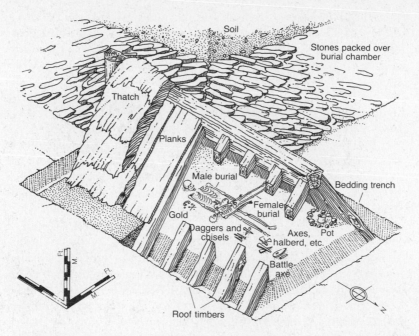

Figure 3.3 A wooden burial house from Leubingen, Germany. The two burials were deposited in a wooden house under a mound. The archaeologist recovers not only the burials and the objects with which they were buried, but also reconstructs the burial layout and sequence of construction of the burial house. Further, the archaeologist tries to infer the funerary rituals from the artifact patterning and the structures under the mound.

environment. The links between cultural and environmental systems are such that a change in one system is linked to changes in the other. Thus, a major objective of archaeology is to understand the linkage between the various parts of cultural and environmental systems as they are reflected in archaeological data. It follows that archaeologists studying cultural systems are more interested in the *relationships* between activities and tools within a cultural system than in the activities or tools themselves. They are profoundly interested in cultural systems within their environmental context.

To be workable, any human cultural system depends on its ability

Figure 3.2 Cultural systems are, of course, theoretical formulations used by archaeologists to interpret the past. This systems model illustrates a systems approach to understanding human culture. It is an attempt to document the relationship between cultural and environmental variables that led to state-organized societies in Mesopotamia between 5000 and 2000 B.C. (From *The Rise of Civilization* by Charles L. Redman. Copyright © 1978 W.H. Freeman and Company. Reprinted with permission.)

to adapt to the natural environment. A cultural system can be broken down into all manner of subsystems: religious and ritual subsystems, economic subsystems, and so on. Each of these is linked to the others Changes in one subsystem, such as a shift from cattle herding to wheat growing, will cause reactions in many others. Such relationships give the archaeologist a measure of the constant changes and variations in human culture that can accumulate over long periods as cultural systems respond to external and internal stimuli.

By examining the systematic patternings of archaeological finds, we can discover more about the intangible aspects of human behavior. By dropping their possessions on the ground or burying their dead in certain ways, people have left vital information about many more elements in their cultural system than merely their tools or skeletal remains (Figure 3.3). One can examine the relationship between individual households by comparing the artifacts left by each; one can study trading practices by analyzing the products of metalsmiths; one can discover religious beliefs by mapping temple architecture. Also, the carefully arranged grave offerings in a royal cemetery tell much about the ranked members of a royal court buried in a communal grave. And the precise and sophisticated recovery of such data is crucial for analysis and interpretation in modern prehistoric archaeology.

CULTURAL PROCESS

Every cultural system is in a constant state of change. Its various political, social, and technological subsystems adjust to changing circumstances. We ourselves live in a time of rapid cultural change, in which measurable differences set apart different ten-year periods. We would find it hard to identify the thousands of minor daily cultural changes that occur, but we can easily recognize the cumulative affects of these minor changes over a longer period.

Consider the many minor changes in automobile design over the past decades. In themselves the changes are not very striking, but if one looks at the *cumulative* effect of several years' steady change toward safer cars—energy-absorbing bumpers, padded steering wheels and dashboards, air bags, seat belts, more aerodynamic shapes—the change is striking. The automobile of today is different from that of the 1960s, and many of the changes are due to stricter governmental safety regulations, which in turn are due to greater public safety consciousness. Here we see a major cumulative change in part of our enormous technological subsystem. By examining the relationship between technological and political subsystems we can understand the processes by which culture changed.

The word **process** implies a patterned sequence of events, one event leading to another. A three-bedroom house is built in an ordered sequence of events, from foundation footings up to final painting. (Archaeological research itself has a process—research design and formulating objectives in the form of hypotheses, collecting and interpreting data to test those hypotheses, publishing the results.) To analyze cultural process, we attempt to consider all the factors that cause changes in human culture and how they affect one another.

How did human cultures change in the past? What cultural processes came into play when people began to cultivate the soil, or when complex and elaborate urban states developed 5000 years ago? As we saw in Chapter 1, new discoveries were thought to have spread throughout the world by mass migrations or by long-distance trading over continents and oceans. But as more and more archaeological data have been accumulated in all corners of the world, people have realized that such straightforward explanations of cultural process as universal evolution, or the spread of all ideas from one place of invention, are simplistic and do not reflect reality.

Most changes in human culture have been cumulative, occurring slowly over a long period of time. Processes of culture change in prehistory were the result of constantly changing adaptations to myriad external environments. Cultural systems were constantly adjusting and evolving in response to internal and external feedback.

Clearly, no one element in a cultural system is a primary cause of culture change, because a complex range of factors—rainfall, vegetation, technology, social restrictions, and population density, to mention only a few—interact with one another and react to a change in any element in the system. From the ecologist's point of view, therefore, human culture is merely one element of the ecosystem, a mechanism whereby people adapt to this environment. This viewpoint provides a useful framework for much modern archaeological research and for studying cultural process.

We shall look more closely at ways in which people have sought to interpret cultural process in prehistory in Chapter 8.

GOALS OF ARCHAEOLOGY

Whatever time period they specialize in, whether that of primeval hominids or of recent centuries, most archaeologists agree that their research has three broad goals:

Studying culture history.

Reconstructing past lifeways.

Explaining why cultural change has taken place.

In practice each objective usually complements the other, especially when archaeologists design their research to answer specific questions rather than merely digging a site as a preliminary to describing rows of excavated objects.

Culture History

Culture history means, quite simply, the description of human cultures as they extend back thousands of years into the past. Culture history is derived from the study of sites—and the artifacts and structures in them—in a temporal and spatial context. By investigating groups of prehistoric sites and their many artifacts, it is possible to erect local and regional sequences of human cultures that extend over centuries, even millennia (see Chapters 8, 12). Most of this activity is descriptive, and an essential preliminary to any work on lifeways or cultural process.

Past Lifeways

The study of past lifeways, the ways in which people have made their living in the past, involves the study of prehistoric cultures within their environmental context. Environmental data come from many sources, including ancient plant remains, fossil pollen grains, and animal bones. Ancient subsistence patterns, and even diet, can be reconstructed from food residues such as animal bones, carbonized seeds, and fish remains recovered during the course of meticulous excavations. This is another form of descriptive archaeology, but one that relates archaeological contexts in time and space to the complex interplay of changing patterns of human settlement, subsistence strategies, and ancient environments (Chapter 9). The theoretical framework for this kind of research is one that sees human cultures as complicated, ever-changing systems that interact with one another as well as the natural environment.

Cultural Process

How can one explain why human cultures in all parts of the world reached their various—and diverse—stages of cultural development? What were the processes of cultural change that caused this diversity, that triggered widely differing rates of culture change in different places, even in very similar environments? Many early archaeologists were content to talk generally of migrations, the diffusion of ideas, and revolutionary inventions. In fact, cultural processes were much more complicated than this. Today, processual archaeology involves the application of rigorous scientific methodology to the archaeological record, developing propositions that can be tested using meticulously collected archaeological data. Processual archaeology is based on the notion that archaeology is far more than merely a descriptive activity, and that it is possible to explain cultural change in the past.

These three broad goals provide the basis for all archaeological research, for the ultimate objective of archaeology is very simple—to describe, understand, and explain human behavior of the past.

THEORY IN ARCHAEOLOGY

Theory is the overall framework within which the archaeological scholar operates. Over the past century and a half, archaeologists have devised many theoretical approaches to the past, approaches that relate a body of theory to a battery of ever more sophisticated methods and techniques for describing the past. Archaeologists are constantly at work devising new theoretical approaches to expand the scope of their research. These evolving theoretical frameworks are a means for archaeologists to look beyond the facts and material objects for explanations of cultural developments and changes that took place during our long history. Ideally, research in archaeology would be a constant, interactive dialogue between theory and observation, a more or less self-critical procedure based on inference about the past built on phenomena in the contemporary world.

ARCHAEOLOGICAL SITES

Archaeology is based on the scientific recovery of data from the ground, on the systematic excavation and recording of the archaeological record. The archaeological **site** is a place where traces of ancient human activity are to be found. It is the archaeologist's archive, in much the same way as government files can yield a day-by-day record of historical events. Sites are normally identified through the manufactured tools, or artifacts, found in them.

Archaeological sites can range in size from a huge prehistoric city, such as *Teotihuacán*, in the Valley of Mexico, to a small meat cache used by hunter-gatherers at Olduvai Gorge, Tanzania. An archaeological site can consist of a human burial, a huge rockshelter occupied over millennia, or a simple scatter of stone tools found on the floor of Death Valley, California. Sites are limited in number and variety by preservation conditions and the activities of the people who occupied them. Some were used for a few short hours, others for a generation or two. Some, like Mesopotamian city mounds, were major settlements for hundreds, even thousands, of years and contain many separate occupation layers. The great mounds of *Ur-of-the-Chaldees* in Mesopotamia, contain many occupation levels, which tell the story of a long-established, ancient city that was abandoned when the river Euphrates changed its course away from the settlement.

Archaeological sites are most commonly classified according to the activities that occurred there. Thus, cemeteries and other sepulchers, like Tutankhamun's tomb, are referred to as *burial sites*. A 20,000-year-old Stone Age site in the Dnieper Valley of the Ukraine, with mammoth-bone houses, hearths, and other signs of domestic activity, is a habitation site. So too are many other sites, such as caves and rockshelters, early Mesoamerican farming villages, and Mesopotamian cities—in all, people lived and carried out greatly diverse activities. Kill sites consist of bones of slaughtered game animals and the weapons that killed them. They are found in East Africa and on the North American Great Plains. Quarry sites—where people mined stone or metals to make specific tools—are another type of specialist site. Prized raw materials, such as obsidian, a volcanic glass used for fine knives, were widely traded in prehistoric times and are of profound interest to the archaeologist. Then there are such spectacular religious sites as the stone circles of Stonehenge in southern England, the Temple of Amun at Karnak, Egypt, and the great ceremonial precincts of lowland Maya centers in Central America at *Tikal*, Copán, and Palenque (Figure 3.4). Art sites are common in southwestern France, southern Africa, and parts of North America, where prehistoric people painted or engraved magnificient displays (see Figure 9.5, p. 159). Some French art sites are more than 30,000 years old.

Each of these site types reflects a form of human activity, which is represented in the achaeological record by specific artifact patterns and surface indications found and recorded by the archaeologist.

Artifacts

Artifacts are objects found in archaeological sites that exhibit features resulting from human activity. The term covers every form of portable archaeological find, from stone axes to gold ornaments, as well as food residues such as broken bones. **Features** are nonportable structures such as houses, hearths, storage pits, and so on.

Artifacts are distinguished from nonartifacts simply because artifacts display patterns of humanly caused features, or attributes.* These objects can be classified according to their distinctive attributes. Artifacts are the product of human ideas, ideas that people had about the way objects should look or be used. Every culture has its own rules, which limit and dictate the form of artifacts. Our own society has definite ideas of what a fork should look like, or an automobile, or a pair

---

*In this book, an artifact is a formal tool. Elsewhere in archaeological literature the word is often given broader meaning.

Figure 3.4 Temple I at Tikal, Guatemala, dating to about A.D. 700, part of a religious site.

of shoes. We are so familiar with the artifacts of other cultures that, seeing a kayak, we at once identify it as "Eskimo."

Most craft skills, such as stone toolmaking, pottery manufacture, basketry, and metallurgy, are learned by each new generation. The skills are passed from one generation to the next, usually resulting in relatively slow, sometimes very slow, changes in artifacts and artifact technology. This inborn conservatism, which we might call tradition, strongly influences perpetuation of artifact forms.

The variation in a group of similar artifacts, such as stone projectile points, may reflect varied ideas behind them. Archaeologists study and classify artifacts, as we discuss in Chapter 8. These classifications are really research devices, by means of which we study the products of human behavior and, indirectly, human behavior itself.

For the archaeologist, every artifact has a number of **attributes,** identifiable properties that combine to give the object its distinctive form. The pots illustrated in Figure 3.5 have several obvious attri-

Figure 3.5 Painted vessels from the American Southwest. Each of these pots has distinctive attributes, some of which are shared with others; others are unique. Attributes include rim shape, height, paint colors, design motifs, clay composition, and so on.

butes: different painted motifs, rounded bases, handles, and so on. Each of these attributes contributes to the form of the pot and was part of the mental template that produced it. Each attribute has a different reason for being there. The band of decoration is purely ornamental, part of the decorative tradition among the people who made it. The shape of the pot is determined by its function—it was designed for carrying liquids and for cooking, for which a bag-shaped, round-bottomed body is essential. Attributes can be present because of traditional, functional, technological, or other reasons. Just occcasionally a new attribute will appear, a new decorative motif perhaps, which may vanish just as fast as it appeared. Why? Because it did not catch on with other potmakers. Occasionally, too, a new attribute may achieve wide popularity and be adopted by everyone. Then the innovation becomes part of the pottery tradition.

The dictates of fashion and style play an important role in the changes that occur in attributes over short and long periods of time. These fashions and the styles associated with them are a major factor in studying culture change. To take a relatively modern analogy, Victorian explorers who penetrated deep into the East African interior traveled in caravans laden with cheap imported goods such as glass beads, cotton cloth, and china vessels. Sometimes they would find that the trade goods they brought with them to barter for food, once thought to be prime commodities, were no longer of interest to peoples in the interior. Fashions had changed, and different bead colors had assumed greater desirability. If one were to investigate sites where such trade was taking place over several centuries, one would find changes in proportions in different bead types, shapes, and colors. In this case, they are the result of changing fashions.

The archaeologist is deeply concerned with how artifacts vary and with the changing forms of the many manufactured objects found in archaeological sites. Variation in the form of artifacts is a complex subject, but one of critical importance to archaeologists. It is the cumulative result of thousands of minor changes in the mental templates of dozens of different artifacts that provide the tangible evidence for culture change in the prehistoric past. And that, as we have seen, is a major concern to anyone studying prehistory.

CONTEXT

Artifacts are found in archaeological sites. Archaeological sites are far more than just a concentration of artifacts, however. They can hold the remains of dwellings, burials, storage pits, craft activities, and sometimes several occupation levels. Each artifact, each broken bone or tiny seed, every dwelling, has a relationship in space and time to all of the other finds made in the site. An artifact can be earlier, contemporary with, or later than its neighbors in the soil. A thousand obsidian flakes and half-completed projectile heads scattered over an area several square feet in diameter are, in themselves, merely stone fragments. But the spatial patterning of all the fragments is significant, for it tells us something of the various manufacturing activities carried out by the person who flaked the thousand fragments from chunks of obsidian. In this instance, and many others, the **context** of the artifacts in time and space is vital (see the section on Site Formation Processes in Chapter 6).

To every archaeologist, an artifact is of limited value without this context. The museums and art galleries of the world are filled with magnificent artifacts that have been collected under circumstances that can only be described as highly unscientific. Generations of treasure hunters have ravaged ancient Egyptian cemeteries and dug up thousands of pre-Columbian pots for museums and private collectors. Few of these objects have any archaeological context. Any expert can look at a pre-Columbian pot and say at once, "Classic Maya." But, tragically, rarely will our expert be able to consult excavation records and say, "Classic Maya, Level VIB from Temple of the Inscriptions, Palenque, excavation C, 1976, associated with burial of an adult male, 35 years old, date about A.D. 680." An artifact removed from its context in space and time in an archaeological site is merely an object that yields only limited cultural information. An artifact carefully excavated from a recorded archaeological context is an integral part of history, and as such has far more significance. This context of space and time lies at the very foundations of modern archaeology. We must now look at ways in which we tell how old something is, and what its spatial associations may be.

4

TIME

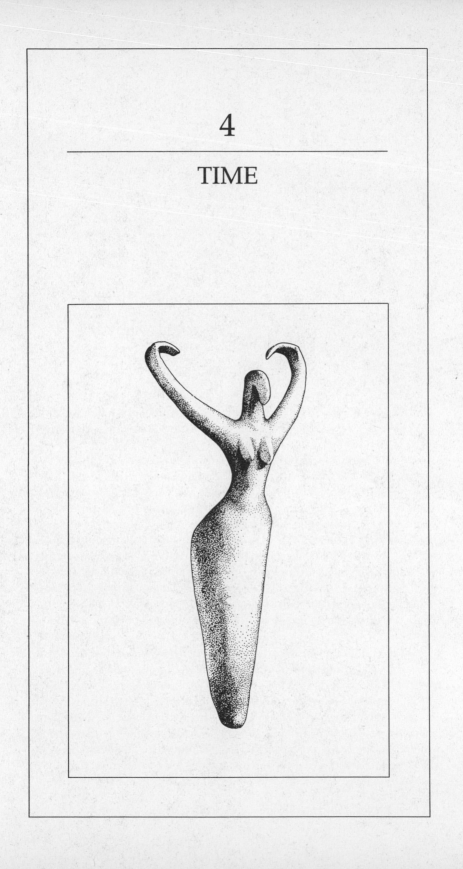

What seest thou else in the dark backward and abysm of time?

William Shakespeare, *The Tempest*

This chapter is about time, about the ways in which archaeologists date projectile points and all the other myraid finds that come from their excavations and surveys.

Human prehistory spans at least two million years of cultural evolution, a vast landscape of sites with long-abandoned food remains, artifacts, burials, and prehistoric dwellings. Each of these sites and their contents has a precise context in time and an exact position in space as well. Some sites, like the great city of *Teotihuacán* in Mexico, were occupied for hundreds of years. Other localities, such as Olduvai Gorge, were inhabited for hundreds of thousands. The chronology of prehistory worldwide is made up from thousands of careful excavations and many types of dating tests used to determine hundreds of local sequences of occupation layers and archaeological sites. Without dates, prehistory would be a jumble of confusing sites and cultures devoid of order.

Our lives are governed by time—by working hours and tax deadlines, bus schedules and calendars. Everyone in our society needs access to a timepiece simply to keep up with everyone else. Precise time measurement is, however, a recent phenomenon. Accurate historical records extend back only 5000 years, to the beginning of ancient Egyptian and Mesopotamian civilizations. Both these societies developed calendars and astronomical predictions to a fine art. The Maya peoples of Mesoamerica devised an astronomically based calendar that they used to regulate cycles of years upon which the prosperity of society depended.

Looking earlier than 3000 B.C., however, we enter a chronological vacuum, a blank that archaeologists have labored to fill with carefully assembled sequences of sites and artifacts. Except in a very few areas, such as the American Southwest, where tree rings can be used to date prehistoric sites very accurately, prehistoric time must be measured in centuries and millennia, rather than individual years. We know that Washington, D.C., was founded in A.D. 1790. We will be lucky if we can ever date the beginnings of Teotihuacán to closer than 200 ± 100 years B.C. Some idea of the scale of the problem can be gained by piling up a hundred quarters to represent the time that humankind has been on earth. The length of time covered by historical records will be considerably less than the thickness of one quarter. Ninety-nine and nine-tenths percent of human experience lies in prehistoric times. Small wonder time is important in archaeology.

RELATIVE CHRONOLOGY

Every event or object has a time relationship to other events and objects. If we place a book on a table, and then put another on top of it, clearly the upper one of the two was placed on the table after—at a later moment in time than—the original volume. The second book became part of the pile after the first, but how long afterward we have no means of telling. This example illustrates the principle of superposition, the cornerstone of **relative chronology.**

Superposition, the notion that underlying levels are earlier than those that cover them, came to archaelology from geology. The geological layers of the earth are superimposed one upon another almost like layers of a cake. Easily viewed examples are cliffs by the seashore or road cuts along the highway, which show a series of geological levels. Obviously, any object deposited in the lower horizons usually got there before the upper strata were accumulated. In other words, the lower levels are relatively earlier than the later strata. The deposition of a series of occupation levels or geological strata in order can be achieved by many processes: wind, water, earthquakes, and other factors.

Superposition is fundamental to the study of archaeological sites, for many settlements, such as desert caves in western North America or Near Eastern mounds, were occupied more or less continuously for hundreds, even thousands, of years. Human occupation of any site results in the accumulation of all kinds of rubbish. Objects are lost and become imbedded in the ground. Buildings fall into disrepair and are leveled to make way for new ones. A flood may wipe out a village and deposit a thick layer of silt. A new village may rise on the same spot years later. The sequence of these superimposed occupation levels is carefully recorded as the excavation of a site proceeds. Of course, not all settlements were occupied several times. Single-occupation sites, even very temporary camps, are studied just as carefully.

The sequence of natural and humanly accumulated layers on an archaeological site is the basis for all stratigraphic observations in archaeology. But as Figure 4.1 shows, it is not only the carefully observed layers, but their detailed contents as well, which provide us with relative cultural chronologies. Each level in a settlement has its associated artifacts, objects that the archaeologist uses as indicators of technological, economic social, or even religious change.

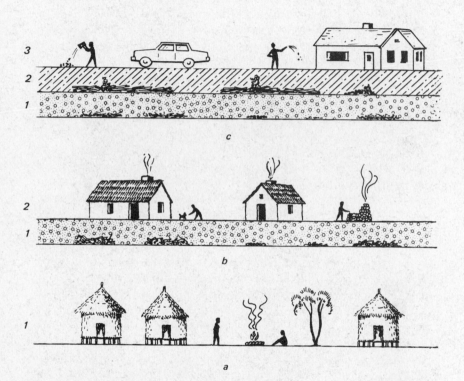

Figure 4.1 The principle of superposition. (a) A flourishing farming village 5000 years ago. After a time, the village is abandoned and the huts fall into disrepair. The ruins are covered by accumulating earth and vegetation. (b) After an interval, a second village is built on the same site, with different architectural styles. This village in turn is abandoned; the houses collapse into piles of rubble and are covered by accumulating earth. (c) Twentieth-century people park their cars on top of both village sites and drop litter and coins that, when uncovered, reveal to the archaeologist that the top layer is modern.

An archaeologist digging this site would find that the modern layer is underlain by two prehistoric occupation levels, that square houses were in use in the upper of the two, which is the later (law of superposition), and that round huts are stratigraphically earlier than square ones here. Therefore, village 1 is earlier than village 2, but when either was occupied or how many years separate village 1 from 2 cannot be known without further data.

Artifacts and Relative Chronology

Manufactured artifacts are the fundamental data archaeologists use to study past human behavior. These artifacts have changed with passing time in radical ways. One has only to look at the humble stone chopper of the earliest humans and compare it with the latest electric carving knife to get the point. Most artifact changes in prehistory are extremely small; minor changes in such characteristics as the shape, decoration, or lip angle of clay pots accumulate slowly as they lead ultimately to a vessel form that is hardly recognizable as originating from its ancestors.

Archaeologists such as the celebrated Egyptologist Flinders Petrie have long been fascinated by the gradual changes in artifacts. Petrie, who worked on a huge prehistoric cemetery at Diospolis Parva, Egypt, in 1902, was confronted with the problem of arranging a large number of tombs in chronological order. He eventually placed them in sequence by studying the groups of pots buried with each skeleton, arranging the vessels in such a way that features, for example handle design, reflected gradual change. The earliest handles were useful for lifting the pot. But the latest vessels bore no handles at all, merely painted lines that represented the once useful handle. Petrie used his pots to create a series of "sequence dates," each characterized by a vessel form. Whenever a vessel form similar to Petrie's was found anywhere in Egypt, the pot itself and the objects found with it could be dated within his series. So effective was this relative chronology based on artifacts that it was used for many years.

Recent studies of changing artifacts are based on the observation that the popularity of any artifact form is a fleeting thing. The miniskirt becomes the midi or the maxi; clothing styles change from month to month. Records hit the Top 40 but are forgotten in a short time. Other artifacts have a far longer life. The stone choppers of the earliest humans were a major element in early toolkits (basic set of tools used by a culture) for hundreds of thousands of years. People used candles for centuries before they turned to kerosene and gas lamps. But each has its period of maximum popularity, or frequency of occurrence, whether it lasts for millennia or only a few months. Figure 4.2 shows how each distribution of artifacts, when plotted, has a profile that has been described as resembling a large battleship's hull when viewed from above.

The relatively unsophisticated methods used by Flinders Petrie have been refined into sophisticated **seriation** (ordering) **techniques** based on the assumption that the populartity of pottery types, stone artifact forms, and other objects peaks at a specific moment in time. If we plot the frequencies with which these objects occur as a set of bars, they will look like the hull of a battleship glimpsed from an aircraft (Figure 4.2). The center of the hull bulges outward amidships,

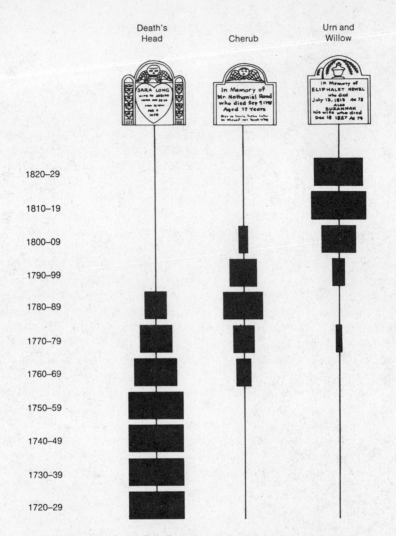

Figure 4.2 Seriation. The changing styles of New England grave-stones, from Stoneham, Massachusetts, between 1720 and 1829, seriated in three styles. Notice how each style rises to a peak of maximum popularity and then declines as another comes into fash-ion. The cherub style shows the "classic battleship curve." Each horizontal bar represents the percentage of a gravestone type at that date; for example, between 1720 and 1729 death's heads were at 100 percent.

where the armor is thickest, coinciding with the period of greatest pop-ularity. This phenomenon is sometimes called the "battleship curve." Thus, it is argued, when sites within a restricted geographic area contain similar pottery and other artifacts at an equivalent rate of popu-larity, they are of approximately the same age. If the samples are statis-tically reliable, a series of sites can be linked in a relative chronology, even though, without dates in years, one cannot tell when they were occupied.

Edwin Dethlefsen and James Deetz tested this battleship-curve assumption against the changing decorative styles on dated gravestones in New England Colonial cemeteries. They found that the changing styles of death's-heads, cherubs, and urns succeeded one another in an almost perfect series of battleship curves. Since the dates of the gravestones were known from their inscriptions, the experiment could be conducted and tested within a precise chronological context.

A series of archaeological sites may contain many different artifacts that appear and vanish over relatively short periods. By applying seriation, it is possible to place the different forms of artifacts in a series of relative chronologies, such as that from the *Tehuacán* Valley in Mexico illustrated in Figure 4.3. Each occupation level of each site will contain different proportions of each artifact form manufactured during that period. And once you have a sequence of changing artifact frequencies, it is possible to fit isolated, newly discovered sites into a relative chronology.

Cross-Dating

Seriation is effective for **cross-dating** sites as well. As we have seen, it can be used to assign a newly discovered settlement to a precise position in the relative chronology of a well-studied area, as Flinders Petrie did. In some cases, too, a series of sites may contain objects such as European coins whose date of minting is known. Hence, we have access to dates in years. Let us assume that an English coin dating to 1825 is traded in a California Indian village. The coin falls onto a hut floor and is lost in the dust. In the 1990s, archaeologists find this dated coin in a stratified level of the ancient village. They know it was traded into the settlement *no earlier than its date of minting,* and so the village was flourishing in, or after, 1825. They may find more sites with the same Indian artifacts in similar proportions—but no coins—a few miles away. When they seriate the finds, they will be able to cross-date the undated settlements because their artifact frequencies are the same. This cross-dating technique has been widely applied to central European prehistoric sites whose inhabitants traded with literate civilizations in the Mediterranean basin, exchanging copper and other raw materials for ornaments and other luxuries whose age is known.

Relative Chronology and the Ice Age

The story of human prehistory has unfolded against a backdrop of massive climatic changes (Figure 4.4). The Ice Age or Pleistocene is the most recent of the great geological epochs, sometimes called the Age of Humanity. It is remarkable for dramatic swings in world cli-

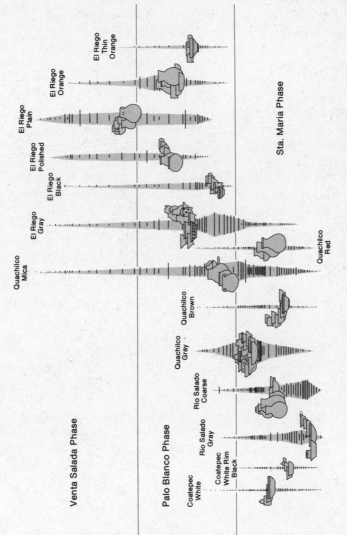

Figure 4.3 Seriation of pottery styles from the Tehuacán Valley, Mexico, showing many sites ordered into a single sequence.

mate. On numerous occasions during the Pleistocene, great ice sheets covered much of western Europe and North America, bringing arctic climate to vast areas of the nothern hemisphere (Figure 4.4b). These climatic fluctuations have been documented from deep-sea sediment cores from the world's oceans. Minute foraminifera (protozoa) in these cores are evidence of periods of cooler and warmer ocean waters that coincided with major climatic changes ashore.

The Ice Age began about 1.6 million years ago, during a long-term cooling trend in the world's oceans. These more than 1.6 million years have been ones of constant climatic change. The Pleistocene epoch is conventionally divided into three periods.

Lower Pleistocene times lasted until about 700,000 years ago. Deep-sea cores tell us that climatic fluctuations between warmer and colder regimens were still relatively minor. These were critical millennia, for it was during this long period that humans emerged in Africa, and spread from tropical regions into temperate latitudes in Europe and Asia.

Middle Pleistocene times began with a reversal in the earth's magnetic polarity about 730,000 years ago. The study of paleomagnetism has shown that the earth's geomagnetic field has reversed its polarity many times in the past, reversals that can be studied in volcanic rocks. During the so-called Matuyama epoch, the polarity was reversed. It reverted to normal with the onset of the Brunhes epoch about 730,000 years ago, a change that has been recognized geologically not only in deep sea cores, but in volcanic rocks ashore, where it can be dated by the potassium argon method (see p. 71). Since then, there have been at least eight cold (glacials) and warm (interglacial) cycles, the last cycle ending about 12,000 years ago. (Strictly speaking, we are still in an interglacial today). These cycles were so constant that it can be said that the world's climate has been in transition from cold to warm and back again for over 75 percent of the past 700,000 years. Typically, cold cycles have begun gradually, with vast continental ice sheets forming on land—in Scandinavia, on the Alps, and over the northern parts of North America. These expanded ice sheets locked up enormous quantities of water, causing world sea levels to fall by several hundred feet during glacial episodes. The geography of the world changed dramatically, and large continental shelves were opened up for human settlement. When a warming trend began, deglaciation occurred very rapidly and rising sea levels flooded low-lying coastal areas within a few millennia. During glacial maxima, glaciers covered a full one-third of the earth's land surface, while they were as extensive as they are today during interglacials.

Throughout the past 700,000 years, vegetational changes have mirrored climatic fluctuations. During glacial episodes, treeless arctic steppe and tundra covered much of Europe and parts of North America, but gave way to temperate forest during interglacials. In the

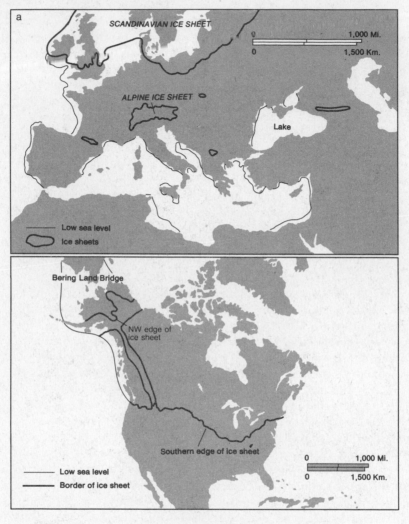

a

Figure 4.4 Pleistocene relative chronology. (a) Distribution of the major ice sheets in Europe and North America during the last glaciation of the Pleistocene, and the extent of land exposed by low sea levels; (b) provisional Ice Age chronology; (c) surroundings of a hunter-gatherer camp from Northern England, occupied about 10,000 years ago, reconstructed by pollen analysis.

tropics, Africa's Sahara Desert may have supported grassland during interglacials, expanding dramatically during dry, cold spells.

The *Upper Pleistocene* stage began about 128,000 years ago, with the beginning of the last interglacial. This period lasted until about 118,000 years ago, when a slow cooling trend brought full glacial conditions to Europe and North America. This Würm glaciation, named

Temperature Lower ← → Higher	Date B.C.	Epoch	Old World Glaciations	New World Glaciations	Prehistory
		Holocene	Post Glacial Period		Cities Agriculture Post Glacial Hunter-Gatherers
	8,000 —				
	18,000 —		Würm Glaciation	Wisconsin Glaciation	First Americans Modern Humans Settle Europe, Eurasia, Australia
	45,000 —				
	100,000 —				Neanderthals
			Last Interglacial	Last Interglacial	
			Riss Glaciation	Illinoian Glaciation	Emergence of Modern Humans
	200,000 —	Pleistocene			Archaic *Homo sapiens*
	400,000 —		Uncertain Climatic Fluctuations		
	500,000 —				
	730,000 —		— Brunhes/Matuyama Boundary —		*Homo erectus*
	1 Million —				
		Pliocene			Origins of Humanity *Homo habilis*
	3 million —				

b

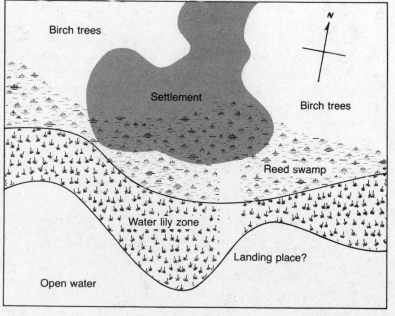

Birch trees

Settlement

Birch trees

Reed swamp

Water lily zone

Landing place?

Open water

N

c

after a river in the Alps, lasted until about 10,000 years ago, when there was a rapid return to more temperate conditions.

The final Würm glaciation was a period of constantly fluctuating climatic change, with several episodes of more temperate climate in northern latitudes (Figure 4.4b). It served as the backdrop for some of the most important developments in human prehistory, notably the spread of anatomically modern *Homo sapiens sapiens* from the tropics to all parts of the Old World and into the Americas. Between about 25,000 and 15,000 years ago, Nothern Eurasia's climate was intensely cold. A series of brilliant Stone Age hunter-gatherer cultures evolved both on the open tundra and in the sheltered river valleys of southwestern France and nothern Spain, cultures famous for their fine antler and bone artifacts and exceptional artwork.

The world's geography was dramatically different 20,000 years ago. These differences had a major impact on human prehistory—one could walk from Siberia to Alaska across a flat, low-lying plain, the Bering Land Bridge. This was the route by which humans first reached the Americas some time before 12,000 years ago. The low-lying coastal zones of Southeast Asia were far more extensive 15,000 years ago than they are now, and they supported a thriving population of Stone Age hunter-gatherers. The fluctuating distributions of vegetational zones also affected the pattern of human settlement and the course of human history.

From the archaeological perspective, the major climatic events of the past 1.5 million years provide a broad framework for a relative chronology of human culture. Although almost no human beings lived on, or very close to, the great ice sheets that covered so much of the Nothern Hemisphere, they did live in regions affected by geological phenomena associated with the ice sheets: coastal areas, lakes, and river floodplains. When human artifacts are found in direct association with Pleistocene geological features of this type, it is sometimes possible to tie in archaelogical sites with the relative chronology of Pleistocene events derived from geological strata. And thanks to sophisticated botanical methods such as pollen analysis, it is often possible to reconstruct local environments during the Ice Age with remarkable precision.

Many early hunter-gatherer bands camped on the shores of Pleistocene lakes, now long dried-up. The sealed deposits of these lakes are rich in organic materials that provide a wealth of information on the environment at the time the site was occupied. Millions of tiny fossil pollen grains from the trees and undergrowth that once grew near the lake are preserved in the lake filling. These pollen grains are highly distinctive and readily identified, because each tree species, even each kind of grass, has a different form. By taking samples from the lake deposits, it is possible to reconstruct the vegetation around a Pleistocene lake by identifying and counting the fossil pollens.

This technique is **palynology,** the science of pollen analysis, about the only means of gaining an accurate picture of prehistoric environments in any detail. Pollen samples have shown how hunter-gatherers living in central Africa 50,000 years ago were exploiting dense rainforests. In 10,000 B.C., present western Europe was covered with treeless arctic plains swept by icy winds. It has taken only a few thousand years for northern Europe to change from arctic climate to the temperate environment of today. Minute changes in vegetational cover accompanied these climatic shifts, changes that can be traced by studying pollens in the lake clays and muds in which many archaeological sites lie (Figure 4.4c), and each vegetation type can be assigned to a dated zone of post-Pleistocene time.

The relative chronology of the Pleistocene provides a general framework for the major events of prehistory. This framework becomes much more accurate after 100,000 B.C., when many more sites are found near lakes and other localities, and pollen analysis can be used to study vegetational and environmental changes.

DATING IN YEARS (CHRONOMETRIC DATING)

People have tried everything to date the past in calendar years. Today, a battery of such **chronometric,** or **absolute, dating** methods are available to the archaeologist. Some are reliable, well-tried techniques, such as tree-ring dating and potassium–argon dating. Others are most experimental, including amino acid racemization, obsidian hydration, and thermoluminescence. We do not have the space to discuss all these methods here, and so we shall confine ourselves to the more widely used chronometric techniques. Fortunately, these straddle most of prehistoric time (Figure 4.5). For the more experimental methods, consult the "Further Reading" section at the back of the book.

Historical Records and Objects of Known Age

In the Near East, 5000 years of history are recorded in government archives, in inscriptions, and on thousands of clay tablets. As we saw in Chapter 1, archaeology provides a means for checking and expanding historical records. But the lists of kings and genealogies in early Egyptian and Mesopotamian archives give us dates in years that go back to at least 3000 B.C. Recorded history starts in about 750 B.C. in the central Mediterranean, about 55 B.C. in Britain. The first historical records for the New World began with the Spanish Conquest, and parts of Africa entered "history" in A.D. 1890. Historical records cover but the very smallest fraction of the human experience.

Date	Method	Major developments
Modern times (after A.D. 1)	Historical documents; dendrochronology; imported objects	Columbus in the New World; Roman Empire
2,500 B.C.		Origins of cities
40,000 B.C.	Radiocarbon dating (organic materials)	Origins of agriculture
75,000 B.C.	Still no chronometric dating method	Colonization of New World *Homo sapiens sapiens*
100,000 B.C.	Potassium–argon dating (volcanic materials)	
500,000 B.C.		
		Early humans
5,000,000 B.C.		

Figure 4.5 Major chronological methods in prehistory. Experimental methods eliminated for clarity.

Fortunately, the literate civilizations of three or four thousand years ago traded their products far and wide. The Egyptians traded fine ornaments to Crete, the Cretans sent wine and fine pottery to the Nile. When archaeologist Arthur Evans discovered the magnificent Minoan civilization of Crete in 1900, he dated the Palace of Knossos by means of Minoan pottery fragments that had been excavated in faraway Egypt, in levels whose precise historical date was known. Coins and other imports of known age can be used to date buildings or refuse pits in which they were dropped centuries earlier. A bewildering array of dated objects are used by archaeologists dealing with the recent periods of prehistory. These include glass bottles and beads, seals, imported Chinese porcelain, even military buttons. Each of these objects has the advantage that its age is known exactly.

Tree-Ring Dating (Dendrochronology)

Everyone is familiar with the concentric growth rings that can be seen in the cross-section of the trunk of a felled tree. These rings, formed in most trees, are of special importance to archaeologists in areas such as the American Southwest, where the seasonal weather changes markedly and growth is concentrated during a few months of the year. Normally trees produce two growth rings each year, which are formed by the cambium between the wood and the bark. Each year's growth forms a distinct ring that varies in thickness according to the tree's age and annual climatic variations. Weather variations in the Southwest tend to run in cycles of dry and wet years, which are reflected in patterns of thicker and thinner rings on the trees.

The tree-ring samples are taken with a borer from living or felled trees. The ring sequences from the borer are then compared to each other and to a master chronology of rings built up from many trees with overlapping sequences tied to a known terminal date. The patterns of thick and thin rings for the new sequences are matched to the master sequence and are dated on the basis of their accurate fit to the master sequence. By using the California bristlecone pine, tree-ring experts have developed a master chronology over 8000 years back into the past (Figure 4.6).

Tree-ring dating can be practiced on long-felled wood beams from Indian pueblos to date the buildings of which they are a part. Tree-ring experts have been able to develop an extremely accurate chronology for southwestern sites that extend back as long ago as 322 B.C. It was a difficult task, for they had to connect a prehistoric chronology from dozens of ancient beams to a master tree-ring chronology connected to modern times obtained from living trees of known age. The dates of such famed southwestern sites as Mesa Verde and Pueblo Bonito are known to within a few years.

Dendrochronology has been used in other areas of the world as well—in Alaska and the American Southeast, and with great success in Greece, Ireland, and Germany. The bristlecone pine is to the Southwest as oaks are to Europe. European tree-ring experts have collected large numbers of tree-ring records from oaks that lived 150 years or so. By visual and statistical comparison they have linked living trees to ancient ones from bogs and prehistoric sites, and also farmhouse and church beams, providing a tree-ring sequence that goes back 7272 years in northern Ireland and 6000 years in Germany. Dutch tree-ring experts have even tried dating the oak panels utilized by old masters as backing for their oil paintings as a way of authenticating paintings.

Unfortunately, tree-ring dating is limited to relatively recent settlements in restricted regions of markedly seasonal rainfall. But, as we shall see, dendrochronology is also useful for calibrating radiocarbon dates. Radiocarbon dates throughout Europe can now be calibrated to as early as 5200 B.C.

Thermoluminescence

Thermoluminescence is a method used for dating baked prehistoric materials such as clay vessels. Although it is still at an experimental

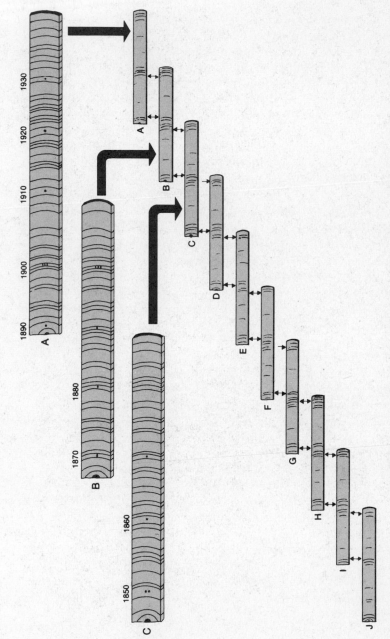
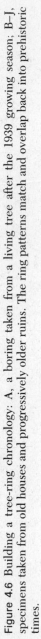

Figure 4.6 Building a tree-ring chronology: A, a boring taken from a living tree after the 1939 growing season; B-J, specimens taken from old houses and progressively older ruins. The ring patterns match and overlap back into prehistoric times.

stage, thermoluminescence shows promise as a means of dating geological strata as well. The principle is simple: The materials from which pottery is made store energy by trapping electrons as atomic defects or impurity sites. This stored energy can be released by heating the pottery, at which time visible light rays, known as thermoluminescence, are emitted. All pottery and ceramics contain some radioactive impurities at a concentration of several particles per million. These materials emit alpha particles at a known rate, depending on how densely concentrated they are in the sample. When an alpha particle is absorbed by the pottery minerals around the radioactive impurities, it causes mineral atoms to ionize. Electrons are then released from their binding to the nuclei and later settle at a metastable (relatively unstable) stage of higher energy. This energy is stored, unless the parent material is heated—as when the pot is being fired. Such heating allows the trapped electrons to be released, subsequently causing thermoluminescence. After the pot is fired, alpha particles are again absorbed by the material and the thermoluminescent potential increases until the pot is heated again. Thus, a clay vessel is dated by measuring the thermoluminescence of the sample as well as its alpha radioactivity and its potential susceptibility to producing thermoluminescence. In the laboratory, the trapped electrons are released from a powdered pottery fragment by sudden and violent heating under controlled conditions.

Thermoluminescence has been used to date heat-altered stone, burned hearths, and pottery with considerable success. Several investigators claim accuracies of ± 10 percent for prehistoric dates. Someday it may also be possible to date Ice Age geological strata that contain human artifacts, such as those in Australia, Africa, and other tropical regions.

Radiocarbon Dating

Radiocarbon dating, developed by physicists J. R. Arnold and W. F. Libby in 1949, is the best known of all chronometric methods. Cosmic radiation produces neutrons that enter the earth's atmosphere and react with nitrogen to produce the carbon isotope carbon-14 (^{14}C, or radiocarbon), which has eight rather than the usual six neutrons in its nucleus. With these additional neutrons, the nucleus is unstable and is subject to radioactive decay. Arnold and Libby calculated that it took 5568 years for half of the ^{14}C in any sample to decay, the so-called half-life of ^{14}C. (The half-life is now more accurately measured at 5730 years.)

The ^{14}C isotope is believed to behave just like ordinary carbon (^{12}C) from a chemical standpoint. Together with ^{12}C it enters into the carbon dioxide of the atmosphere. Because living vegetation builds up its own organic matter by photosynthesis and by using atmospheric carbon dioxide, the ratio of ^{14}C to ^{12}C in living vegetation and the animals that eat it is equal to that in the atmosphere. As soon as an organism dies, no further radiocarbon is incorporated into it. The radiocarbon present in the dead organism will continue to disintegrate, so that after 5,730 years half the original amount will be left; after about 11,400 years, a quarter; and so on. Thus, measuring the amount of ^{14}C still present in plant and animal remains and emitting radiation enables us to determine the time that has elapsed since death. By calculating the difference between the amount of ^{14}C originally present and that now present, and comparing the difference with the known rate of decay, we can compute the time elapsed in years. The amount of ^{14}C in a fresh sample emits particles at a rate of about 15 particles per minute per gram of carbon. A sample with an emission rate of half that amount would be approximately 5730 years old, the time needed for one-half the original radioactive material to disintegrate (the half-life of ^{14}C).

Radiocarbon samples can be taken from many organic materials, about a handful of charcoal, burned bone, shell, hair, wood, or other organic substance is needed for analysis. This requisite means that few actual artifacts may be dated, because wood and other organic artifacts are rare. But charcoal from hearths is frequently used for dating. The samples themselves are collected with meticulous care from particular stratigraphic contexts so that an exact location, or a specific structure, is dated.

The laboratory converts the sample to gas and pumps it into a proportional counter. The beta particle emissions are measured, usually for 24 hours. The results of the count are then converted to an age determination. When a ^{14}C date comes from a laboratory, it bears a statistical plus or minus factor. For example, 3600 ± 200 years (200 years represents one standard deviation) means that chances are two out of three that the correct date is between the span of 3400 and 3800. If we double the deviation, chances are 19 out of 20 that the span 3200 to 4000 is correct. Radiocarbon dates should be recognized for what they are—statistical approximations.

The conventional radiocarbon method relies on measurements of a beta ray decay rate to date the sample. A new approach uses accelerator mass spectrometry, which allows radiocarbon dating to be carried out by direct counting of ^{14}C atoms rather than by counting radioactive disintegrations. This has the advantage that one can date even tiny samples, especially ones dating to between 10,000 and 30,000 years ago. The samples required are so small that it is possible, for example, to date an individual tree ring. Accelerator dating is especially useful for dating the amino acids from bone collagen, but one can date almost any material, even tiny wood fragments preserved in the haft sockets of metal spearheads, for example. Another major advantage is the ability to date materials such as charcoal from an artifact associated with a hearth; very often tiny fragments of organic material still adhere to the actual object one wishes to date. This makes it possible, for example, to date an actual corn cob in a Southwestern cave, a much better way of dating early agriculture than by merely using the law of association to link a cob with a dated feature or isolated charcoal sample. At present about one-third of all radiocarbon dates are accelerator-generated dates, which often achieve high precision.

The practical limits of radiocarbon dating with beta decay approaches are between 40,000 and 60,000 years. Researchers have tried detecting ^{14}C atoms directly with a particle accelerator, a technique that would extend the limits of radiocarbon dating to as much as 100,000 years, although at present its limits, mainly because of contamination carried into soil by roots, are around 70,000 years.

When J. R. Arnold and W. F. Libby first developed radiocarbon dating in the late 1940s, they compared their ^{14}C readings with dates from objects of known age, such as ancient Egyptian boats. These tests enabled them to claim that radiocarbon dates were accurate enough for archaeologists' purposes. But about 25 years later, just when archaeologists thought they at last had an accurate and reliable means for dating the past, some radiocarbon dates for dated tree rings of long-lived California bristlecone pines were published. They turned out to be consistently younger—for trees dating to before 1200 B.C.

It turned out that Libby had incorrectly assumed that the concentration of radiocarbon in the atmosphere has remained constant through time, so that prehistoric samples, when they were alive, would contain the same amount of radiocarbon as living things today. But, in fact, changes in the strength of the earth's magnetic field and alternations in solar activity have considerably varied the concentration of radiocarbon in the atmosphere and in living things.

Fortunately, however, it is possible to correct ^{14}C dates back to about 4500 B.C. by calibrating them with tree-ring chronologies, for dendrochronology provides absolutely precise dates. Some idea of the changes in accuracy of ^{14}C dating over the past 6000 years can be gathered from Figure 4.7. Calibration of dates earlier than 4500 B.C. is impossible because three-ring chronologies are lacking, but extreme accuracy is less important for earlier periods anyway because time scales are less precise.

Despite its chronological and technical limitations, radiocarbon dating is of enormous significance. ^{14}C samples have dated some African hunter-gatherers to more than 50,000 years ago and Paleo-Indian bison kills on the Great Plains to more than 11,000 years ago and they have provided chronologies for the origins of agriculture and civilization in the New World and the Old. Radiocarbon dates provide a means for developing a truly global chronology that can equate major events such as the origins of literate civilizations in such widely separated areas as China and Peru. The prehistory of the world from some

Radiocarbon age A.D./B.C.	Calibrated age range A.D./B.C.
A.D. 1500	A.D. 1300 to 1515
1000	870 to 1230
500	265 to 640
1	420 to 5 B.C.
500 B.C.	820 to 400
1000	1530 to 905
1500	2345 to 1660
2000	2830 to 2305
2500	3505 to 2925
3000	3950 to 3640
3500	4545 to 3960
4000	5235 to 4575
4500	5705 to 5205
5000	6285 to 5445
5300	6585 to 5595
before 5500	Outside calibration range

Figure 4.7 Widely agreed-upon calibrations for radiocarbon dates at 500-year intervals, from A.D. 1500 to 5300 B.C.

40,000 years ago up to historic times is dated almost entirely by the radiocarbon method. But most "finite" ^{14}C dates earlier than 40,000 years ago (and a lot of younger ones) are, in fact, minimum dates.

Early Prehistory

Earlier than 40,000 years ago, we find a long period of prehistory that is poorly dated. Some experimental dating methods such as uranium–thorium and other uranium series methods are being tried to fill this gap, but their archaeological applications are still very limited. Consult the references in "Further Reading" for a description of this and other experimental techniques.

The period between 75,000 and 500,000 years ago was one of slow human cultural evolution, when *Homo sapiens* first appears in the archaeological record. At present, we have no idea exactly when, or how, modern human beings first evolved. Obviously, such information must await new dating methods and additional archaeological sites.

Potassium–Argon Dating

Some very early archaeological sites can be dated by a radioactive counting technique known as **potassium–argon dating.** Geologists use this method to date rocks as early as 4 to 5 billion years old and as recent as 100,000 years before the present. Potassium (K) is one of the most abundant elements in the earth's crust and is present in nearly every mineral. In its natural form, potassium contains a small proportion of radioactive ^{40}K atoms. For every 100 ^{40}K atoms that decay, 11 percent become ^{40}Ar, an inactive gas that can easily escape from its present material by diffusion when lava and other molten rocks are formed. As volcanic rocks form by crystallization, the concentration of ^{40}Ar drops to almost nothing, but the decay of ^{40}K continues, and 11 percent of every 100 ^{40}K atoms will become ^{40}Ar. It is possible therefore, using a spectrometer, to measure the concentration of ^{40}Ar that has accumulated since the rock formed.

Many archaeological sites, such as those at Olduvai Gorge, Tanzania, were formed during periods of intense volcanic activity. Dates have been determined for contemporary volcanic ashes, sometimes stratified above and below places where human tools and broken animal bones lie. Louis and Mary Leakey were able to determine potassium–argon dates for artifact and bone scatters at Olduvai, where early human fossils were found. The samples gave readings of about 1.75 million years.

Even earlier dates have come from sites at *Hadar* in Ethiopia and *Laetoli* in Tanzania, both in East Africa, where volcanic materials associated with early human fragments have been dated by potassium–argon techniques to more than three million years ago. Stone flakes and chopping tools have come from *Koobi Fora* in northern Kenya, dated to about 2.3 million years.

Like ^{14}C, potassium–argon dates have a standard deviation, a few tens of thousands of years for early Pleistocene sites. On the other hand, because some of the world's most important early archaeological sites are found in volcanically active areas, we are fortunate in having at least a provisional chronology for the earliest chapters of human evolution, one far more accurate than the educated guesses of earlier generations. Potassium–argon dating is getting ever more accurate, and 1- to 3-million-year-old East African dates now have standard deviations in the 20,000- to 50,000-year range. Recent improvements in dating techniques have both reduced statistical errors and extended the range of potassium-argon dates into the past 100,000 years. Perhaps, one day, potassium-argon will take over where radiocarbon dating leaves off, dating sites as recent as 40,000 years old. In recent years, a number of experimental dating methods such as fission track dating of minerals and some natural glasses like obsidian have helped confirm the reliability of early potassium argon dates.

Archaeologists base their studies of time on precise stratigraphic excavations and records and on proven as well as experimental dating techniques. These data and analyses provide a provisional time scale for world prehistory. Potassium–argon dates place human origins at least as early as 2.5 million years ago, the appearance of *Homo erectus* to about 1.5 million. Radiocarbon dates assign the earliest cave art of western Europe to earlier than 20,000 B.C., the origins of agriculture in the Near East to before 8000 B.C. We know that Mesopotamians were living in sizable city-states by 3200 B.C., the Olmec of Mexico flourishing before 1000 B.C. Tree-ring chronologies date Mesa Verde, Colorado, to A.D. 1150, and historical records and artifacts of known age enable us to cross-date hundreds of sites in Europe and the Americas within the recent millennia of prehistory. Hence, we have developed the first provisional chronology for a truly global world history and prehistory.

5

SPACE

After an artifact has been exposed, its position must be recorded. This information is as significant as the artifact itself.

Robert Heizer, 1958

Space—not the limitless space of the heavens, but a precisely defined location for every find made during an archaeological survey and excavation—is another vital dimension of archaeological context. Every archaeological find has an exact location in latitude, longitude, and depth measurement, which together identify any point in space absolutely and uniquely. When carrying our surface surveys or excavations, archaeologists use special methods to record the precise positions of artifacts, dwellings, and other finds. They tie in the position of each site to accurate survey maps so that they can use the grid coordinates on the map to define the location precisely on the landscape. When investigating a site, they lay out recording grids made up of equal squares over the entire site, using the grids to record the exact position of each object on the surface or in the trenches (see Figure 7.1 on page 112 for a site grid).

In Chapters 1 and 3, we saw that human behavior is patterned. Thus, it leaves patterns in the archaeological record that we can detect and interpret through the archaeologist's *spatial analysis*—the analysis of spatial relationships.

Spatial location is indispensable to archaeologists because it enables them to establish the distances between objects or dwellings, or between entire settlements, or between settlements and key vegatational zones and landmarks. Such distances may be a few inches of level ground between a fine clay pot and the skeleton of its dead owner, or 10 miles separating two seasonal camps. A team of fieldworkers may record the distance measurements between dozens of villages that traded luxury goods such as seashells over hundreds of miles. We

can now distinguish two spatial considerations: the distribution of artifacts *within* a settlement, and the distribution of the *settlements themselves.* We return to this topic—settlement archaeology—in Chapter
10.

Context in space is closely tied to peoples' behavior. Archaeologists examine both an artifact itself and its association with other artifacts to gain insight into human behavior. The patterning of artifacts
around an abandoned iron-smelting furnace or near the bones of a
slaughtered bison is good evidence for specific human behavior. An
isolated projectile head can tell you only that it was used as a weapon;
but the patterning of projectile heads, scraping tools, and large boulders associated with a bison skeleton supply a spatial relationship that
allows much more detailed inferences.

Collections of similar artifacts at contemporary sites within a reasonable geographic range are likely to have been made by people with
the same culture. Such consistent patternings of artifact collections are
the basis for classifying "archaeological cultures" and for studying how
prehistoric cultures differ over space and through time (Chapter 8).

Space involves archaeologists in two directions of inquiry. The first
is part of the process of describing one's finds, of determining the cultural origins of artifacts. This procedure of ordering is described more
fully in Chapter 8, where we discuss some of the arbitrary analytical
devices that archaeologists use. The second aspect of space involves
studying specific activities—economic, religious, social, technological—within a human settlement. These patternings may reflect the
activities of a person, a household, or an entire community.

THE LAW OF ASSOCIATION

In the first analysis, context in space is based on **associations** between
artifacts and other evidence of human behavior around them. Let us
say you find a beer can opener in a plowed field. An expert on such
artifacts—and they can be found—usually can date your opener to
within a few years of its manufacture by going to manufacturers' files
or U.S. Patent Office records. But your beer can opener was an isolated find. No other signs of human activity were discovered nearby.
How could you infer, if you were not a twentieth-century American,
that the artifact was used for opening a can? But had you found the
can opener in association with a dozen punctured beer cans of similar
age, you could then infer the general activity that took place and you
could draw some conclusions about the purposes for which the artifact
in question was designed.

The law of stratigraphic association is based on the principle that
an artifact is contemporary with the other objects found in the precise
archaeological **horizon** in which it is found (Figure 5.1). The proof that

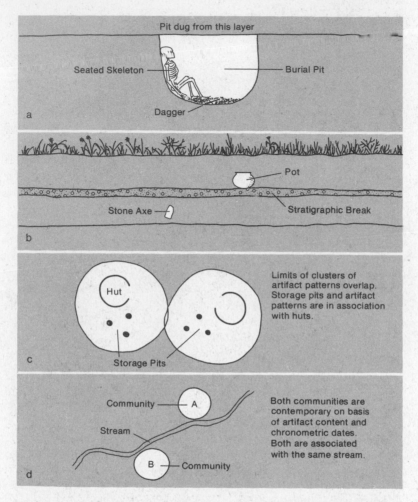

Figure 5.1 The law of association: (a) a skeleton associated with a dagger; (b) a pot and a stone axe, separated by a stratigraphic break, which are not in association; (c) two contemporary household clusters associated with each other; (d) an association of communities that are contemporary.

humanity was far older that the 6000 years of Biblical chronology came when scientists found ancient stone axes in association with the bones of apparently older extinct animals. The mummy of Egyptian Pharaoh Tutankhamun was associated with an astonishing treasury of household possessions and ritual objects. This association provided unique information on Egyptian life in 1342 B.C. The mummy alone would have been far less informative.

The law of association is of great importance when one is ordering artifacts in chronological sequences. Many prehistoric societies buried their dead with grave furniture—clay pots, bronze ornaments, seashells, or stone axes. In some cases, the objects buried with a corpse were obviously in use when their owner died. Occasionally, they may be prized heirlooms, passed down from generation to generation. Together they are an association of artifacts, a grave group that may be found duplicated in dozens of other contemporary graves. But later graves may be found to contain quite different furniture, vessels of a

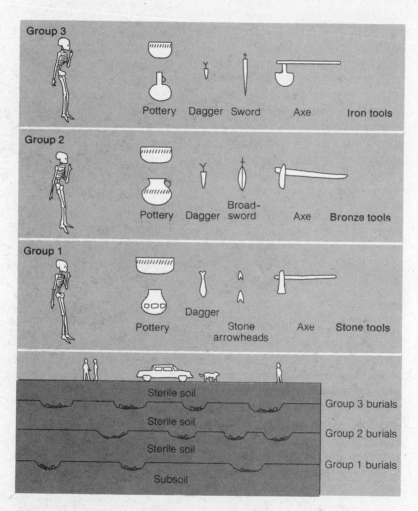

Figure 5.2 Burial groups divided into chronological groups by assessing associated artifacts. Group 1 burials contain no metal artifacts, but simple decorated shallow bowls that were made by all burial groups and show cultural continuity through time. The stone arrowheads of Group 1 are replaced by metal swords; daggers continue in use, made successively in stone, bronze, and iron. Continuity of artifacts is sufficient to place groups in sequence using the law of association; this grouping was in fact confirmed by stratigraphic observation, shown at the bottom.

slightly altered form. Obviously some cultural changes had taken place. When dozens of burial groups are analyzed in this way, the asso ciations and changing artifact styles may provide a basis for dividing the burials into different chronological groups (Figure 5.2).

Archaeological context can be both primary and secondary, as best illustrated with a burial mound. Someone important dies. His or her kinfolk bury the important personage in a lavishly decorated grave covered with a large earthen mound, visible from a long distance. This is the **primary context** of the burial mound. Many centuries later, some other people come along and bury a series of bodies in shallow pits dug into the higher levels of the mound. These are *intrusive* burials, in a secondary context. If one of the later graves impinges upon the original grave pit, perhaps disturbing the body, archaeologists speak of primary and secondary burials.

SUB-ASSEMBLAGES AND ASSEMBLAGES

Human behavior can be individual and totally unique, shared with other members of one's family or clan, or common to all members of the community. All these levels of cultural behavior should, theoretically, be reflected in artifact patterns and associations in the archaeological record. The iron projectile point found in the backbone of a British war casualty of A.D. 43 is clearly the consequence of one person's behavior, but that behavior is clearly related to the common cultural behavior of the warrior's society (Figure 5.3).

When more than one artifact is found in a patterned association that reflects the shared cultural behavior of a group of individuals, the artifacts are grouped in **sub-assemblages,** part of a toolkit that reflects a specific activity. A hunter uses a bow and arrows, which are carried in a quiver. An auto mechanic uses wrenches, screwdrivers, and gauges. Such sub-assemblages of artifacts are confined to particular individuals in society.

But what happens when quite dissimilar subassemblages of artifacts—let us say, hunting weapons and baskets and also digging sticks used in collecting plant foods—are found in a contemporary association? The artifacts together reflect in their patterning the shared activities of a total community and are known as an **assemblage.**

This shared behavior is reflected in the remains of houses—in the nonportable artifacts such as storage pits and hearths, inside and outside of them—and in community settlement patterns. Some early prehistoric Mexican villages consisted of groupings of square, thatched houses. Each house contained sub-assemblages that reflected the behavior of individual males and females, sub-assemblages inferred from artifact associations and patternings. The patterned household groups

Figure 5.3 An iron arrowhead embedded in the backbone of a British warrior killed during a battle with Roman soldiers at Maiden Castle, England, in A.D. 43.

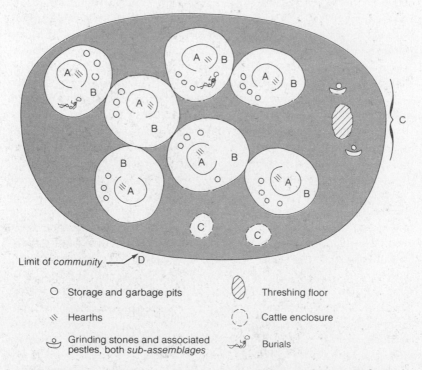

Figure 5.4 A hypothetical prehistoric farming village: A, houses; B, household areas; C, activity areas; D, the community; E, sub-assemblages.

in the village—that is, the associations of those sub-assemblages and the features associated with them—make up the larger assemblage of human behavior in space that constitutes the entire community (Figure 5.4).

HOUSEHOLDS, COMMUNITIES, AND ACTIVITY AREAS

Archaeological sites can be classified in several ways. One way is by location: hilltop site, cave, rockshelter, hot-spring village, and so on. They can also be classified by the types of activity that took place in them. These activities are distinguished by patterning of artifacts and food remains within households and within the settlement. A kill site is identified by the presence of dismembered bison skeletons associated with scattered stone projectile heads and butchering tools. We find no houses, workshop areas, burials, or storage pits at a kill site; this is simply where the people cut their prey.

Some sites defy such classification. The 1.75 million-year-old scatters of human artifacts and broken animal bones at Olduvai Gorge, Tanzania, lie in clusters of stone flakes and bones, with occasional gaps between them. Originally, Louis and Mary Leakey believed these were campsites, places where very early humans had dwelt for a few days while butchering game. But more recent research rejects this hypothesis, for close examination of the weathering on the bones shows that many had lain on the ancient land surface for between four and ten years. Most of them are limb bones from a very diverse group of mammals, large and small. Many of the bones bear both stone tool cut marks and telltale gnawings by carnivores such as hyenas. It may be that the accumulations of bones and stone tools marked places where early humans brought meat-rich bones they grabbed from lion and other predator kills. At such locations, they hastily cut off meat and marrow before abandoning the bones to prowling carnivores. The Olduvai "campsites" may, in fact, be bone caches, locations used again and again over long periods to dump bones from animal carcasses.

Many later settlements contain the remains of individual houses, each occupied by a group of people who were members of a **household unit.** In these instances, we can examine the artifacts, hearths, and broken bones within, and around, the confines of one dwelling, and then compare the activities of individual households. Each house had its own storage areas, garbage pits, and so on, in much the same way as every suburban household today has its own garage and garbage cans (Figure 5.4). All the households in one settlement make up a **community.**

Activity areas are identified from characteristic artifact patternings preserved in the ground that reflect a set of tasks carried out by one or more members of a community (Figure 5.4). Activity areas can usually be identified by mapping a scatter of tools characteristic of a specialist activity such as bead making or stone-tool manufacture. Such activities usually took place within a limited area. Under favorable archaeological conditions, these artifact distributions can be used to compare differences in activities between separate households within a community. Some families may have been specialists in stone knife making, and others made shell beads or were expert metalworkers. The activity areas in these households may reflect such skills.

The behavior of an entire community is reflected in the distribution of houses and households, activity areas, and individual artifacts.

CULTURE AREAS AND SETTLEMENT PATTERNS

But what happens when one considers several communities that share activities? Big-game hunting, long-distance trade, major religious ceremonies, and other such activities are often shared by entire cultures and societies. But these behavior patterns can be identified only by patterning in a number of assemblages at different sites. Such consistent patternings of assemblages represent an **archaeological culture,** the archaeological equivalent of a human society (Chapters 3 and 8). Archaeological cultures consist of material remains of human culture preserved at a specific space and time at several sites. A **culture area** is the geographic area over which the assemblages that make up a unique culture are defined in time and space. An example from New Zealand might be the Maori culture area, the region over which the characteristic toolkits of these remarkable people are found.

To see how behavior in a prehistoric society as a whole was patterned requires analyzing the ways in which communities and their associated assemblages are distributed on the landscape. Such distributions form **settlement patterns,** which we study with the aid of distribution maps. Many factors interact to determine settlement paterns. These include the natural environment with its seasonal changes, the distribution of plant and animal food resources, peoples' economic practices, and technological skills. Learned cultural patterns and established relationships between different peoples have a compelling influence on settlement patterns in some societies.

The !Kung* San hunter-gatherers of the Kalahari Desert live in small camps of a few families by small water holes (Figure 5.5). They move campsites through the year as water supplies become more plentiful or scarcer and vegetable foods within walking distance of each

---

*The ! symbol denotes a click sound made with the tongue.

Figure 5.5 A San nuclear family group; a few families live together in camp-sites near water holes, moving as water supplies increase or diminish.

home base are exhausted. Each group of families has a regular set of localities they camp at each year. The amount of time they spend at each varies. The resources of their hunting-and-gathering territory can support only a few people per square mile, and so the different camps are widely dispersed over the landscape. Because the San have no large containers for carrying water or great quantities of food, they return home most nights having ventured out only as far as they can walk, forage comfortably, and return in daylight. Thus, the !Kung settlement pattern of widely dispersed campsites by water holes results from many interlinked variables.

A settlement pattern and a culture area do not necessarily coincide. The settlement patterns of the Maya in Mesoamerica consisted of large ceremonial centers with elaborate pyramids, temples, plazas, and houses, surrounded by, and linked with, secondary ceremonial centers, which in turn were related to a hierarchy of lesser settlements. But this Maya settlement pattern is merely one part of the Maya cultural system and culture area, the larger area through which characteristic Maya artifact assemblages can be recognized in time and space.

The concepts of culture, time, and space in archaeology are absolutely inseparable. A minimal definition of archaeology is the study of the interrelations between the form of artifacts found in a site and their date and spatial location. All scientific archaeology, whether survey, excavation, laboratory analysis, or sophisticated theoretical argument encompassing thousands of artifacts, is based on the two critical concepts—time and space—that make up archaeological context.

6

PRESERVATION AND SURVEY

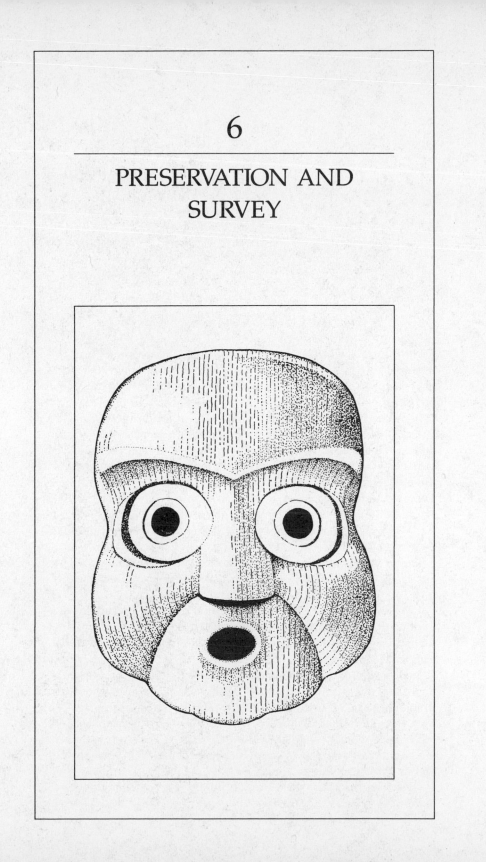

*Antiquities are history defaced, or some remnants of history
which have casually escaped the shipwreck of time.*

Francis Bacon, 1605

THE ARCHAEOLOGICAL RECORD

Prehistoric archaeologists study ancient human behavior by way of the traces of such behavior that survive in food remains, structures, and manufactured objects. These material remains form the *archaeological record*, the archives of human history before written records.

The archaeological record comprises all kinds of archaeological finds, from the pyramids of Giza to an early human butchery site at Olduvai Gorge, Tanzania, occupied nearly two million years ago. California shell mounds, Ohio earthworks, Inca cemeteries, all are part of the archaeological record. So too are isolated artifacts—the throne of Tutankhamun ("King Tut"), a wooden religious mask from a midwestern burial mound, and a Polynesian stone adze.

We seek to find out about prehistoric people from the traces of their activities. The carcass of a mammoth butchered 20,000 years ago is a mine of information on ancient hunting practices. Analysis of dried-out seeds or ancient human body waste found in archaeological sites tells us much about prehistoric diet.

What we can find out about the past is severely limited, however, by the state of preservation of archaeological finds. Some substances, such as baked clay or stone, will survive indefinitely. But wood, bone, leather, and other organic materials soon vanish except under water-logged, frozen, or exceptionally dry conditions. Everyone has heard of the remarkable tomb of Egyptian Pharaoh Tutankhamun, whose astonishing treasure survived almost intact in the dry climate of the Nile Valley for more than 3000 years (Figure 6.1). This archaeological record is exceptionally complete and informative. We even know, from the bouquet of wildflowers laid on his inner coffin, that Tutankhamun's funeral took place in the spring.

But most archaeological sites are found where only a few durable materials survive. Constructing the past from these finds is a chal-

Figure 6.1 The throne of Egyptian Pharaoh Tutankhamun, one of the many wood artifacts recovered from the richest royal sepulcher ever found.

lenge, the sort of problem faced by the detective piecing together the circumstances of a crime from a few fragmentary clues. The analogy is close: Take two spark plugs, a fragment of a china cup, a needle, a grindstone, and a candlestick. Imagine someone from Patagonia digging them up in 1000 years' time and trying to tell you how the makers used the objects. This analysis is precisely what the archaeologist does in going about the work of being a special type of anthropologist.

The data we amass from **surface survey** (looking for sites) and **excavation** (digging) make up the archaeological record. The two basic units studied by archaeologists are **sites** and **artifacts.**

Site-Formation Processes

"The time machine, which has enchanted generations of readers and moviegoers, is a fictional artifact for transporting people through time. Although archaeologists would welcome a time machine, we are satisfied by the remarkable fact that objects made, used, and deposited in the past survive into the present. We need not go to the past, for it comes to us." Archaeologist Michael Schiffer's point is well taken, for the objects from the past that survive come down to us in two forms, either as historically documented artifacts, such as, for example, Orville and Wilbur Wright's first airplane, or in the archaeological record as abandoned artifacts that are no longer part of a living society. The past in the form of artifacts does not come down to us unchanged, for complex processes have acted upon these objects, be they tools, dwellings, burials, food remains, or other manufactured or humanly modified items. Archaeologists have not only to study these artifacts but to untangle the many events and processes that contribute to the great variability in the archaeological record. The factors that create the historic and archaeological records are known as site-formation processes. Site-formation processes are those agencies, natural or cultural, that have transformed the archaeological (or historical) record since a site was abandoned. There are two basic forms of site-formation processes: cultural processes and noncultural processes.

Cultural processes are those where human behavior has transformed the archaeological record. They can vary widely in their impact and intensity. For example, later occupants of a surface that was a hunter-gatherer camp in the Near East may have been farmers and goat herders rather than hunters. The foundations of their houses cut deeply into underlying soil, while the hooves of their penned goats trampled on, and scattered, small stone artifacts lying on the surface.

People also reuse artifacts. To conserve prized tools and valuable raw materials, one may change the use of an artifact from a knife to a scraper or recycle a projectile point to another use. Sometimes prestigious or valuable objects become prized heirlooms passed down from generation to generation, or are buried with the dead—as soapstone pipes and other artifacts were with Hopewell kin leaders in the Midwest more than 2000 years ago. Reuse, especially of such commodities as building materials, can become a potent factor in settlements that are occupied for longer periods of time, where people recycle old bricks and other materials for new dwellings. Then there is the dumping of trash. Whether underfoot or, in secondary locations, trash heaps may form. These heaps often tend to cluster in specific locations that can be used for many generations, perhaps in a convenient, abandoned storage pit or an old dwelling. Disposal of the dead can also be viewed as another form of discard behavior. It is a great mistake to think of any form of human discard behavior as random. The archaeologist must decipher the complicated behavioral processes—perhaps the logic, if you will—behind the accumulation of trash heaps, the disposal of the dead, and many other activities.

In short, the archaeological record is not a safe place for artifacts, for myriad human activities can disturb them after deposition—plowing, mining, digging of foundations, land clearance, and even artillery bombardment, to say nothing of pot hunting and site looting.

Noncultural processes are the events and processes of the natural environment that affect the archaeological record. The chemical properties of the soil or bacteria may accelerate the decay of organic remains such as wooden spears or dwellings or even increase the chances of superb preservation. Rivers may overflow and inundate a settlement, mantling the abandoned remains with fine silt. A great earthquake can topple a settlement in a few minutes, as happened to the Roman port at *Kourion* in Cyprus in A.D. 365. Windblown sands, ice, and even earthworms can disturb the archaeological record.

Whether site-formation processes are cultural or noncultural, the important point is that one can never take the archaeological record at face value. What the archaeologist sees in the ground is not necessarily a direct reflection of human behavior. The archaeologist has not only to record, analyze, and interpret the archaeological record at face value; he or she also must investigate the formation processes that altered the record from the moment of its deposition.

Site-formation processes must be identified before behavioral or environmental inferences are made about any archaeological site. It is not enough to observe conditions of unusually good preservation or to describe the complex layers of a prehistoric rockshelter. One must also analyze and interpret the ways in which the archaeological record was formed—site-formation processes. As Michael Schiffer put it: "The real time machine, then, is the archaeological process: the principles and procedures that we as scientists apply to material traces in the historical and archaeological records. If we desire to obtain views of the past that are closer to reality . . . then we must build into our time machine a thorough understanding of formation processes." This chapter examines some exceptional preservation conditions for archaeological remains and discusses some of the ways in which archaeologists find archaeological sites.

The environment is a hostile place for human artifacts. The process of interacting with it causes deterioration and drastic modification to many properties of artifacts, affecting everything from color and texture to weight, shape, and chemical composition. The environmental agents of deterioration can be grouped into chemical, physical, and biological categories. Chemical agents are universal, for the atmosphere contains water and oxygen, which create many chemical reactions, for example, corrosion of some metals, Different water temperatures, irradiation of materials by sunlight, and atmospheric pollutants all cause chemical reactions. Buried objects are often subject to rapid chemical change, especially as a result of dampness. Soils also contain reactive compounds such as acids and bases, which contribute to deterioration—acid soils dissolve bones, for example. Many archaeological deposits are somewhat salty, a condition caused by salts derived from wood ash, urine, and the neutralization of acids and bases. Such saline conditions can retard some decay, but react severely with cooper, iron, and silver.

Physical agents of deterioration such as water, wind, sunlight, and earth movement are also universal. Water is especially potent, for it can tumble artifacts on the shoreline sometimes even fracturing them in ways that suggest human intervention. Rainwater can cascade off roofs and tunnel deep grooves into walls. Cycles of wetness followed by dryness can crack wood and cause rot, while melting and freezing ice cracks rocks and concrete. Physical agents operate on small and large scales alike. For example, the effects of the Kourion earthquake in Cyprus not only flattened the small port, but affected the landscape for miles around.

Living organisms are the main agents of biological decay. Bacteria occur almost everywhere, and are usually the first to colonize dead organic matter and to begin the processes of decay. Fungi also occur widely, and are especially destructive to wood and other plant matter, particularly in warm, damp climates. Beetles, ants, flies, and termites infest archaeological sites, especially middens and abandoned foods. Dogs, hyenas, and other such animals gnaw, chew, and scavenge bones and other organic materials from the surface of abandoned sites and game kills.

Not only artifacts but the actual physical sites as well are affected by the processes within the natural environment of which they are part. Archaeologists who spend most of their time in the field are often known as "dirt archaeologists," because they are always working with one of the primary constituents of an archaeological site—the soil. The first human activity at any site takes place on a natural surface, on natural sediments sitting on underlying bedrock. Sometimes this underlying sediment was weathered over a long time, and may contain pollen grains, plant remains, or other sources of environmental information. Some Bronze Age burial mounds in Europe were erected on undisturbed soils that contained forest pollen grains, giving a picture of the local environment at the time of construction. After a site is abandoned, additional sediments usually accumulate on top of the archaeological remains, sediments accumulated by wind or water action, such as the windblown sands that accumulate in the rooms of southwestern pueblos. The footsteps of humans and animals as well as burrowing animals, earthworms, wall flakings from overhanging cliffs, and the deteriorating elements of artifacts and structures contribute to the alteration of archaeological deposits. Stone Age rockshelters in southwestern France, for example, were occupied intermittently by hunter-gatherer groups between 30,000 and 15,000 years ago. Some of the larger ones contain densely packed layers of hearths, ash accumulations, boulders, and decaying structures. Untangling how these levels were formed is a complex process. A myriad of different environmental processes contribute to site formation and can transform the archaeological record in ways that can be mistaken for traces of human behavior.

The preservation of such fragile organic archaeological remains as bone, leather, skin, textiles, and wood depends on their physical environment. Soil and climatic conditions very strongly influence archaeological materials. The inorganic artifacts—stone, baked clay pots, mud bricks, gold, copper, and bronze—are preserved best. Much of the surviving archaeological record consists of such durable materials in the form of human tools (Figure 6.2).

Prehistoric peoples used many organic substances, materials that survive at relatively few locations. Bone and antler were commonly used by early hunter-gatherers, especially in Europe some 15,000 years ago. The desert peoples of western North America relied heavily on plant fibers and baskets for their material culture. Both hard and soft woods were used for digging sticks, bows and arrows, and other tools and weapons. Cotton textiles were much prized in coastal Peru 2000 years ago. Nearly every human society collected wild vegetable foods for part of their livelihood. These and traces of broken animal bones and other food remains are sometimes found when preservation conditions are favorable.

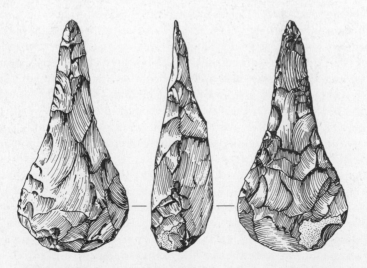

Figure 6.2 Three views of an Acheulian stone axe from Swanscombe on the River Thames, England.

FAVORABLE PRESERVATION CONDITIONS

What are the most favorable conditions for preservation of archaeological finds? The fantastically rich tomb of the Egyptian Pharaoh Tutankhamun, who died in 1342 B.C., yielded incredible finds, including his personal wooden furniture, much of his clothing, and the perishable ritual objects that accompanied the dead king to the next world (see Figure 6.1). Tutankhamun's tomb is the only pharaoh's burial ever to be discovered intact, undisturbed by tomb robbers. The richness of the grave furniture came as a complete surprise. And the survival of the funeral bouquets, which showed that the king had died in the spring, was certainly exceptional. Dry conditions like those of the Nile Valley have led to remarkable discoveries in the desert of the western United States as well, where caves in Utah and Nevada have yielded not only sandals, bows and arrows, and other wood and fiber objects, but thousands of seeds, and even human excrement (coprolites or feces), which can be analyzed to give information on prehistoric diet (Chapter 9).

Waterlogged, flooded sites too aid preservation. They can seal off organic finds in an oxygen-free atmosphere. Danish archaeologists have found prehistoric dugout canoes deep in ancient peat bogs, along with leather clothing, traps, and wood spears. Their most famous finds are the corpses of sacrificial victims buried in the bogs more than 2000 years ago. We can gaze on the serene countenance of Tollund man. His corpse is in such excellent condition that we know he did not eat for at least 24 hours before his death, and that his last meal was a porridge of barley and wild grasses (Figure 6.3).

Richard Daugherty gained unusual insights into prehistoric whale hunting on the Northwest coast of North America by digging a Makah Indian village at *Ozette*, Washington, long buried by sudden mudslides. The wet mud crushed cedar plank houses by the ocean, sealing their contents from the destructive effects of the atmosphere. The Ozette village was occupied for more than 2000 years, right into the twentieth century. Daugherty's buried houses provided a wealth of information about Makah life and artistic traditions of centuries ago. The thick mud preserved walls and beams, sleeping benches, and fine mats. Wood fish hooks, seal-oil bowls, cedar storage boxes, and whaling harpoons were uncovered by fine water jets from pressure hoses washing mud from soft wood. The most remarkable find of all was a whale fin carved of red cedar and inlaid with sea otter teeth, a unique ritual object without parallel in North America (Figure 6.4). Fortunate is the archaeologist who finds a site with conditions as good as those at *Ozette*. They are very much the exception rather than the rule.

Arctic cold has frozen the past, often literally refrigerated human behavior in dramatic ways. For example, archaeologists have been able

Figure 6.3 Tollund Man, a remarkably well-preserved corpse discovered in the peat bogs of Denmark.

to solve the mystery of a vanished Victorian expedition. On May 19, 1845, veteran Arctic explorer Sir John Franklin left London in command of the most completely equipped arctic expedition ever to search for the famed Northwest Passage across far northern Canada. *H.M.S. Erebus* and *H.M.S. Terror* sailed into the remote north from western Greenland in July of the same year, and were never seen again. De-

Figure 6.4 Richard Daugherty examining a whale fin carved of cedar wood, found at the Ozette site, and inlaid with 700 sea otter
teeth. The teeth at the base are set in the design of a mythical
bird with a whale in its talons.

spite lengthy searches, the cause for the disaster was never established
until the 1980s, when modern forensic medicine came into play.

In 1981, physical anthropologist Owen Beattie applied for permission to exhume the remains of Franklin's men—Petty Officer John
Torrington, Able Seaman John Hartnell, and Marine Private William
Braine—who had been interred on Beechey Island in the Canadian
arctic. Their caskets were well preserved, Torrington's covered with
blue wool fabric decorated with white tape. A handpainted, wrought-
iron plaque, perhaps fashioned from a tin can, bore the inscription
"John Torrington, died January 1st, 1846, aged 20 years." The excavators had to thaw the ice around the coffin lid and shear the nails. The
body was encased in a block of ice, which was melted with buckets of
heated water. Soon Torrington's perfectly preserved toes and the front
of his shirt came into view. The head was covered with a fold of blue
wool. When the cloth was drawn back with tweezers, John Torrington's perfectly preserved countenance stared at them (Figure 6.5). For
the first time, scientists gazed not at a crude drawing or a primitive
photograph of their forebears, but at the face of an actual nineteenth-
century human being. It was a startling and emotional experience.

John Torrington had been buried in simple, gray linen trousers

Figure 6.5 The well-preserved burial of Petty Officer John Torrington, Royal Navy, Beechey Island, Canada, who died January 1, 1846.

and a white shirt with blue stripes with a high collar and pleated waist. A white, polka-dotted kerchief covered his medium brown hair. An on-site autopsy revealed that he had stood 5 feet 4 inches (138 cm) tall, and had been very emaciated at the time of death. Laboratory tests on his organs told a tale of serious medical problems for such a young man. His lungs were blackened by inhalation of coal dust and smoke, and other atmospheric pollutants. Since Torrington was a stoker, this is hardly surprising. He was suffering from emphysema and tuberculosis, and had probably died of pneumonia. However, the real cause of death was probably the severe mental and physical problems caused by lead poisoning, for trace element analyses of his hair gave readings of more than 600 parts per million, evidence of acute lead poisoning.

The bodies of John Hartnell and William Braine were exhumed in 1986, and also bore signs of serious lead poisoning. Beattie's detailed autopsies painted a picture of an expedition plagued by catastrophic health problems, almost certainly resulting from lead poisoning. Loss of energy and poor appetites, neurotic and illogical behavior, acute depression—these symptoms, especially the mental ones, were especially deadly in the stressful conditions of the arctic. The lead concentrations probably came from the solder used to seal the tinned foods consumed by members of the expedition, and many of the foods may have been spoiled owing to poor sealing.

There were, of course, many causes of the ultimate failure of the Franklin expedition, but the near-perfect preservation conditions of the arctic have provided modern science with a possible underlying cause for one of the great tragedies of nineteenth-century exploration.

Eskimo archaeology has benefited greatly from frozen soils, for beautiful ivory and bone artifacts have survived almost intact for thousands of years. The Arctic artistic traditions of the North have been dated back, by means of changing motifs and styles of harpoons, thousands of years ago (Figure 6.6). And near Barrow, Alaska, permafrost conditions literally refrigerated an Eskimo family buried in their driftwood house centuries ago by a sudden ice surge from the nearby ocean. The sleeping women were preserved so completely that it was possible to establish that both suffered from lung diseases caused by the soot from oil lamps.

But most archaeological sites yield only a fraction of the organic materials buried in them. The fortunate archaeologist may recover not only manufactured tools but some food remains as well—animal bones or a handful of shells, seeds, or other vegetable remnants. Obviously the picture one obtains of the inhabitants at such a site is incomplete compared with that from Ozette, *Ipiutak,* and elsewhere. And, because of archaeologists' constant preoccupation with ancient environments and prehistoric lifeways, sites with exceptional preservation conditions are obviously of paramount importance.

Figure 6.6 A walrus ivory object of unknown use of the Ipiutak culture, about 1500 years old, 26 centimeters long. The Arctic artistic traditions of North America have been dated by means of changing motifs and styles on bones and ivory artifacts.

FINDING ARCHAEOLOGICAL SITES

How do you know where to dig? How do you find sites or conduct an archaeological survey? Many people are amazed at how archaeologists seem to have an uncanny ability to choose the place for their excavations. Yet, most often they have merely used common sense or well-tried survey techniques to locate their site.

Finding archaeological sites involves far more than merely locating a prehistoric settlement to dig. Some archaeological sites are so conspicuous that people have always known of their existence. The pyramids of Giza in Egypt have withstood the onslaught of tourists, treasure hunters, and quarrymen for thousands of years. The Pyramid of the Sun at *Teotihuacán*, Mexico, is another easily visible archaeological site (see Figure 10.1). The eastern United States is dotted with hundreds of burial mounds and earthworks, which are easily distinguished from the surrounding countryside. Sites of this type are obviously simple to identify, and have been known for centuries.

Most archaeological sites are far less conspicuous. They may consist of little more than a scatter of pottery fragments or a few stone tools lying on the surface of the ground. Other settlments may be buried under several feet of soil, leaving few surface traces except when exposed by moving water, wind erosion, or burrowing animals. Cemeteries may be marked by piles of stones, and the deep accumulations of occupation deposits at the mouths of rockshelters or caves or the huge piles of abandoned shells left by collectors are more readily located. Finding archaeological sites depends on locating such telltale traces of human settlement. Once the sites have been found, they have to be recorded, and surface collections must be made at each locality to assemble a general impression of the activities of the people who lived there.

ACCIDENTAL DISCOVERIES

Whole chapters of the past have been retrieved by accidental discoveries of sites, spectacular artifacts, or skeletons. Dramatic finds have resulted from despoiling of the environment. Deep plowing and freeway and dam construction have led to the uncovering—and damaging—of priceless sites. When Mexico City's Metro (subway) was tunneled under the modern city, the 28 miles of tunnels yielded a wealth of archaeological material. Mexico City is built on the site of the Aztec city of Tenochtitlán, overthrown by Hernán Cortés in 1521. Little remains of the Aztec city on the surface today, but the contractors for the Metro recovered 40 tons of pottery, 380 burials, and even a small temple dedicated to the wind god Ehecatl-Quetzalcoatl. The temple is now preserved on its original site as part of the Pino Suarez station of the

Metro system. All the tunneling operations were under the supervision of expert archaeologists, who were empowered to halt construction whenever an archaeological find was made.

Even more dramatic was the accidental rediscovery of the great Templo Mayor in the heart of Mexico City. Modern construction activity revealed the most sacred shrine of Aztec Tenochtitlán, the temples of the gods Huitzilopochtli and Tlaloc. Mexican archaeologist Eduardo Matos Moctezuma's excavations subsequently unearthed at least five successive temples and many rebuildings going back to as early as A.D. 1390, if not earlier. The temple visited by Spanish conquistador Hernán Cortés had 114 steps, with a drum so loud it could be heard 6 miles away. The conquistadors pulled it down to build a Catholic cathedral nearby. The abandoned shrines were forgotten until the 1970s.

The fields of the Western world have yielded many caches of buried weapons, coins, smith's tools, and sacrificial objects, valued treasures that were buried in times of stress by their owners. For whatever reason, the owners never returned to recover their valuables. Thousands of years later, a farmer comes across the hoard and, if a responsible citizen, reports the find to archaeological authorities. If not, yet another valuable fragment of the past is lost to science.

Nature itself sometimes uncovers sites for us, which are then located by a sharp-eyed archaeologist looking for natural exposures of likely geological strata. Olduvai Gorge is a great gash in the Serengeti Plains of northern Tanzania. An ancient earthquake eroded a deep gorge, exposing hundreds of feet of lake beds that had been buried long before. These buried lake deposits have yielded early tool and bone concentrations dating back at least 1.75 million years. They would never have been found without the assistance of an earthquake and subsequent erosion. The Olduvai area is but one of many examples from all over the world where nature has revealed the incredible bounty of the past.

DELIBERATE ARCHAEOLOGICAL SURVEY

An archaeological survey can vary from spending an afternoon searching a city lot for traces of historical structures to a large-scale survey of an entire river basin or drainage area over several years. In all cases, the theoretical ideal is easily stated: to record all traces of ancient settlement in the area. But this ideal is impossible to achieve. Many sites leave no traces above ground. And no survey, however thorough and however sophisticated its remote sensing devices, will ever achieve the impossible dream of total coverage. *The key to effective archaeological survey lies in carefully designing the research before one sets out and in using techniques to estimate the probable density of archaeological sites in the region.*

Archaeological surveys are most effective in terrain where the vegetation is burned off or sparse enough for archaeologists to be able to see the ground. In lush vegetation areas such as those of the American South, only the most conspicuous earthworks will show up. And, of course, thousands of sites are buried under housing developments, parking lots, and artificial lakes, which have radically altered the landscape in many places.

A great deal depends on the intensity of the survey in the field. The most effective surveys are carried out on foot, when the archaeologist can locate the traces of artifacts, the gray organic soil eroding from a long-abandoned settlement, and the subtle colors of rich vegetation that reveal long-buried houses. Plowed fields may display revealing traces of ash, artifacts, or hut foundations. Scatters of broken bones, stone implements, potsherds, or other traces of prehistoric occupation are easily located in such furrowed soil. *Observation is the key to finding archaeological sites and to studying the subtle relationships between prehistoric settlements and the landscape on which they flourished.*

Archaeologists have numerous inconspicuous signs to guide them. Gray soil from a rodent burrow, a handful of humanly fractured stones in the walls of a desert arroyo, a blurred mark in a plowed field, a potsherd—these are the signs they seek. And often, information on possible sites is provided by knowledgeable local inhabitants.

There is far more to archaeological survey than merely walking the countryside, however. Such surveys can be of varying intensity. The least intensive survey is the most common, the investigator examining only conspicuous and accessible sites, those of great size and considerable fame. Heinrich Schliemann followed just this procedure when he located the site of ancient Troy at Hissarlik in Turkey in the 1870s. John Lloyd Stephens and Frederick Catherwood did the same thing when they visited Uxmal, Palenque, and other Maya sites in Mesoamerica in the early 1840s. Such superficial surveys barely scratch the archaeological surface.

A more intensive survey involves collecting as much information about as many sites as possible from local informants and landowners. Again, the sites located by this means are the larger and more conspicuous ones, and the survey is necessarily incomplete. But this approach is widely used throughout the world, especially in areas where archaeologists have never worked before.

Many more discoveries will be made if archaeologists undertake a highly systematic survey of a relatively limited area. This type of survey involves not only comprehensive inquiries among local landowners, but actual systematic checking of the site reports on the ground. The footwork resulting from the checking of local reports may lead to more discoveries. But, again, the picture may be very incomplete, for the survey deals with known sites and does not cover the area systematically from one end to the other or establish the proportions of each type of site known to exist in the region.

The most intensive surveys have a party of archaeologists covering a whole area by walking all over it, often in straight lines, with a set distance between the fieldworkers. Such surveys are usually based on carefully formulated research designs. The investigators are careful to check that their site distributions reflect actual prehistoric settlement patterns rather than where archaeologists walked. Between 1979 and 1981, a group of archaeologists headed by Garth Sampson surveyed several thousand square miles of the Seacow River Valley in South Africa, looking for late-Stone-Age hunting-and-gathering activity. Sampson noticed that most sites lay on low hills and ridges in dense clusters. Did these clusters reflect a concentration of archaeologists or prehistoric reality?

The Sampson team developed a comprehensive survey plan that assessed every part of the study area with aerial photographs, maps, and on the ground. They then decided which areas they would eliminate on the grounds that they were unlikely to yield many sites. An 85-square-kilometer area was randomly selected and covered by a grid of 2.47-acre (1 hectare) squares. Then 66.75 percent of the test area was searched on foot, the reminder, mainly steep slopes and flats, was not visited. Only 6.1 percent of the searched squares yielded sites, suggesting that the observed site clusters were real ones, occupied areas surrounded by zones where no camps or other activity areas were sited. Sampson was able to show that 64 percent of the sites in the test area occurred on 30 percent of the land, all of it within 0.62 mile (1 km) of a dependable water hole. Statistically, this distribution is highly significant. This survey provided valuable information on ancient hunting and settlement practices.

Clearly, most archaeological surveys can record only a sample of the sites in the survey area, even if the declared objective is to plot the position of every prehistoric settlement. Such has been the purpose of an ambitious survey of the Basin of Mexico, home of the Teotihuacán and Aztec civilizations of the past 2000 years. The investigators have managed to chronicle the changing settlement patterns in the Basin since long before Teotihuacán rose to prominence after A.D. 100 right up to the Spanish Conquest and beyond. But they would be the first to admit that they have recovered only a fraction of the Basin's sites. For a start, most of the Aztec capital, Tenochtitlán, and its outlying suburbs lie under the foundations of Mexico City.

In the early days, archaeologists concentrated on conspicuous, easily found sites. Now, with so many sites endangered by all kinds of industrial development, they hurry to locate as many prehistoric locations as possible. Often, a survey is designed to make an inventory of an archaeological resouce base in a specific area. When an area is to be deep-plowed or covered with houses, the burden of proof that archaeological sites do or do not exist in the endangered zone is the responsibility of the archaeologists. Often, time is short and funds are very limited. The only way the archaeologists can estimate the extent of the site resource base is to survey selected areas in great detail. Those areas are determined by careful research design and knowledge of the variables that affect site location. The density and distribution of sites in these areas are then used as a basis for generalizing from the sample survey areas to larger regions. The reliability of these vital generalizations is tested by routine statistical procedures. This approach to archaeological survey, often called predictive modeling, is still relatively new, and is somewhat controversial. It is assuming weight as a weapon to counter the wholesale destruction of archaeological sites by industrial activity. Archaeologists cannot stop the destruction of every threatened site. The best they can hope for is a chance to make decisions on which sites in the archaeological resource base are to be preserved, which excavated before destruction, and which are to be destroyed in the name of progress.

All archaeologists have the responsibility for managing the priceless resource base of sites that is our legacy from the past. More and more archaeology in North America results from efforts to conserve sites and to manage a diminishing resource base. This activity is known as **cultural resource management,** and involves not only finding sites and investigating them, but making decisions about their fate as well— managing the past.

Obviously, accurate maps and record keeping are essential to any archaeological survey. And locating sites is pointless without making some attempt to establish their probable content and age. No one has the resources to excavate every site located in a survey, but, in areas where nothing is known, a representative surface collection from all located sites is essential. The artifacts on the surface of a site can give an idea of the occupations and activities that took place there. Surface collections can give little more than a general impression of site contents, for the effects of pot hunting, erosion and weathering, and burrowing animals can bias surface scatters of artifacts. The site may have been occupied more than once, or may have been the location of some specialist activities such as hunting or stone tool making. In such sites, every object on the surface must be collected according to a carefully formulated design. But even then, surface collection is no substitute for excavation.

AERIAL PHOTOGRAPHY

The building of today's inventories of archaeological sites would never have been possible without aerial survey techniques. Aerial photography gives an overhead view of the past. Sites can be photographed from many directions, at different times of day, and at various seasons. Numerous sites that left almost no surface traces have been discovered by analyzing aerial photographs. Many earthworks and other complex structures have been leveled by plows or erosion, but their original layout shows up clearly from the air (Figure 6.7). The rising or setting sun can make large shadows, emphasizing the relief of almost-vanished banks or ditches; the features of the site stand out in oblique light. Such phenomena are sometimes called shadow sites.

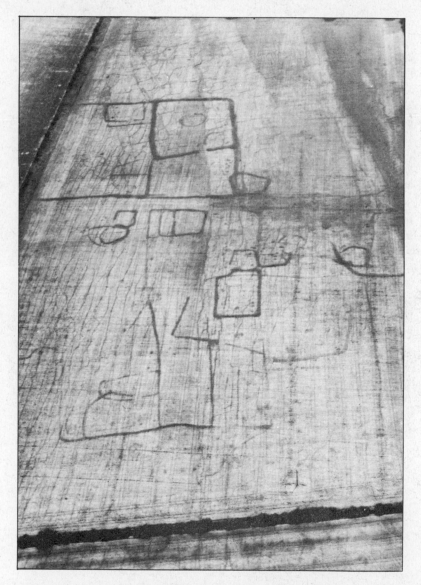

Figure 6.7 A long-lost archaeological site revealed by dark crop marks.

In some areas, it is possible to detect differences in soil color and in the richness of crop growth on a particular soil. Such marks are hard to detect on the surface but often show up clearly from the air. The growth and color of a crop are greatly determined by the amount of moisture the plant can derive from the soil and subsoil. If the soil depth has been increased by digging features such as pits and ditches, later filled in, or because additional earth has been heaped up to form artificial banks or mounds, the crops growing over such abandoned structures are high and well nourished. The opposite is also true, where soil has been removed and the infertile soil is near the surface, or where impenetrable surfaces such as paved streets are below ground level and the crops grow less thickly. Thus, a dark crop mark can be taken for a ditch or pit, and a lighter line will define a more substantial structure.

Much of the world has been photographed from 24,000 feet by military photographers. Such coverage has been put to use by archaeologists to survey remote areas such as the Virú Valley in Peru, where a team of archaeologists led by Gordon Willey plotted 315 sites on a master map of the valley. Many of the sites were stone buildings or agricultural terraces, others were refuse mounds that appeared as low hillocks on the photographs. By using aerial surveys, Willey saved days of survey time, for he was able to pinpoint many sites before going out in the field. When the settlements were visited, the fascinating story of shifting settlement patterns in Virú over thousands of years was made visible by a combination of foot survey and air photography.

REMOTE SENSING

Aerial remote-sensing devices of many types have become available in recent years to complement the valuable results of black-and-white photography. Infrared film, which has three layers sensitized to green, red, and infrared, detects reflected solar radiation at the near end of the electromagnetic spectrum, some of which is invisible to the naked eye. The different reflections from cultural and natural features are translated by the film into distinctive "false" colors. Vigorous grass growth on river plains shows up in bright red. Such red patterns have been used in the American Southwest to track shallow, subsurface water sources where springs were used by prehistoric peoples. The infrared data could lead the archaeologist to likely areas for previously undetected hunting camps and villages.

In some areas, exuberant vegetation hampers archaeological surveys, especially in the Maya lowlands. For years, archaeologists have wondered how the Maya civilization managed to feed itself and have puzzled over the incompletely known distribution of its cities and ceremonial centers. Originally they believed that the Maya population was supported by slash-and-burn cultivation, a system still used today, in which people burn off and clear the forests, then cultivate the land for three or four years before leaving it fallow and moving on to new virgin plots. But so many sites are now known that we can be certain that the population was far larger than such a simple agricultural system could handle. Some surveys and excavations suggested that the Maya may have drained swamps and used irrigated lands, but no large-scale fieldwork was possible in the hot and densely overgrown rainforest.

A group of archaeologists, looking for a sensor system that would penetrate the dense forest cover of the area and see through silt and root cover to map ancient roads, causeways, and other humanly made structures invisible on the surface, discovered an unexpected archaeological payoff in the imaging radar developed by NASA for spaceborne lunar sounders and in synthetic aperture radar. (The radar chosen for the Maya experiment was, in fact, developed for imaging the surface of the planet Venus.) On flights made over the Maya lowlands in 1978 and 1980, black-and-white and color infrared film were used to capture indications of archaeological sites and ancient landscape modifications. When the features discovered were plotted onto topographic maps, they revealed not only shadows of large mounds and buildings, but irregular grids of gray lines within swampy areas near known major sites. These lines were found to form ladder-and-lattice as well as curvilinear patterns, which very closely matched conventional aerial views of known canal systems from the Valley of Mexico and the lowlands. Investigators believe that further radar surveys will reveal that the Maya grew large food surpluses using large-scale swamp agriculture, developing field systems that are nearly invisible on the ground today. The radar method is still experimental, however.

AERIAL SENSOR IMAGERY

Aerial sensor imagery using aricraft, satellites, and even manned spacecraft, is prohibitively expensive and still rarely used in archaeology. The best-known source of aircraft-borne sensor imagery is Sideways-Looking Airborne Radar (SLAR), which senses the terrain on either side of an aircraft's track, with the instrumentation tracking the pulse lines in the form of images, whether or not clouds obscure the ground. This approach has been used not only for tracing Maya agricultural systems, but also to detect buildings under dense rainforest canopy. Ground-penetrating radar now shows promise as an important tool for subsurface detection and has been used with great success on historical sites in Pennsylvania and on Anglo-Saxon settlements in Britain. Satellite sensor imagery is used for both military and environmental monitoring. The best-known satellites are the Landsat series, which scan the earth with readers that detect the intensity of reflected light and infrared radiation from the earth's surface. These data are converted electronically into photographic images and mosaic maps, normally at a scale of about 1:1,000,000, too imprecise except for the most general of archaeological surveys. But Landsat imagery has great potential for studying present and past environments, as a backdrop for more detailed aerial and ground reconnaissance. Aircraft and satellite scanning imagery will be more commonly used in archaeology, but the high cost will probably limit their application for the foreseeable future.

OTHER SURVEY TOOLS

Fortunately, some geophysical prospecting tools are available at a more moderate cost. They are of great use when a site has been located and the archaeologist wants to find buried subsurface features such as stone walls. A resistivity survey meter is sometimes used to measure the variations in the resistance (resistivity) of the ground to electric current. Stone walls or hard pavement retain less dampness than a deep pit filled with soft earth or a silt-filled ditch. These differences can be measured accurately with a resistivity meter, which records the resistivity "contours" across a grid of squares laid out on the site. On well-drained soils, resistivity surveys can locate their drier areas where buried ditches and walls lie.

Most people are familiar with the metal detector, a device used by many beachcombers and treasure hunters to search for loot. Although the companies selling such devices often promote them as a means for finding wealth in the ground, archaeologists have turned such electromagnetic detection devices to good use to find iron objects, fired clay furnaces, hearths, and pottery kilns. A proton magnetometer is used to measure the differences between the remanent magnetism of undisturbed soil and that of nearby subsurface features such as pottery kilns, which have been heated in the past. The heated features retain a weak magnetism different from that of the earth's magnetic field. Magnetic detecting has been used very successfully to record pits, walls, and other features in the middle of large fortified towns and in ceremonial centers where total excavation of a site is clearly uneconomical.

The archaeologist of today cares not only about the discovery of sites but their preservation and management as well. The archaeological record consists of thousands of sites that can never be replaced. In a sense, all archaeologists are managers of this archive. More and more archaeological surveys are conducted in advance of bulldozers and major construction projects. Often archaeologists have to estimate how many sites in an area remain undiscovered after their survey and then recommend to federal or state agencies what measures, if any, should be taken to minimize the effects of a major land-use project on the archaeological resources they have discovered. This type of archaeological survey results from recent local, state, and federal legislation recognizing that archaeological sites are an important natural resource. And the stakes are high. Without adequate surveys and efforts at resource management, the future of archaeology in some parts of the world, especially North America and western Europe, would be in grave doubt. There would simply be nothing left to explore.

7

EXCAVATION

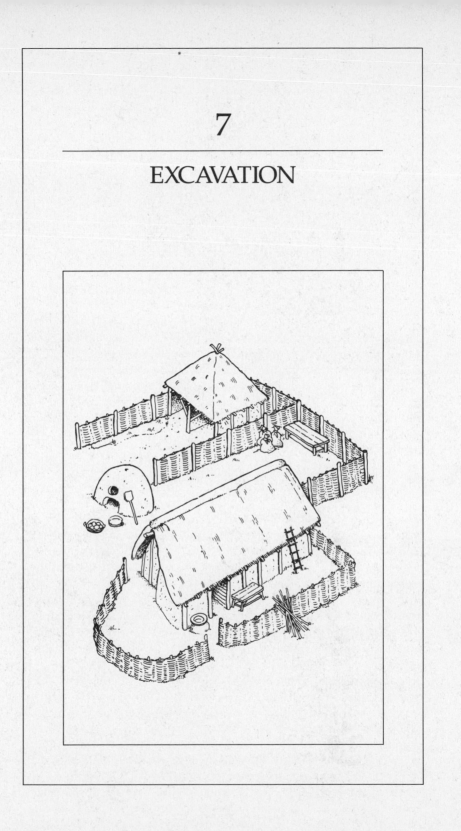

A mere hole in the ground, which of all sights is perhaps the least vivid and dramatic, is enough to grip their attention for hours at a time.

P. G. Wodehouse, 1919

Modern archaeological excavation is a precise and demanding science whose objective is recording archaeological sites and their contents in exact detail. In this chapter we describe some of the basic principles of excavation and some of the many excavation problems that archaeologists can encounter in the field. Realize, though, that each site presents distinctive problems and requires modification of the basic principles enumerated in this chapter.

ARCHAEOLOGICAL PROCEDURES

There was a time when archaeologists concentrated most of their efforts on excavating single sites. They would choose a promising site, excavate it, and study the recovered artifacts without worrying too much about the environmental setting or the broader context of their excavation. Today, archaeologists think in terms of cultural and ecological systems, of interactions between humans and their natural environment. With the new calls for scientific methods in archaeology, the focus has shifted toward regional studies, studies with specific, problem-oriented perspectives, and also toward formal research design.

Regional archaeology is a much more complex process than mere site investigation. Thus, research problems, often involving entire teams of scholars from different disciplines, dictate the creation of systematic, detailed research designs. These designs are created through a formal process that acts as the driving mechanism for the entire research project. In a sense, a research design is like a flow chart, for it is created both to monitor the validity of research results and to maximize efficient use of money, people, and time.

A **research design** divides the research process into specific stages, each of which, in turn, is carefully designed to carry out certain functions. Together they form a sequence of investigation that divides the flow chart into stages—not that the stages necessarily follow one upon the other in close order. Several may be carried out simultaneously. The design may be a formal process, but it must be flexible and fluid enough to accommodate ever-changing circumstances in the field as well as individual needs. It must also accommodate the diverse needs of every participant in the project and bring together all relevant research for final publication.

Archaeological research is thought of in the following general stages:

Design and Formulation. The problem is defined, its feasibility tested, and the entire background for the project researched very carefully. Background research is especially important, as it provides an opportunity to refine research questions. The finished research design includes not only a definition of the research problem, but also a statement of specific goals, including sampling stategies to be used and specific hypotheses to be tested. It is also an accurate definition of the kinds of data the research team will be looking for to test its hypotheses. However, flexibility is essential if the research is not to be shackled too tightly.

Implementation. Fund-raising, an eternal problem for archaeologists, gaining permission for access to land and to excavate, acquiring equipment and a work force—all these are important ingredients of the implementation stage.

Data Acquisition. This is accomplished when field research takes place, and can be merely a preliminary reconnaissance of the research area, a full-scale survey, or an excavation.

Processing and Analysis. Archaeological finds come in many forms—as artifacts, food remains, remains of houses, human skeletons, and so on. These finds are usually cleaned, rough sorted, and cataloged in the field before packing for transport to the laboratory. Once back from the field, these data, including not only finds, but the detailed notes, drawings, and other recorded data acquired in the field, are analyzed. This is the stage at which some specific materials, such as radiocarbon samples and pollen grains, are sent to specialists for analysis. Most laboratory analysis involves detailed artifact classification and study of animal bones and other food remains—the basis for the later interpretation of data (Chapters 8, 9).

Interpretation. During this phase, everything is brought together into an interpretative synthesis to answer the research questions posed in the original design. Anthropological and historical models usually provide the most consistent interpretations of the archaeological record (Chapter 12).

Publication. No research project is complete until the final results are published in a form accessible to other scholars. Unfortunately, many archaeologists neglect publication, forgetting that an unpublished site is effectively destroyed, not only by the excavations, but by the absence of any permanent record of the findings.

The research design is complete only after the results of the work have been published, for only then can the archaeologist move on to another project or use the results from this research design as a foundation for further inquiry in the same region.

PLANNED EXCAVATION

The first principle of excavation is that digging is destructive. As archaeologist Kent Flannery once remarked, archaeologists murder their informants (their sites) when they question them! The archaeological deposits so carefully examined during a dig are destroyed forever. Site contents are removed to a laboratory, permanently divorced from their context in time and space in the ground. And this is a radical difference from other disciplines: A chemist can readily recreate the conditions of a basic experiment, a biographer can return to the archives to reevaluate the complex events in a politician's life, but an archaeologist's archives are destroyed during the dig. All that remains from an excavation are the finds from the trenches, the unexcavated portions of the site, and the photographs, notes, and drawings that record the excavator's observations for posterity. One of the tragedies of archaeology is that much of the available archaeological data have been excavated under far from scientific conditions. Our archives of information are uneven at best.

The treasure hunter destroys a site in search of valuable finds, and keeps no records. Archaeologists destroy sites as well, but with a difference: They create archives of archaeological information that document contexts for the objects they take back to the laboratory with them. Although they have destroyed the site forever, they have created a data bank of information in its place, the only archive their successors will be able to consult to check their results. Archaeologists have serious responsibilities: to record and interpret the significance of the layers, houses, food remains, and artifacts in their sites, and to publish the results for posterity. Without accurate records and meaningful publication of results an excavation is useless. Regrettably, far too many interesting and important excavations have never been recorded in print and the results are lost forever.

A generation ago, archaeologists' first inclination was to dig sites to solve problems. Nowadays, there is increased awareness among archaeologists that excavation destroys irreplaceable evidence of the past and they dig only when they must. Anyone who digs without serious attention to record keeping and all the other processes of excavation is committing vandalism of an unforgivable kind.

At the core of every modern archaeological excavation lies a sound research design, a design that very often has a regional rather than a specific site focus (Chapter 3). The research design is developed to answer specific questions, to acquire a maximum information with a minimum disturbance of finite archaeological resources. It is, of course, a flexible, ever-changing plan, modified as hypotheses are tested, proved wrong, validated, or refined as a result of knowledge acquired in the ongoing excavation.

The design is formulated to extend beyond the excavation itself. The end products of even a month's excavation on a moderately productive site are boxes upon boxes of potsherds, stone tools, animal bones, and other finds that have been cleaned, sorted, and bagged in the field. Rolls of drawings and stacks of computer disks hold valuable stratigraphic information. So also do slides, photographs, and hundreds of pages of field notes compiled by excavation staff as the long days of toil continue. At the same time, radiocarbon and soil samples are collected for later analysis. Freshwater shells and charcoal fragments are packed for shipment to specialist investigators. It takes a minimum of six months to analyze the notes from a month's excavation. The dozens of boxes, hundreds of notebook pages, and the piles of computer disks contain a vast array of data that must be collated to reconstruct what happened at the site. It follows, then, that the excavation research design is constantly reevaluated to determine the future course of the dig and to monitor the long months of analysis and interpretation that follow. The days when a site was dug simply because it "looked good" are long gone.

The organization of even a moderate-sized excavation requires careful planning at the implementation stage of the research design. One classic example of such planning comes from the Midwest. Illinois archaeologists Stuart Struever and James Brown spent many field seasons excavating the *Koster* site in the lower Illinois River Valley. Here, at least 12 human occupations are represented at one site, the earliest of which dates to before 5100 B.C. Koster is a deep site, probably abandoned before A.D. 1000 after generations of Indians had settled at this favorable locality. It offered Brown and Struever a unique opportunity to examine the changing cultures of the inhabitants over more than 6000 years. But the organizational problems were enormous. Koster is more than 30 feet deep, with each of the 12 cultural horizons separated from its neighbor by zones of sterile soil. Brown and Struever were fortunate in that they were able to treat each occupation level of this mammoth site as an entirely separate digging operation.

The archaeologists had two options. One was to dig small test tren-

ches and obtain samples of pottery and other finds from each stratigraphic level. But this approach, although cheaper and commonly
used, was inadequate for the problems to be investigated at the Koster
site. The excavators were interested in studying the origins of agriculture in the lower Illinois Valley. Brown and Struever therefore decided to excavate each living surface on a sufficiently large scale to
study the activities that had taken place there. This procedure would
enable them to examine minute economic changes. Thus, the emphasis in the Koster excavations was on isolating the different settlement
types that lay one on top of the other.

In developing the Koster research design, Brown and Struever
needed to control a mass of complex variables that affected their data.
They had to invent special procedures to ensure the statistical validity
of their excavations. In order to acquire immediate feedback on the
finds made during the excavations, they organized an elaborate data-
processing system that sorted the animal bones, artifacts, vegetable
remains, and other discoveries on location in the field. The tabulated
information on each sorted find was then fed by remote access terminal
to a computer many miles away. Within a few days, the excavators had
instant access to the latest data from the dig. This system means that
overall research design can be modified while an excavation is still in
progress (Figure 7.1).

The Koster site is a fine example of elaborate research design that
uses complex computer technology. The dig employed dozens of people each field season. Most excavations operate on a far smaller scale,
but the ultimate principles are the same: sound research design, very
careful recording of all data, and scientifically controlled excavation.
The Koster excavation was designed, like all good digs, to solve specific
research problems formulated in the context of a sound research design.

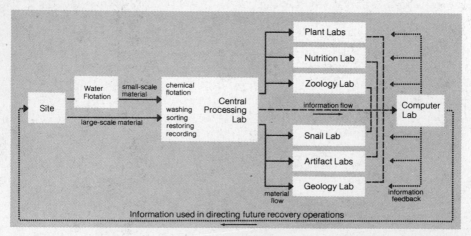

Figure 7.1 Organization of the Koster excavation.

TYPES OF EXCAVATION

People commonly ask the same questions when they visit an excavation. How do you decide where to dig? What tools do you use? Why are your trenches in this shape? How deep do you excavate? In the following we discuss different types of archaeological sites and the problems they create for excavators.

You can decide where to dig on a site by simple, arbitrary choice of a spot that has yielded a large number of surface finds or one where traces of stone walls or other ancient structures can be seen above ground. When Richard Daugherty dug the *Ozette* site on the Washington coast, he began by digging through the place where the largest occupation sequence seemed to be. Why? He needed to obtain as complete a cultural sequence as possible. The logical way to do so was to dig through the deepest part of the site. There was, of course, no guarantee that his trench would penetrate to the earliest part of the whale-hunters' site. But his choice was a logical way to start attacking the fundamental questions of when and for how long the whale hunters lived at Ozette. Similar decisions have been made at thousands of other sites all over the world.

In these days of high digging costs, archaeologists rely more heavily on statistical sampling than their predecessors did. Sampling is used in digging shell heaps or dense accumulations of occupation debris containing thousands of artifacts. Obviously only a small sample of a large garbage heap can be dug and analyzed. To ensure validity of the statistical samples, some form of unbiased sampling must be used to choose which part of a site is to be dug.

Sampling has been defined as the "science of controlling and measuring the reliability of information through the theory of probability." Sampling techniques allow us to ensure a statistically reliable basis of archaeological data from which we can make generalizations about our research data. Most archaeologists make use of probabilistic sampling, a means of relating small samples of data in mathematical ways to much larger populations. The classic example of this technique, commonly used in the disciplines of statistics and statistical theory, is the political opinion poll, testing national feelings from tiny samples, perhaps as few as 1500 people. In archaeology probablistic sampling improves the likelihood that the conclusions reached from a survey or excavation on the basis of the samples are relatively reliable.

The use of formal sampling techniques in archaeology is still in its early stage. Simple random sampling is quite commonly used, for example, when an archaeologist wishes to obtain an unbiased sample of artifacts from an ancient shell mound. One can arrive at this result by laying out a rectangular grid of squares on a site and then selecting the squares to be dug by using a table of random numbers (Figure 7.2). The excavated samples are thus chosen at random, rather than on the basis of surface finds or other considerations. **Stratified sampling,**

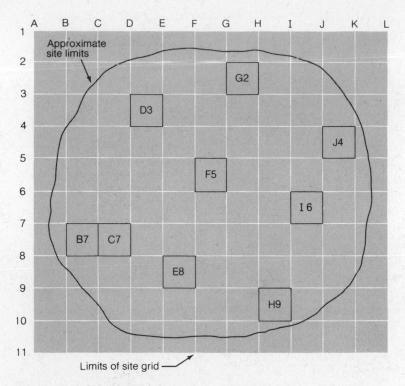

Figure 7.2 A hypothetical dig with trenches laid out by referring to a random sampling table. That is, the trench layout is completely by chance, with the cuttings to be dug selected by a table of randomly selected numbers.

whereby the investigator uses previous knowledge of an area, such as its topographic variation, to structure further research, enables one to sample some selected units intensively, others less thoroughly. Archaeological sampling, based as it is on descriptive and inferential statistics, is a complex subject that is still in its infancy. I urge you to consult the references at the back of this book.

Vertical Excavation

The layout of small digs is determined not only by surface features, density of surface finds, or sampling techniques, but by available funds as well. Most excavations are run on a shoestring, and so small-scale operations have to be used to solve complex problems with minimal expenditure of time and money. Some of the world's most important sites, such as Coxcatlán Cave in the *Tehuacán Valley*, Mexico (Figure 7.3), have been excavated on a small scale by vertical excavation, digging limited areas for specific information on dating and stratigraphy. Vertical trenches can be used to obtain artifact samples, to establish

Figure 7.3 Vertical excavation in Coxcatlán Cave in Tehuacán Valley, Mexico. The large pits result from the excavation of alternate squares as separate units. Coxcatlán has yielded some of the earliest evidence of maize cultivation in the world.

sequences of ancient building construction or histories of complex earthworks, and to salvage sites threatened with destruction. The small trenches are often dug in areas where the deposits are likely to be of maximal thickness or where important structures may be found. Much vertical excavation is test trenching, designed to establish the cultural sequence at, and extent of, a site before area excavation begins.

Area Excavation

Large-scale excavations are normally used to uncover wider areas of a site. These horizontal, or area, excavations used to uncover house plans and settlement layouts are expensive (Figure 7.4). The only sites that are completely excavated are very small hunter-gatherer camps, isolated huts, and burial mounds. With larger settlements, all one can do is excavate several portions of the settled area in order to sample areas representative of the entire settlement.

Area excavations expose large, open areas of ground to a depth of

Figure 7.4 Area excavation of an Iroquois long house near Onondaga, New York. The small stakes indicate positions of house wall posts; placement of hearth areas and support posts can be seen inside the walls.

several feet. A complex network of walls or abandoned storage pits may lie within the area to be investigated. Each of these ancient features relates to other structures, a relationship that must be carefully recorded if the site is to be interpreted correctly. If the area excavated is large, we immediately have a big recording problem. The excavators use a grid of squares, each with its own letter and number, to aid in digging and recording the site (Figure 7.5a). For excavating the surviving remains of an Indian long house or a scatter of artifacts left by a prehistoric craftsman, accurate recording techniques are obviously essential (Figure 7.5b).

Digging, Tools, and People

How do you do the digging? Much depends on the type of site you are excavating. A huge burial mound on the Ohio River may be more than 20 feet deep. Much of the sterile deposit covering the burial levels is removed with picks and shovels. But as soon as the archaeologists reach layers in which finds are expected, they dig with meticulous care, removing each layer in turn, recording the exact position of their finds upon discovery. Smaller caves or cemeteries are excavated inch by inch. The earth surrounding the finds is passed through fine screens so that tiny beads, fish bones, and myriad small items can be found.

   Excavation is in part a recording process and accuracy is essential.

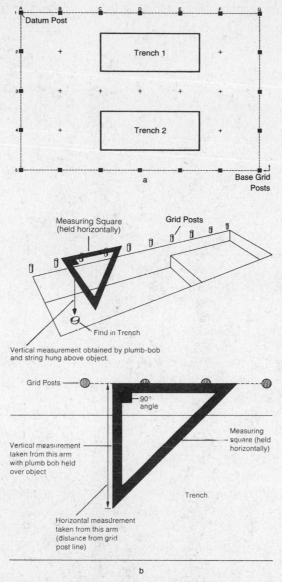

Figure 7.5 (a) Two trenches laid out with a grid. (b) Three-dimensional recording of the position of an object using the grid squares.

The records will never be precise unless the dig is kept tidy at all times. The trench walls must always be straight. Why? So that you can record the layers you are digging and follow them across the site. Surplus soil is dumped well away from the trenches so that it does not cascade into the dig or have to be shifted when new areas are opened. The excavation is a laboratory and should be treated as such.

All archaeological digs are headed by a director, who is responsible both for organizing the excavation and for overseeing the specialists and diggers. Many larger digs will involve a team of specialist experts who work alongside the excavators. At the *Ozette* site, Richard Daugherty had the cooperation of a geologist and a zoologist who visited the site regularly. They studied the geological background of the settlement and the many animal bones found as the dig proceeded. A really large excavation in Mesopotamia or Mesoamerica can involve dozens of people—specialist archaeologists, a team of resident experts in other fields including after an architect, graduate student trainees, and volunteer or paid workers who do much of the actual excavation. We describe some of the ways in which you can obtain digging experience in Chapter 11.

Archaeologists use many digging tools in their work. Picks, shovels, and long-handled spades carry the brunt of the heavy work. But the most common archaeological tool used in North America is the diamond-shaped trowel, with its straight edges and sharp tip. With it, soil can be eased from a delicate specimen or an unusual discoloration in the soil scraped clean. Trowels are used for tracing delicate layers in walls, clearing small pits, and other exacting jobs. They are rarely out of the digger's hand.

Household and paint brushes often come in handy, the former for soft, dry sediments and for cleaning trenches, the latter for freeing fragile objects from the soil. Even fine artists' brushes have their uses cleaning beads, decaying ironwork, or fine bones. Enterprising archaeologists visit their dentists regularly, if only to obtain regular supplies of worn-out dental instruments, which make first-rate fine digging tools! And so do 6-inch nails ground to different shapes. A set of fine screens for sifting soil for small finds, several notebooks and graph paper, tapes, plumb bobs, surveyors' levels, and a compass are just a few of the items that arhaeologists need to record their excavations and process their finds.

RECORDING

No dig is worth more than its records. The excavation notebooks provide a day-to-day record of each trench, of new layers and significant finds. Before any trench is measured out, the entire site is laid out on a grid of squares. Important finds, or details of a house or a storage pit, are measured in on the site plan by simple, three-dimensional recording techniques (Figure 7.5b). It is information from your records, as well as the artifacts from the dig, that form the priceless archive of your excavation. If the records are incomplete, the dig is little better than a treasure hunt.

Let us now turn from general principles to some specific excavation problems that will give you an insight into the multitude of challenges awaiting field workers. As we indicated in Chapter 3, archaeological sites, in all shapes and sizes, are the basis for all field investigations. All contain traces of human activity, in the form of artifacts, structures, and food remains. Archaeologists most commonly classify sites by their functions, that is to say, by the activities that took place within them. It is no coincidence that these various site categories present different excavation problems.

HABITATION SITES

Open Campsites and Villages

Small sites, often little more than scatters of artifacts, that were once places where specific tasks were performed are probably the most common archaeological sites. However, the most obvious and most interesting locations are habitation sites, places where people have lived and carried out many activities. Hunter-gatherers have occupied temporary camps for short periods since the very earliest millennia of prehistory. Where preservation conditions are good, archaeologists can sometimes identify such settlements, represented by concentrations of stone artifacts and broken animal bones, as well as the stone foundations of long-abandoned brush shelters. Such concentrations have been found in the Great Basin of the American West, in the arctic North, and also in sub-Saharan Africa.

Many hunter-gatherer camps are hard to identify from the surviving archaeological record (Figure 7.6). The same is not true of later farming villages, which were usually occupied longer, resulting in the accumulation of considerable quantities of occupation debris as well as substantial house foundations. Some 8000 years ago, the villagers of *Ain Ghazal* in Jordan lived in a large settlement of small huts and stock compounds covering several acres. The house foundations and numerous animal bones, as well as other artifacts, enabled the excavators to trace the extent and nature of the settlement.

Numerous prehistoric agricultural settlements in North America were occupied over long periods, and in them varied domestic and industrial activites as well as food preparation and household life took place. (Figure 7.4).

Caves and Rockshelters

Favored home sites for prehistoric peoples included the mouth of a cave or beneath a cliff overhang. Huge accumulations of occupation debris extending over thousands of years are to be found in the great rockshelters and caves of the Dordogne Valley in southwest France,

Figure 7.6 Excavation of an artifact and bone concentration at Olduvai Gorge, Tanzania. The interpretation of such locations as
habitation sites has caused considerable controversy. Recent research suggests that many such early "campsites" may, in fact,
have been places where early hominids cached and processed
meat and bones scavenged from nearby predator kills.

where prehistoric hunter-gatherers flourished from 40,000 to 10,000
years ago and painted exquisite pictures of the animals they hunted.
The Danger and Hogup caves in Utah reflect thousands of years of
hunter-gatherer occupation. The dry environment of the desert preserved wood objects and basketry as well as minute details of economic
life. And the dry caves of *Tehuacán Valley* in south-central Mexico
provide a unique history of how maize cultivation developed in the
New World (Chapter 9).

Cave and rockshelter excavations are some of the hardest digs to
carry out successfully. The ground below cliff overhangs usually consists of ash and other debris piled up through successive human occupations. Sterile soils may interrupt this sequence of habitation, representing periods when the site was abandoned. Excavating such
complicated sequences is slow and meticulous work. The trenches are

usually restricted by the size of the shelter. Each hearth and small occupation layer has to be isolated from the others during excavation.

Many cave and rockshelter excavations deal purely with dating and stratigraphy but others are more ambitious. When Hallam Movius dug the Abri Pataud rockshelter in France, he had to record at least six layers of human occupation dated to between 40,000 and 19,000 years ago, extending through more than 20 feet of stratified deposit. The site was excavated following a coordinated master plan that involved not only archaeologists but botanists, geologists, and other specialists as well. Movius was able to record minute changes in tool types as well as record many details of the changing hunting and gathering practices of Abri Pataud's inhabitants.

Mounds

Occupation mounds (often called **tells** in the Near East) are common in many parts of the world. Mound sites result when the same site is occupied for centuries, even thousands of years. Successive generations lived atop their predecessors' settlements. The result is a gradual accumulation of occupation debris, which, when excavated, provides a complicated picture of occupation levels.

Even a small mound can cost a fortune to excavate, simply because the lowest levels are so deeply buried below the surface. A huge mound such as that of *Ur-of-the-Chaldees* in Mesopotamia, or even a relatively small mound like Tepe Yahya in Iran, can be sampled only by large trenches that cut into the sides of the mound in a series of great steps, or by very large-scale excavation indeed, using a combination of vertical and area trenches (Figure 7.7). There is far more to

Figure 7.7 Tepe Yahya, Iran, a typical Near Eastern city mound, or *tell*. The stepped trenches of the excavation can be seen in the slope of the mound.

excavating an occupation mound than merely stripping off successive layers. So many natural and artificial processes, ranging from wind erosion to human activity, can change the stratigraphy of a site of this type that each presents a challenging new excavation problem.

Earthworks and Forts

Many peoples—Iron Age peasants in western Europe, Maori warriors in New Zealand, Hopewell Indians in Ohio—built extensive earth fortifications to protect their settlements and sacred places. The Ohio earthworks enclose large areas of ground, but no one knows exactly why such earthworks were undertaken. To excavate them would require both vertical excavation to record cross-sections across the earthworks, and area investigation to uncover the layout of the structures built inside the earthworks. Such excavations were indeed carried out on the great prehistoric fortress at Maiden Castle, England, many years ago. The massive earthworks of Maiden Castle were stormed by a Roman legion in A.D. 43. By careful excavation and use of historical data, the excavator Mortimer Wheeler was able to provide a blow-by-blow description of the battle for the fortress (Figure 7.8).

Shell Middens

Shell middens—vast accumulations of abandoned shells, fish bones, and other food remains—are common in many coastal areas of the world. Remarkable results can be attained by studying these dense heaps, especially in reconstructing prehistoric diets (Chapter 9). The excavation problem is twofold: first, to identify the stratified levels in

Figure 7.8 The Iron Age hill fort at Maiden Castle, Dorset, England; its extensive earthworks were excavated by Mortimer Wheeler.

Figure 7.9 An exemplary area excavation of a shallow shell midden at Galatea Bay, New Zealand.

the middens, and second, to obtain statistically reliable samples of food remains and artifacts from the deposits. Most shell midden digs are laid out by random cuttings, described very briefly earlier. We illustrate an example of an area excavation on a New Zealand shell midden (Figure 7.9), where much information on ancient diet was found by using a carefully laid-out grid of trenches. The excavation of a shell midden is mostly rather unspectacular, for the detailed statistical results come from laboratory analysis of artifacts rather than from actual digging. One hopes to look at ways in which the inhabitants utilized different communities of shellfish, such as oysters of different sizes, through time.

CEREMONIAL AND OTHER SPECIALIST SITES

Some of the world's most famous archaeological sites are ceremonial centers, such as the pyramids of *Giza* in Egypt or the Maya ceremonial center at Copán, Honduras. Many ceremonial sites are enormous, and, like occupation mounds, present great difficulties for the excavator. *Teotihuacán* in the Valley of Mexico is, of course, far more than a ceremonial center (see Figure 10.1). It was a great city as well, which flourished from 200 B.C. to as late as A.D. 750. Discovering the true significance of the site has involved not only extensive area excavation designed to help reconstruct pyramids and major buildings, but sophisticated mapping and surface survey combined with small-scale excavation as well. René Millon and other archaeologists have mapped more than 12.5 square miles of Teotihuacán in a survey program combined with some excavation. Their aim is to give a comprehensive picture of the huge city as it rapidly developed into a religious and ceremonial center of wide importance.

With trading sites, quarries, and other specialized sites as well as with ceremonial centers, indeed all sites, one major question is the artifact patternings coming from the excavations. Do these patterns reflect long-distance trading activity in, say, copper ornaments or seashells? Are marine stingray spines, which are present in ruins that appear to be temples built hundreds of miles inland, artifacts of great religious significance in Mexico? It is questions like these that can be answered only by careful studies of spatial associations.

BURIALS AND CEMETERIES

Human burials are the stereotypic finds of archaeology, reflecting humanity's abiding concern with the afterlife. The earliest human burials were left by Neanderthal peoples more than 70,000 years ago. Most human societies have paid careful attention to funerals and burials ever since. Burials were deposited with simple or elaborate grave furniture designed to accompany its owner to the afterlife.

People have buried their dead in isolated, shallow graves within their settlement, in special cemeteries, in caves, as cremated remains in jars, and in vast burial mounds. Some burials consist of the body alone, others lie with a few beads or a handful of clay pots (Figure 7.10). Royal personages have been buried in all their glory: Shang kings in China with their chariots; the rulers of early Ur-of-the-Chaldees, Mesopotamia, with their entire court; Maya nobles with their prize treasures.

By studying a group of burials from one cemetery it may be possible to distinguish different social classes by the grave furniture buried with the remains. The common people may take nothing with them; merchants or priests may be buried with distinctive artifacts associated with their status in society. The Adena and Hopewell peoples of North America were much concerned with the afterlife during their heyday 2000 years ago. From the distribution of the burials and cemeteries in their burial mounds, and from the cult objects and ornaments associated with the skeletons, it may be possible to gain some insights into the social organization of Adena and Hopewell societies (Chapter 10). And, of course, burials are a fruitful source of information on personal ornamentation and appearance, too, for people were (and still are) often buried in the clothes and ornaments they wore in life. The physical

Figure 7.10 A classic Maya collective tomb at Gualan in the Mota-
gua Valley, Guatemala.

characteristics of the skeletons themselves can provide valuable data
on age, nutrition, sex, and ancient disease.

How does one excavate a burial? Whether one is digging a large
cemetery or a lone burial, each skeleton and its associated grave, ornaments, and grave goods are considered a single excavation problem.
Each burial is exposed as a unit that has both internal associations with

its accompanying goods and external associations with other burials in the same and other levels. The first step is to identify the grave, either by locating a gravestone or a pile of stones, or from the grave outlines, which may appear as a discoloration in the surrounding soil. Once the grave outlines have been found, individual bones are exposed. The main outline of the burial is traced first. Then you uncover the fingers, toes, and other small bones. You leave the bones in place and take care not to displace any ornaments or grave furniture associated with them. Once the skeleton is exposed and fully cleaned where it lies, the layout of the burial and grave furniture is recorded by drawings and photographs before the skeleton is lifted bone by bone or encased in a cocoon of plaster of paris and metal strips (Figure 7.10).

Burial excavation may seem very romantic. In reality it is not only technically demanding, but raises important ethical questions as well. For years, archaeologists casually dug up Indian burials and prehistoric graves all over the world, some of them even of people of known tribal or historical identity. Now both Australian Aborigines and American Indians, among others, are objecting strenuously to excavation and destruction of ancient burial grounds—and with good reason. They argue: Why should their ancestors be dug up and displayed in museums? Many surviving communities retain strong emotional and religious ties with their ancestors, and excavation of their remains flies in the face of their religious beliefs. There are now demands for reburial of human remains stored in museums, especially of those that can be documented to have direct historical links with modern American Indian groups. Recent federal legislation has empowered the Smithsonian Institution to return human remains stored in the museum to their historical descendants, if such links can be scientifically established. Several states have, or are passing, somewhat similar legislation. Both archaeologists and physical anthropologists watch these developments with concern; they argue that priceless scientific information about early human biology, prehistoric disease, and other topics will be lost to science. The ongoing and far from resolved controversy pits scientists against native peoples, science against taditional religion. Certainly, any excavations of human skeletons must now be conducted with complete regard for the feelings of local American Indian communities, something that was never a factor, even a generation ago.

8

ORDERING THE PAST

Order is Heav'n's first law.

Alexander Pope, *An Essay on Man*

BACK FROM THE FIELD

Archaeologists spend much more time in their laboratories than they do excavating and surveying. They must, for the finds from even a brief excavation can take months to sort, clean, label, classify, and analyze. The field crew returns from the dig with truckloads of boxes and bags of unsorted stone tools, pot fragments, broken animal bones, and other finds. Cartons contain precious human skeletons and rows of radiocarbon and soil samples for specialists to examine. It can take some days simply to organize these piles of boxes in the laboratory before the real work begins. Then, once the tables are clear, the long work of describing and ordering all the finds from the dig starts.

The laboratory crew—usually graduate students and undergraduates working under supervision—begins by sorting all the finds into very broad categories. Soil and radiocarbon samples are sent off to experts. Animal bones, seeds, and other food remains are separated from manufactured artifacts and handed over to the members of the team who are skilled in identifying such finds. The manufactured artifacts are sorted into broad classes, pot fragments separated from stone implements, metal tools handled separately from shell beads, and so on. The labeling of every bag and box is carefully checked. Properly marked containers must specify the three-dimensional unit of space and time in which the materials were found (see Figure 7.5). Only then is everything ready for basic classification and ordering of the manufactured artifacts. In this chapter we describe some of the ways in which archaeologists tackle these complex tasks.

CLASSIFICATION, TAXONOMY, AND SYSTEMATICS

Our attitude toward life and our surroundings involves constantly classifying and sorting massive quantities of data. We classify types of eating utensils: knives, forks, and spoons; each type has a different use and is kept in a separate compartment in the kitchen drawer. We group roads according to their surface, finish, and size. A station wagon is classified separately from a truck. As we classify artifacts, life-styles, and cultures, we make choices among them. Most Westerners eat rice with a fork, but the Chinese and other Asian people use chopsticks, and still others have decided that a spoon is more suitable for the purpose. There are myriad choices. The final decision is often dictated by cultural usage rather than functional pragmatism.

Everyone "classifies" because doing so is a requirement for abstract thought and language. Archaeological classification is something quite different, for classification is used as a research tool. All classifications used by archaeologists follow directly from the problems that they are studying. Let us say that a prehistorian is studying changes in pottery designs over a 500-year period in the Southwest. The classification he or she uses will follow not only from what other people have done, but also from the problems being studied. How, and even what, you classify stems directly from the research questions asked about the data.

Taxonomy is a system for classifying materials, objects, and phenomena used in many sciences, including archaeology. The taxonomies of biology, botany, geology, and some other disciplines are highly sophisticated and often very rigid systems that were created in the nineteenth century and early in the twentieth. Many are now dated by today's sophisticated standards. In contrast, archaeology has built its own taxonomy of specialist terminologies and concepts quite haphazardly. British archaeologists refer to "cultures," North American scholars to "phases" (see page 143), and the French to "civilizations." Each term has basically the same meaning, but the subtle differences stem from cultural traditions and from different field situations.

Systematics is essentially a way of creating units that can be used to categorize things as a basis for explaining archaeological or other phenomena. It is a means for creating units of classification within a scientific discipline. Biologists classify human beings within a hierarchy of classification constructed by Carl Linnaeus in the eighteenth century. Human beings are grouped in the *Kingdom* Animalia, in a classificatory hierarchy that passes through the *Class* Mammalia, ending with the *Subspecies Homo sapiens sapiens*. This biological classification consists of empirically defined units, each precisely described and related to the others. Archaeologists use systematics in much the same way, but their classifications are closely related to the problem being studied.

OBJECTIVES OF CLASSIFICATION

As we have stated, classification in archaeology depends on the problem being studied. However, four major objectives can be identified:

1. *Organizing data into manageable units.* This step is part of the
   preliminary data-processing operation, and it commonly involves separating finds on the basis of raw material (stone,
   bone, and so on) or separating artifacts from food remains. This
   preliminary ordering allows much more detailed classification
   later on.

2. *Describing types.* By identifying the individual features (attributes) of hundreds of artifacts or clusters of artifacts, the archaeologist can group them by common attributes into relatively few types. These types represent patterns of separated
   associations of attributes. Such types are economical ways of
   describing large numbers of artifacts. Which attributes are chosen depends on the purpose of the typology.

   Artifact types (sometimes called archaeological types) are
   based on criteria set up by archaeologists as a convenient way
   of studying ancient toolkits and technology. They are a useful
   scientific device that provides a manageable way of classifying
   small and large collections of prehistoric tools and the byprod-
   ucts from manufacturing them.

3. *Identifying relationships between types.* Describing types provides a hierarchy which orders the relationships between artifacts. The relationships stem, in part, from the use of a variety
   of raw materials, manufacturing techniques, and functions.

These three objectives are used a great deal in culture-historical
research (see page 194). Processual archaeologists may use classification for:

4. *Studying assemblage variability in the archaeological record.*
   These studies are often combined with middle-range research
   on dynamic, living cultural systems (see Chapter 11).

TYPOLOGY

Typology is a system of archaeological classification based on the construction of types. It is a search for structure among either objects or
the variables that define these objects, a search that has taken on
added meaning and complexity as archaeologists have begun to use
computer technology and sophisticated statistical methods.

Originally, archaeological typology involved dividing up objects
and variables arbitrarily. I remember sitting in a Cambridge archaeological laboratory many years ago and learning the basics of stone tool
classification. Our instructor laid out a series of Acheulian hand axes
in front of us, magnificent specimens from the gravels of the Thames
River (Figure 6.1). He divided them into different categories. "These
are pointed axes, these ovates (oval-shaped), these ovates with twisted

edges, these linguate, with tongue-shaped ends," he declared. One of us pointed out that some of the axes in the pointed category were far from ideal examples of the form; in fact, one or two were distinctly oval. "They are pointed handaxes," pronounced our instructor firmly, brooking no disagreement. The arbitrariness of his classifications was just like that used by a stamp collector classifying postage stamps. It was as if prehistoric handaxes were all standardized productions turned out by an impersonal stone flaking machine. One lost the opportunity to examine the underlying patterns of human design and behavior, which is what interests archaeologists more than mere classification.

Typology enables one to construct objectively defined units of analysis that apply to two or more samples of artifacts, so that these samples can be compared objectively. These samples can come from different sites, or from separate levels of the same site. Typology is classification to permit comparison.

Archaeological Classification

As we have emphasized, archaeological classification is the ordering of data according to shared characteristics. But how do archaeologists go about this organizing?

Typology is based on the archaeologist's "concept of types," a subject that is one of the great controversies in archaeology.

On a formal level, a **type** can be defined as a group or class of items that is internally cohesive and separated from other groups by one or more discontinuities. Most now argue that types are identified by combinations of attributes that distinguish and isolate one artifact type from another. In the final analysis, the idea is to organize data in such a way as to reveal continuities and breaks between groups of artifacts that display internal cohesion and are isolated from other such groups.

Attributes are the physical characteristics used to distinguish one artifact from another. As archaeologists work out their typologies, they find themselves examining hundreds of individual fragments, each of which bears several distinctive attributes (Figure 8.1). Every commonplace artifact we use can be examined by its attributes. The familiar glass beer mug has a curved handle that extends from near the lip to the base, often fluted sides, a straight, rounded rim, and dimensions that are set by the amount of beer it is intended to contain. It is manufactured of clear, relatively thick glass (the thickness can be defined by precise measurement). You can find numerous attributes on any human artifact, be it a diamond ring or a prehistoric pot. For example, a collection of 50 potsherds lying on a laboratory table may bear black-painted designs, while eight have red panels on the neck, 10 are shallow bowls, and so on. An individual potsherd may come from a vessel made of bright red clay that was mixed with powdered sea shells so

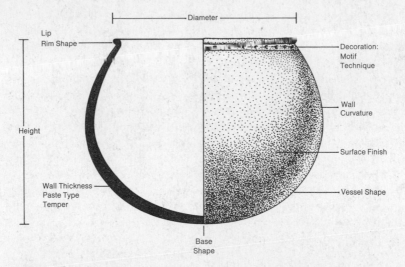

Figure 8.1 Some common attributes of a clay vessel. Specific attributes that could be listed for this pot are concave shoulder, dot and drag decoration, mica temper, round base, and thickness of wall at base.

that the clay would fire better. It may come from a pot with a thick rim made by applying a rolled circle of clay before firing, and a criss-cross design cut into the wet clay with a sharp knife during manufacture. Each of the many individual features is an attribute, most of which are obvious enough. Only a critically selected few of these attributes, however, will be used in classifying the artifacts. (If all were used, then no classification would be possible: each artifact would be an individual object identified by an infinite number of attributes.) Thus, the archaeologist works with only those attributes considered most appropriate for the classificatory task at hand.

A number of broad groups of attributes are in common use:

Formal attributes are features such as the shape of the artifact, its measureable dimensions, and its components. Normally, they are fairly obvious.

Stylistic attributes include decorations, color, surface finish, and so on.

Technological attributes are those covering the material used to make an artifact and the way it was made.

The selection of attributes and the entire process of archaeological classification involves many hours of laboratory work, working with large numbers of artifacts that are laid out on tables and examined individually. Today the archaeologist relies heavily on quantitative methods for both describing and comparing artifacts, and for recording and manipulating attribute data. A discussion of these approaches lies beyond the scope of this short book. Attribute-based classifications of artifacts are based on large numbers of attributes, selected by the classifier and usually coded on a computer. Statistical typologies are often derived from attribute clusters, the archaeologist using statistically derived attribute clusters as a way of dividing artifact collections into categories. This approach gives one an insight into the most important artifact clusters; there are, however, many different criteria that can affect such clustering. For example, a classification of bronze swords based on blade dimensions will give you a very different clustering from one based on the sources and composition of the copper and tin used to fabricate them. Other quantitative approaches, outside the scope of this book, work with entire artifacts. They calculate the similarities between all possible pairs of objects in a collection to produce hierarchies of different artifact clusters.

In the final analysis, quantitative methods enable archaeologists to organize artifact data in intelligent, efficient, and replicable ways, allowing them to discern possible patterns that relate to past human behavior. These same techniques also allow them to evaluate the reliability of their inferences objectively and to make inferences about the interrelationships between different variables in attribute counts. As such, they are an invaluable aid to artifact classification.

Archaeological Types

All of us have feelings and reactions about any artifact, whether it is a magnificent wood helmet from the Pacific Northwest coast (Figure 8.2), or a simple acorn pounder from the southern California interior. Our immediate instinct is to look at and classify these and other prehistoric artifacts from our own cultural standpoint. That is, of course, what prehistoric peoples did as well. The owners of the tools that archaeologists study classified them into groups for themselves, each one having a definite role in their society. We assign different roles in eating to a knife, fork, and spoon. Knives cut meat, steak knives are used in eating steaks. The prehistoric arrowhead is employed in the chase; one type of missile head is used to hunt deer, another to shoot birds, and so on. The use of an artifact may be determined not only by convenience and practical considerations, but by custom or regulation. The light-barbed spearheads used by some Australian hunting bands to catch fish are too fragile for dispatching kangaroo; with the special barbs an impaled fish can be lifted out of the water. Pots are made by women in most African and American Indian societies, which have division of labor by sex; each has formed complicated customs, regulations, and taboos, which, functional considerations apart, categorize clay pots into different types with varying uses and rules in the culture (Figure 8.3).

Figure 8.2 Tlingit carved wood helmet from the Northwest coast, classified as a "natural" type when found in an archaeological context. This artifact would obviously be classified as a helmet from the perspective of our cultural experience. (Height, 9 inches; width, 10 inches.)

Furthermore, each society has its own conception of what an artifact should look like. Until recently, Americans have generally preferred larger cars, Europeans small ones. These preferences reflected not only pragmatic considerations of road width and longer distances in the New World, but also differing attitudes toward traveling. Many Americans still think that their car is a reflection of prestige and social standing. To these people, style changes, aluminum wheel designs, turbos, and other niceties are important. But we all think that a car should have a color-coordinated interior to look "right." The steering wheel is on the left, and it is equipped with turn signals and seatbelts by law. In other words, we know what we want and expect an automobile to look like, even though minor design details change—as do the length of women's skirts and the width of men's ties.

The problem that confronts the archaeologist is to devise archaeological types that are appropriate to the research problems they are tackling, an extremely difficult task. In archaeology, a type is a grouping of artifacts created for comparison with other groups. This grouping may or may not coincide with the actual tool types designated by the original makers. A good example comes from the world-famous Olduvai Gorge site in East Africa, where Louis and Mary Leakey excavated

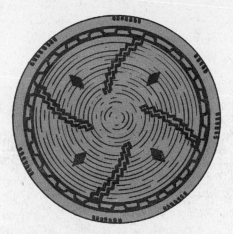

Figure 8.3 This Chumash parching tray is a good example of the difficulties of archaeological classification. This finely made basket was produced by the Chumash Indians of southern California by weaving plant fibers. The design was formed in the maker's mind by several factors, most important of which is the tremendous reservoir of learned cultural experience that the Chumash have acquired, generation by generation, through the several thousand years they lived in southern California. The designs of their baskets are learned, and relate to the feeling that such and such a form and color are "correct" and traditionally acceptable. But there are more pragmatic and complex reasons too, including the flat, circular shape that enables the user to roast seeds by tossing them with red embers.

Each attribute of the basket has a good reason for its presence—whether traditional, innovative, functional, or imposed by the technology used to make it. The band of decoration around the rim is a feature of the Chumash decorative tradition and occurs on most of their baskets. It has a rich red-brown color from the species of reed used to make it. The steplike decoration was dictated by the sewing and weaving techniques but the diamond pattern is unique and the innovative stamp of one weaver, which might or might not be adopted by other craftspeople in later generations. The problem for the archaeologist is to measure the variations in human artifacts and to establish the causes behind the directions of change, and to find what these variations can be used to measure. This fine parching tray is a warning that variations in human artifacts are both complex and subtle.

a series of cache sites used by very early humans, *Homo habilis*. Mary Leakey studied the stone tools and grouped them in the "Oldowan tradition," a tradition characterized by jagged-edged chopping tools and flakes. Her classifications were based on close examination of the artifacts, and the idea that the first human toolkit was based on crude stone choppers soon became archaeological dogma. Recently, Nicholas Toth of Indiana University has taken a radically different approach to classifying Oldowan artifacts. He has spent many hours not only studying and classifying the original artifacts, but also learning Oldowan technology for himself, fabricating hundreds of artifacts identical to those made by *Homo habilis* nearly 2 million years ago. His controlled experiments have shown that *Homo habilis* was not using chopping tools at all. The primeval stone workers were more interested in the sharp-edged flakes they knocked off lumps of lava, for cutting and butchering the game meat they scavenged from predator kills. The "chopping tools" were, in fact, just the end product of knocking flakes off convenient lumps of lava and not artifacts at all. Controlled experiments like Toth's provide useful insights into how prehistoric peoples thought of the raw materials they used, and how they used them to manufacture the tools they needed. Toth and other experts are now trying to study the tell-tale patterns of edge wear on the cutting edges of Oldowan flakes; the scars left by working, for example, fresh bone as opposed to hide or wood are highly distinctive. With controlled experimentation and careful examination of edge wear, they hope to achieve a closer marriage between the ways in which the first humans used stone tools and the classifications devised by the archaeologist hundreds of thousands of years later.

Everyone agrees that a type is based on clusters of attributes or on clusters of objects. Although patterns of attributes may be fairly easy to identify, how do archaeologists know what is a type and what is not? Should they try to reproduce the categories of pot that the makers themselves conceived? Or should they just go ahead and create "archaeological" types designed purely for analytical purposes? This is the hub of the controversy about types in archaeology.

The archaeologist constructs typologies based on the recurrence of formal patterns of physical features of artifacts. Many of these formal types have restricted distributions in space and time, which suggests they represent distinctive "styles" of construction and/or tasks that were carried out in the culture to which they belong. For example, the so-called Chavín art style was widespread over much of coastal and highland Peru after 900 B.C. The characteristic jaguar, snake, and human forms of this art are highly characteristic, and mark the spread of a distinctive iconography over an enormous area that flourished until 200 B.C. Chavín art, and the characteristic styles associated with it, had a specific role in Peruvian society of the time (Figure 8.4).

Archaeologists tend to use four "types of types," which we describe briefly here; in practice they are rarely separated one from another, for experts tend to draw this kind of information from more general classifications of artifacts.

Descriptive types are the most elementary descriptions, based solely on the form of the artifact—physical or external properties. The descriptive type is used when the use or cultural significance of the object or practice is unknown. For example, the excavations at Snaketown in Arizona revealed a "large basin-like depression," a mysterious feature that also turned up at other Hohokam sites in the Southwest. This descriptive type was subsequently proven to be a ball court, and so the noncommittal descriptive classification was abandoned in favor of a functional one that defined the struc-

Figure 8.4 A Chavín carving on a pillar in the temple interior at Chavín de Huantar, Peru. This reconstruction makes the temple walls seem more regular and the background more open than they actually were. The distinctive motifs exhibit the style of Chavín art spread throughout highland and coastal Peru, marking an interval termed the Chavín "Horizon" that cuts across many local sequences.

ture's role in Hohokam culture. Descriptive types are commonly used for artifacts from early prehistory, when functional interpretations are much harder to reach (Figure 8.5). For instance, the famous prehistoric stone circles found throughout Britain are usually classified as just that, because we have no idea what their purpose was, except for a general impression that they had a ritual and symbolic function.

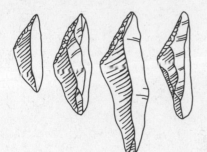 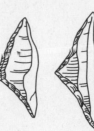 

a Obliquely blunted   b Triangular

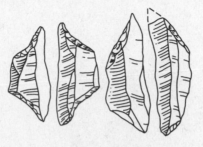

c Elongated trapeze

Figure 8.5 Ten-thousand-year-old Mesolithic artifacts from *Star Carr,* England (shown actual size). You can classify these by—Descriptive type: geometric stone tools; Chronological type: Mesolithic microliths, Star Carr forms; Functional type: microlithic arrowhead barbs.

Chronological types are defined by form, but are time markers. They are types with chronological significance. Like descriptive types, they are part of a culture's inventory as reflected in the archaeological record, but are widely used to distinguish chronological differences. For example, on the Great Plains of North America, *Clovis* and *Folsom* points were used for short periods of prehistoric time, the former for about five centuries from about 9500 to 9000 B.C. Projectile points have long been used as chronological markers in North American archaeology. Pottery is probably the most common form of chronological type, for the clay, decoration, and so on change, and are shown to have noncultural significance and to be significant historical indexes. Chronological types are defined in terms of attributes that do show change over time. When the archaeologist compares artifacts known to be of different ages, certain attributes are observed to be different, so he or she uses them to define the types. Chronological types figure prominently in southwestern archaeology, and were used by Alfred Kidder in his classic excavations at *Pecos.*

Functional types are based on cultural use or role rather than on outward form or chronological position. The same artifacts can be treated as functional or descriptive types. You can classify an assemblage in broad categories: "wood," "bone," "stone," and so on. But a functional classification can be adopted equally as well: "weapons," "clothing," "food preparation," and so on.

Ideally, functional types should reflect the precise roles and functional classifications made by the members of the society from which they came. Needless to say, such an objective is very difficult to achieve, because of incomplete preservation and lack of written records. There are many artifacts—for example, the polished stone ax, the bow and arrow, or the *atlatl*, the prehistoric throwing stick—that were in use for thousands of years, indeed right into modern times. In many cases like these, it is easy to tell what an artifact was used for. However, we have no means of visualizing the complex roles that some artifacts played in prehistoric society, or of establishing the restrictions placed on their use by the society (Figure 8.6). The famous "Venus" female figurines made by Stone Age hunter-gatherers in Europe about 25,000 years ago have always been assumed to be part of an elaborate fertility cult, but, in fact, we have no means of knowing what functional and symbolic role they played in these societies (Figure 10.4).

Stylistic types are best exemplified by items such as dress, because style is often used to convey information by displaying it in public. The Aztecs of central Mexico lived in a ranked society where everyone's dress was carefully regulated by sumptuary laws (Figure 8.7). Thus, a glance at the noble in the marketplace could reveal not only his rank but the number of prisoners he had taken in battle and many other subtle facts. Even the gods had their own regalia and costumes that reflected their roles in the pantheon. Stylistic types can be expected, theoretically at any rate, to have a structure entirely different from that of functional ones. As such, they are not used often in archaeological classification, except when historical records are available. The approach is much debated.

What Do Assemblages and Patternings Mean?

For generations archaeologists studying culture history classified artifacts into assemblages, associations of tools that were thought to be contemporary. This approach assumed that human culture had evolved through the millennia. Thus artifact assemblages were merely traces of contemporary cultural "species" that extended far back into prehistory. This "organic" view of culture history saw assemblages of

PASTE

Tempering   Grit, diameters ranging from −0.5 to 2.0 mm. The appearance and composition (quartz, mica and a little feldspar) suggest that the tempering material is a decomposed granite.

Texture   Medium to coarse.

Hardness   3.0–4.0.

Color   Tan to dark gray; exterior surfaces often heavily carboned.

FORM

Overall shape   Jars with collared rims, constricted necks, rounded shoulders, and rounded bottoms.

Lip   Rounded, occasionally thickened by the addition of a small bracing fillet on the exterior surface.

Rim   All the rims are collared. The collars range from 24 to 55 mm. in height. Interior and exterior profiles are more or less parallel to each other, forming a straight or concave plane which extends downward and outward from the lip. The lower edge of the collar is marked by a fairly abrupt shoulder which forms the junction between the collar and the low curved neck. The bottom of the collar is sometimes scalloped. Below the neck, the vessel wall turns outward toward the shoulder. These rims might be contrasted with the rims of the Foreman types by describing them as Z-rims rather than S-rims, since the surface is flat or concave rather than convex.

Neck   A relatively low, constricted zone below the shoulder of the rim.

Shoulder   Rounded.

Base   Rounded.

HANDLES   One sherd has a short tablike lug extending down from the lower edge of the collar in the same plane as the face of the collar itself. Two others have fractured areas which seem to indicate the presence of loop handles running from the base of the rim collar to the shoulder of the vessel.

SURFACE FINISH   Bodies simple stamped, some with extensive plain areas. The stamping on one of the restored vessels is vertical. Necks are plain or brushed vertically; interior surfaces are plain.

DECORATION   The decoration is confined to the rim and lip. It is preponderantly cord impressed. Patterns consist of a series of horizontal lines, or a series of interlocking triangles filled alternately with horizontal and diagonal cord impressions. The cord-impressed zone is sometimes bordered by a series of punctations. Two pieces were decorated with diagonal broad-trailed lines, and one was plain except for a series of punctations at the base of the rim.

REMARKS   A number of the pieces assigned to Colombe Collared Rim at the Phillips Ranch site show a considerable similarity to some Lower Loup sherds from Nebraska. The most striking difference is in the incised decoration on the Nebraska pieces and the predominantly cord-impressed decoration on the Phillips Ranch rims.

FROM: D. J. Lehmer, *Archaeological Investigations in the Oahe Dam Area, South Dakota, 1950–51*, Bureau of American Ethnology, Bulletin 158, 1954.

Figure 8.6 An archaeologist's type description of a pottery type from South Dakota, "Colombe Collared Rim." This description appears exactly as it was published in 1954 by D.J. Lehmer. This example illustrates the detail required for type description. (Do not be dismayed if you do not understand some of the technical terms used; they are irrelevant to the main discussion of types in this text.)

Figure 8.7 Aztec warriors wearing elaborate uniforms signifying different ranks, awarded according to the number of captives taken in battle. From the Codex Mendoza.

artifacts as distinct categories, like organic species, which did not modify their form from one context to the next. It was assumed in the organic approach that a specific cultural tradition leads to only one characteristic type of industry in the archaeological record, an industry circumscribed in time and space.

The organic view of the past is a highly organized scheme, rather like the Medieval "Chain of Being" in early biology, where every living thing had its place in the general scheme of things.

American archaeologists have generally preferred a more "cultural" perspective, making considerable use of data on artifacts and other culture traits known to have been used by living societies in North America. The observation of these data has shown that there is a strong correlation between the distributions of distinctive cultural forms and different environments. For example, plank houses and an elaborate canoe technology are characteristic of the peoples of the Pacific Northwest coast, where readily split cedar and other trees flourished in abundance. In contrast, desert peoples in the Great Basin lived in much more transitory settlements of brush shelters and houses, using a highly portable toolkit that was adapted to a mobile desert lifeway. It is all very well to say that such correlations were true of historic times, but what about earlier prehistory? Can one say that artifact assemblages from the Great Basin dating to 5000 years ago reflect similar adaptations, similar social groups? Were conditions different in the past from today—can one use modern artifact patternings as a basis for interpreting ancient behavior?

Some archaeologists, among them Lewis Binford, have attacked this problem by studying living hunter-gatherer societies. Binford spent time among the Nunamiut caribou hunters of northern Alaska. There he learned that the only way to understand a living society's subsistence and material culture was to conceive of all their sites as part of a larger system. The Nunamiut had residential sites and other kinds of sites used for specialized purposes. Thus, he argued, archaeologists have to identify the specific function of each site they examine, then fit the sites into a much larger, overall pattern of land use. Archaeology's basic unit is the site; the artifacts in it are part of an assemblage pattern that reveals the different activities that took place there. If archaeologists want to understand the dynamics of cultural systems like that of the Nunamiut in the past, they will have to study and interpret prehistoric living conditions, using such classificatory devices as typology, tool frequencies, and the relationships between tool debris and finished artifacts, as just some of their methods of doing so. Thus, the role of classification in archaeology is shifting away from "organic" viewpoints that see artifacts and cultures as finite in time and space, to new means of problem-oriented classification that concentrate not only on individual tools, but on entire assemblages and their patternings.

But the data for interpreting these patterns must finally come from sources other than stone tools or potsherds. In other words, classification alone is meaningless, unless the classifications are interpreted in terms of other data. And here is where the study of contemporary societies—Middle-Range Research—is coming into its own (Chapter 11). Artifact classifications are still carried out for the most part with approaches meant for reconstructing culture history, formulations of time and space that owed much to functional classifications of artifacts based on common sense. At the same time, however, new explanatory frameworks based on theories of cultural evolution are providing new explanations of the past. They are designed to account for the structure and change that everyone can see in the archaeological record of the ages, phenomena that are far more dynamic and ever-changing than the more rigid classifications of earlier scholars imply. Robert Dunnell and other theorists have pointed out that these new explanatory frameworks render it unimportant when a new element in human culture such as, say, the plow, was invented or first appeared. What matters is how and why it becomes accepted and visible in the archaeological record. The challenge for the archaeologist is to devise new methods for classifying artifacts that enable us to identify processes of cultural evolution in the archaeological record. Research into this most fundamental of problems is still in its infancy.

Units of Ordering

Recall from Chapter 6 that an assemblage is the diverse group of artifacts found together that reflects the shared activities of a community.
This assemblage was found in a single site. Recall too that the site is
the fundamental unit for all stratigraphic studies in archaeology. If
time has passed, one can assume that at least some culture has taken
place at a site.

Many archaeological sites, such as the Olsen-Chubbock site in
Colorado, consist of a single assemblage of artifacts and a single component—another archaeological unit. A **component** is a physically
bounded portion of a site that contains a distinct assemblage, which
serves to distinguish the culture of the inhabitants of a particular level.
Sites that were occupied many times, like Hogup Cave in Utah, contain many components, each of them distinguished by assemblages
that separate them in time and space from other components at the
same site. The social equivalent of the archaeologist's component is
the **community.**

Once the research team's analysis is completed, they may find
they have only one component with which to deal. If the site was occupied several times, they might have two or three. How do they compare these components with those from other, nearby sites? And how
do they develop a sequence of occupation levels and cultures for their
local area?

When all the artifact collections from the local area have been analyzed and classified to everyone's satisfaction, they are ordered in
space and time with the aid of stratigraphic observations, seriation,
cross-dating, and radiocarbon or tree-ring dates. We described both
seriation and cross-dating techniques that place artifacts in chronological order with the help of battleship curves and dated components—
in Chapter 4. Figure 8.8 shows how the team joined ten sites into a
local sequence, a chronological ordering built up from several multi-
component sites and some single-component settlements within the
area. They were also able to obtain some radiocarbon dates to give an
accurate chronology for the sequence.

When the team studied the distribution of their sites, they discovered that two different dated components were repeated at settlements over a considerable area. These were so well dated and precisely distributed in time that two phases in the sequence could be
identified.

A **phase** is a cultural unit represented by like components on different sites or at different levels of the same site, although always
within a well-defined chronological bracket. The characteristic assemblage of artifacts of the phase may be found over hundreds of miles
within the area covered by a local sequence. Many archaeologists use
the term "culture" in the same sense as phase. Both are concepts de-

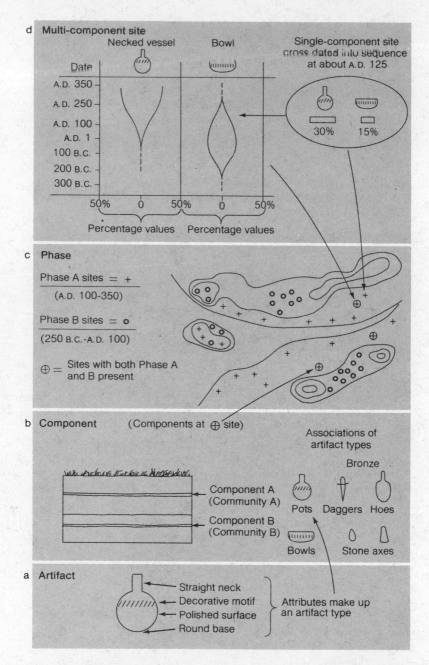

d Multi-component site

Necked vessel   Bowl

Single-component site
cross dated into sequence
at about A.D. 125

Date

A.D. 350
A.D. 250
A.D. 100
A.D. 1
100 B.C.
200 B.C.
300 B.C.

50%   0   50%   0   50%

30%   15%

Percentage values   Percentage values

c Phase

Phase A sites = +
(A.D. 100-350)

Phase B sites = o
(250 B.C.-A.D. 100)

⊕ = Sites with both Phase A
and B present

b Component   (Components at ⊕ site)

Associations of
artifact types

Bronze

Component A
(Community A)   Pots   Daggers   Hoes

Component B
(Community B)   Bowls   Stone axes

a Artifact

Straight neck
Decorative motif
Polished surface
Round base

Attributes make up
an artifact type

Figure 8.8 Archaeological units in use. (a) Patterns of attributes form an artifact type. (b) Cross-section through a hypothetical archaeological site with two stratified components. The two components are radiocarbon dated to between 250 B.C. and A.D. 100 and between A.D. 100 and 350, respectively. Our artifact type is a diagnostic vessel in Component A, the later one. The total artifact content from the site is the assemblage. (c) Now the archaeologists have studied dozens of sites in their archaeological region, which consists of an estuary with an offshore island. Higher ground with

signed to assist in ordering artifacts in time and space. Phases or cultures usually are named after a key site where characteristic artifacts are found. The *Acheulian* culture, for example, is named after the northern French town of St. Acheul, where the stone hand axes so characteristic of this culture are found (Figure 6.1).

Larger Archaeological Units

After many seasons' work, the research team may have studied several local sequences and may be able to describe their finds in a wide context such as that of the dozens of local sequences within the southwestern United States. Some characteristic art styles or artifacts, such as the Chavín art that flourished in Peru between 900 B.C. and 200 B.C., spread over enormous distances (Figure 8.4). Archaeologists sometimes use the term **horizon** to cover such phenomena, where a number of phases in neighboring areas contain rather general cultural patterns in common. The term **tradition** is used to describe a lasting artifact type, assemblages of tools, architectural styles, economic practices, or art styles that last much longer than one phase or even the duration of a horizon. A single toolmaking tradition may continue in use while the many cultures that share it develop in entirely different ways. A good example of a tradition is the so-called Paleo-arctic tradition of Alaska that originated at least as early as 8500 B.C. and lasted for several thousand years. Perhaps the most renowned larger archaeological units are those identified by the Danish archaeologist Christian Jurgensen Thomsen in 1807. His Stone Age, Bronze Age, and Iron Age technological labels are still in wide use.

In this chapter, we have discussed the classification of artifacts and their use in the construction of cultural units, primary activities in archaeology. Before considering the ways in which archaeologists use this information to study culture change, we must examine methods of studying human subsistence in the past, and approaches to changing settlement patterns in prehistory.

---

pine forest overlooks the estuary. When they plotted site distributions, they found that the earlier, Phase B sites were distributed on the higher ground, and the later components were established near the shore where shellfish were abundant. Only three sites contain both components, stratified one above the other. The two distributions are distinctive, both phases defined in space and time, forming a local sequence. (d) At the four 2-component sites, the archaeologists seriated the pottery types and other artifacts and obtained distinctive battleship curves. Then they were able to fit other sites into the same sequence by cross-dating.

9

SUBSISTENCE

There was a noise, and behold a shaking, and the bones came together, bone to his bone.
And when I beheld, lo, the sinews and the flesh came up upon them, and the skin covered them above, but there was no breath in them.

Ezekiel 37:7–8

We now consider one of the most fascinating questions in archaeology: How did prehistoric peoples make their living? Once archaeologists realized that human prehistory was the story of humanity's diverse and constantly changing adaptations to world environments, they could not afford to ignore prehistoric subsistence activities, the ways in which people had fed themselves and achieved a satisfactory diet.

When studying prehistoric subsistence, the archaeologist seeks to answer many fundamental questions, among them: What was the role of domestic animals in a mixed farming economy? How important was fishing to a shellfish-oriented population living by the ocean? Was a site occupied seasonally while the inhabitants concentrated on, say, bird snaring to the exclusion of all other subsistence activities? What agricultural systems were used? How was the land cultivated? In this chapter we review some of the ways in which we seek the answers to these and related subsistence questions.

EVIDENCE FOR SUBSISTENCE

The archaeological evidence for prehistoric subsistence consists of artifacts and food remains. How much survives depends, of course, on preservation conditions on the site. All too often the evidence for ancient diet is incomplete. Stone axes or iron hoe blades may give an indication of hunting or agriculture, but they hardly yield the kind of detail archaeologists need. Many artifacts used in the chase or for agriculture were made from such perishable materials as bone, wood, and fiber (Figure 9.1).

Food remains themselves survive very unevenly. The bones and teeth of larger mammals are the most common economic data, but

Figure 9.1 A reconstructed stone axe used by early Danish farmers for forest clearance. Such artifacts tell us little about prehistoric economic practices.

careful excavation will often reveal remains of such small animals as birds, fish, and frogs as well as invertebrates, such as beetles. Vegetal remains are very perishable and are usually underrepresented.

PREHISTORIC DIET

The ultimate aim in studying prehistoric food remains is not only to establish how people obtained their food, but to reconstruct their actual diet as well. An overall picture of prehistoric diet requires, of course, constructing a comprehensive list of food resources available to the people and then answering questions such as: What proportion of the diet was meat? How diverse were dietary sources? Did the principal diet sources change from season to season? Was food stored? These and many other questions can be answered only from composite pictures of prehistoric diet reconstructed from many sources of evidence.

Just occasionally, however, it is possible to gain insights into actual meals consumed thousands of years ago. The stomach of Tollund man, whose body was buried and preserved in a Danish peat bog, contained the remains of finely ground porridge made from barley, linseed, and several wild grasses (see Figure 6.2). No meat was found in his belly. Human excrement (coprolites or feces) found in dry caves in the United States and Mexico have been analyzed microscopically. The inhabitants of *Lovelock Cave* in the central Nevada desert were eating bulrush and cattail seeds, as well as Lahontan chub from the waters of nearby Humboldt Lake. These fish were eaten raw or roasted over a fire. One coprolite contained the remains of at least 51 chub, calculated by a fish expert to represent a total fish weight of 3.65 pounds. The same people were eating adult and baby birds, as well as water tiger beetles. Human feces from Texas caves near the mouth of the Pecos River have been subjected to pollen analyses so precise that the investigators established the sites to have been occupied regularly during the spring and summer months for 1300 years between 800 B.C. and A.D. 550.

Although coprolite studies are a promising source of dietary information, the food remains from most sites are far too incomplete to allow more than a very general impression of diet. Recently, however, new research using the ratio between two stable carbon isotopes—^{12}C and ^{13}C in animal tissue—has enabled scientists to establish the diet of prehistoric populations as they switched from wild foods to a predominantly maize diet. Carbon is metabolized in plants through three major pathways: ^{4}C, ^{3}C, and by Crussalacean acid metabolism. The plants that make up the diet of animals have distinct ^{13}C values. Maize, for example, is a ^{4}C plant. In contrast, most indigenous temperate flora in North America is composed of ^{3}C varieties. Thus, a population that shifts its diet from wild vegetable foods to maize will also experience a shift in dietary isotopic values. Because ^{13}C and ^{12}C values do not change after death, you can study archaeological carbon from food remains, humus, and skeletal remains to gain insight into ancient diet. This approach is yielding promising results. For example, a study of prehistoric populations in Southeast Missouri and Northeast Arkansas showed a dramatic shift in the ^{13}C value after A.D. 1000, when intensive maize cultivation took hold in the area.

ANIMAL BONES

Broken animal bones can tell us a great deal about ancient hunting, herd management, and butchery practices. One can identify mammal species from their skeletal remains. Unfortunately, however, most animal bones found in archaeological sites are highly fragmentary. Until recently, archaeologists assumed that they were in such small fragments because the inhabitants slashed to ribbons every carcass they butchered. But researches on modern predator kills and controlled experiments on butchered animals, mainly in Africa, have shown that a great many complex and little-understood forces act on bones found in archaeological sites long after they are dropped where archaeologists find them. Weathering as bones decay in the open air, compaction of the sediments in which they are buried, chemistry of the soil, even treading by animals can break up bones and help determine which parts of the body survive and which do not. Add to these accidents the butchering activities of the prehistoric inhabitants and you have an archaeological jigsaw puzzle to piece together (Figure 9.2).

Generally speaking, the older the archaeological site, the more daunting it is to study postdepositional forces. The problem is particularly confusing at locations such as Olduvai Gorge or *Koobi Fora* in East Africa, where hominids chewed and cut bones more than 1.75 million years ago—and probably scavenged their meat from predator

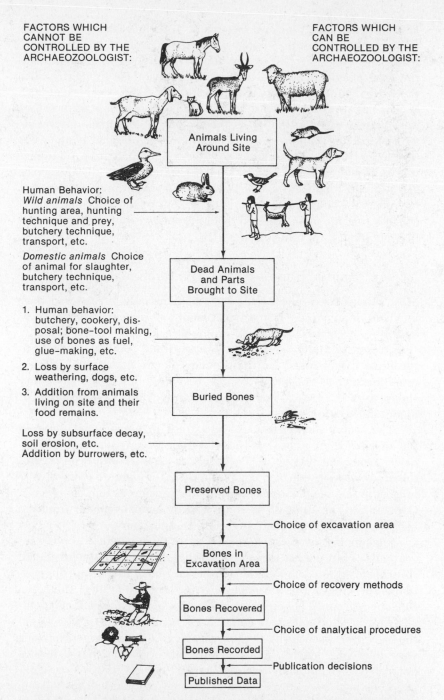

FACTORS WHICH CANNOT BE CONTROLLED BY THE ARCHAEOZOOLOGIST:

FACTORS WHICH CAN BE CONTROLLED BY THE ARCHAEOZOOLOGIST:

Animals Living Around Site

Human Behavior:
Wild animals Choice of hunting area, hunting technique and prey, butchery technique, transport, etc.

Domestic animals Choice of animal for slaughter, butchery technique, transport, etc.

Dead Animals and Parts Brought to Site

1. Human behavior: butchery, cookery, disposal; bone-tool making, use of bones as fuel, glue-making, etc.

2. Loss by surface weathering, dogs, etc.

3. Addition from animals living on site and their food remains.

Buried Bones

Loss by subsurface decay, soil erosion, etc.
Addition by burrowers, etc.

Preserved Bones

Choice of excavation area

Bones in Excavation Area

Choice of recovery methods

Bones Recovered

Choice of analytical procedures

Bones Recorded

Publication decisions

Published Data

Figure 9.2 Some of the factors that affect animal bones found in archaeological sites. On the left are factors over which the archaeologist has no control; on the right, those that can be controlled.

151

kills in the bargain. On more recent sites, one finds that people often utilized the carcasses they butchered to the maximum. Every piece of usable meat was stripped by the inhabitants from the bones of even the smallest animals or the portions of larger mammals brought back to the settlement. Sinews were made into thongs. Skins became clothing, containers, or even part of a shelter. Even the entrails were eaten. The hunters smashed the bones themselves to get at the marrow or for manufacture into arrowheads or other tools. Animal bones were fragmented by many domestic activities, quite apart from trampling underfoot and scavenging by dogs and carnivores. Thus, the archaeologist is faced with the formidable task of identifying from tiny, discarded fragments the animal that was hunted or kept by the site's inhabitants and the role the animal played in the economy, diet, and culture of the community.

Animal Bone Analysis (Zooarchaeology)

Most animal bone collections consist of thousands of scattered fragments from all parts of a site. Occasionally, however, a kill site, perhaps from prehistoric bison kills on the Great Plains or the big game slaughtered by Stone Age hunters in East Africa, provides a chance to reconstruct the hunters' activities in more detail. Apart from such unusual finds, most collections have to be sorted out in the laboratory simply to give a general impression of hunting and stock-raising techniques at the site.

The goal of **zooarchaeology**—the study of animal bones found in the archaeological record—is to reconstruct the environment and behavior of ancient peoples as thoroughly as animal remains allow. But the study of such bones is complicated by the natural and humanly induced processes that operate on organic remains as they lie on or in the ground. The study of this transition by animal remains from the biosphere to the lithosphere is known as **taphonomy.**

Taphonomy involves two related forms of research: observing recently dead carcasses as they are gradually transformed into fossils and studying fossil remains with the knowledge gained from these observations. The crux of the zooarchaeologists' difficulty is their subject: a collection of animal bones, the part of the fossil assemblage that is actually excavated or collected. This fossil assemblage in turn consists of the body parts that survive in the archaeological record, an assemblage very different from the original community of live animals that once populated the natural environment in their "natural" proportions. Animal bone analysis involves two fundamental problems: (1) estimating the characteristics of a fossil assemblage from a collected sample, a statistical problem; and (2) a taphonomic problem, inferring what the original bone assemblage was like before it became a fossil (Figure 9.2).

The first stage in bone analysis is to isolate the diagnostic fragments. Often only a few bones are identifiable to the species level. One 3000-year-old central African hunting camp yielded only 2,128 identifiable fragments out of 195,415 bones! The actual identifications are made by comparing such diagnostic body parts as teeth, jaws, horns, and some limb bones with modern animal skeletons (Figure 9.3). This procedure is not as easy as it sounds. Domestic sheep and

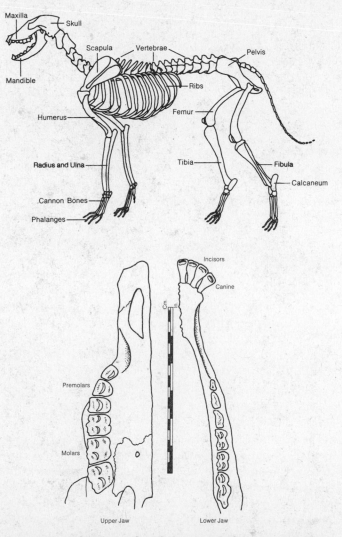

Figure 9.3 At the top, a dog skeleton with the most important body parts labeled from the bone identification point of view. At the bottom, a domestic ox jaw seen from below (upper jaw) and above (lower jaw). Notice the characteristic cusp patterns of molars and premolars that grow as the beast gets older.

goats have skeletons that are almost identical to those of their wild ancestors, the bones of the domestic ox closely resemble those of the African buffalo, and so on. But accurate identifications are vital, for they provide answers to many questions. Are both domestic and wild animals present? If so, what are the proportions of each group? Were the inhabitants concentrating on one species to the exclusion of all others? Are any now-extinct species present?

Comparing Bone Collections

Having identified the animals present, how do you compare the proportions of different species from one site to those from another? The work is fraught with difficulty because it is almost impossible to infer the once-living population from the surviving bones. Zooarchaeologists therefore apply two measures of specimen abundance to study the relative abundance of species:

> *The Number of Identified Specimens* (NISP) is a count of the number of bones or bone fragments. This assay has obvious disadvantages, because it is easy to overestimate one species at the expense of another, especially if its bones are cut into small fragments. The NISP has some limited use in conjunction with:

> *The Minimum Number of Individuals* (MNI), a count of the number of individuals necessary to account for all the identifiable bones. This count is based on careful inventories of such individual body parts as, say, jaws. The MNI is a much more accurate estimate of the number of animals present in a collection.

Using these two counts together brackets the actual number of animals present in a bone sample, but the figure is still but an approximation, even when used with sophisticated computer programs.

Species Abundance and Cultural Change

Climatic change rather than human culture was probably responsible for most long-term shifts in abundance of animal species during the great Ice Age. Some changes in the abundance of animals in bone collections, however, must reflect human activity—changes in the way in which people exploited animals.

Zooarchaeologist Richard Klein has studied two coastal caves in South Africa to document such changes. The Klasies River cave on the Cape coast was occupied by "Middle Stone Age" hunters from about 130,000 to about 70,000 years ago, during a period of progressively colder climate. The people took seals, penguins, and shellfish and lived off the eland, a large antelope. The nearby Nelson's Bay cave was occupied by "Late Stone Age" people, after 20,000 years ago. These people took not only dangerous or elusive land mammals such as the Cape buffalo but birds and fish as well, both quarries requiring some skill to hunt or take successfully.

Did these changes between the two sites reflect cultural change or climatic differences? Were eland more abundant in earlier times, or just easier to hunt? Klein examined the toolkits from each cave, and found that Middle Stone Age artifacts were large and relatively crude, but the later Nelson's Bay people used bows, arrows, and an elaborate toolkit of small, more specialized tools. This more-sophisticated toolkit allowed the Nelson's Bay groups to hunt more dangerous and tricky quarry with great success. Therefore, eland were less plentiful later not because of climatic change, but because other animals were hunted, too. Then too, in later times the population was larger. Klein suggests the growth from his examination of the limpet and tortoise shells from both sites. The Nelson's Bay specimens are smaller, as if these creatures were allowed to grow larger in earlier millennia when fewer people were there to exploit them.

Game Animals

A collection of game animals yields a wealth of information about the great variety of mammals that ancient hunters killed with astonishingly simple weapons. North American Paleo-Indian bands used game drives, spears, and other weapons to hunt herds of now-extinct big game. So effective were early American hunters that some zoologists believe much Plains big game to have become extinct at least partly as a result of overhunting. Twenty thousand years ago, big-game hunters on the banks of the Dnieper and Don rivers in western Russia cooperated in pursuing mammoth and other arctic mammals. They cached supplies of game meat to tide them through the long, bitterly cold winters, which lasted more than eight months.

When the identified game animal bones are counted, one species may appear to dominate. Some hunters concentrate on one or a few species, whether from economic necessity, convenience, or cultural preference. But the dominance can be misleading, for many societies restrict the hunting of particular animals. Others forbid males or females to eat certain species, though others may be consumed by everyone. The !Kung San of the Kalahari today have complicated personal and age- or sex-specific taboos to regulate their eating habits. No one may eat all the 29 game animals regularly taken by the San. Indeed, no two individuals will have the same set of taboos. Such complicated restrictions are repeated with innumerable variations in other hunter-gatherer societies. The simple dietary figure of, say, 40 percent white-tailed deer and 20 percent wild geese may, in fact, reflect much more complex behavioral variables than mere concentration on two species.

Domesticated Animals

Domestic animal bones present even more difficulties. Owners can affect their herds and flocks in many ways—by selective breeding to improve meat yields or to increase wool production, and by regulating the ages at which they slaughter surplus males and old animals. All domesticated animals originated from wild species with an inclination to be sociable, a characteristic that aided close association with humans. Animal domestication may have begun when a growing human population needed a regular food supply to support a greater density of people per square mile. Wild animals lack many characteristics valuable in their domestic relatives. Wild sheep have hairy coats, but their wool is unsuitable for spinning. The ancestors of oxen and domestic goats produced milk for their young but not enough for human consumption. People have bred wild animals selectively for long periods to enhance special characteristics. Often the resulting domestic animals can no longer survive in the wild.

The history of domestic animals must be written from fragmentary animal bones found in sites occupied by prehistoric farmers. The difference between domestic and wild animal bones is often so small that it may be next to impossible to tell the two apart. No one can tell a domestic sheep or goat from a wild one from a single jaw. One has to work with large numbers of animals, studying changing body sizes as the animals undergo selective breeding. Early Near Eastern domestic sheep are smaller and display less variation in size than their wild relatives. Even then, it is, state the Scriptures, "difficult to tell the sheep from the goats."

Aging and Butchery

Prehistoric peoples hunted game animals for food, used their hides for garments and tents, and their stomachs for bags. Domesticated animals provided meat and were used for plowing, riding, or for their milk. Establishing such practices from fragmentary animal bones is difficult, involving close study of both the age of slaughtered animals and the ways in which they were butchered.

Just as with comparing different assemblages, the problem is turning figures and percentages into meaningful interpretations of human behavior. Researches such as Lewis Binford's studies of Alaskan caribou hunters have provided valuable information for such approaches (see Chapter 11).

Determining the sex and age of an animal may provide a way of studying the hunting or stock-raising habits of those who slaughtered it. Many mammal species vary considerably in size and build between male and female. With species such as the North American bison, you can often distinguish male from female by bone sizes, but the determination is much more difficult with animals where the size difference is less.

Teeth and the epiphyses (joints) at the end of limb bones are most commonly used to establish the ages of prehistoric animals. In almost all mammals, the epiphyses fuse to the limb bones at adulthood, so one can immediately establish two categories of animals: immature and fully grown. Teeth and complete jaws are a more accurate way of establishing animal age. Teeth provide an almost continuous guide to the age of an animal from birth to old age. With complete jaws one can study immature teeth as they erupt. Large numbers of them enable you to count with some accuracy the proportions of immature and very old animals with heavily worn teeth.

Richard Klein has used the height of tooth crowns to study the age of mammals taken by Stone Age hunters at Klasies River and Nelson's Bay caves in South Africa. He identified two "mortality distributions" that apply to prehistoric and living animal populations:

> A **catastrophic age profile** is stable in size and structure, and has
> progressively fewer older individuals. This is the normal distri-
> bution for living antelope populations (Figure 9.4). If a group

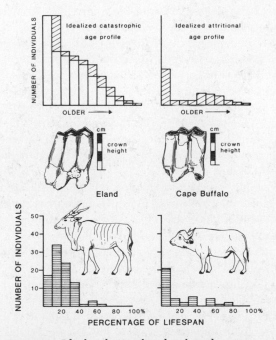

Figure 9.4 Idealized mortality data based on mo-
lar crowns of two common South African mammals, the eland and the Cape buffalo. Left, idealized catastrophic age profile. Right, idealized
attritional age profile (for explanation, see text).

of hunters drives a herd over a cliff, you will find a distribution like this, for they are not being discriminating in their hunting.

An **attritional age profile** shows underrepresentation of prime-age animals relative to their abundance in living populations, but young and old are overrepresented. This profile is thought to result from scavenging or simple spear hunting.

The eland tooth profiles at both Klasies River and Nelson's Bay were close to the catastrophic profile and so Klein argued that they were hunted in mass game drives. In contrast, the more formidable Cape buffalo displayed an attritional profile, as if the hunters had preyed on immature and old beasts over long periods.

These interpretations are fine at a general level, but it is much harder to draw more specific conclusions. Lewis Binford's Nunamiut caribou hunters from Alaska direct much of their hunting activities toward obtaining meat for winter consumption. In the fall, they pursue caribou calves to obtain clothing. The heads and tongues of these young animals provide meat for the people who process the skins.

The fragmentary bones in an occupation level are the end product of the killing, cutting up, and consumption of domestic or wild animals. To understand the butchery process, the articulation of animal bones must be examined in the levels where they are found, or a close study made of fragmentary pieces. Rarely is an entire kill site preserved, like the famed *Olsen-Chubbuck* bison kill in Colorado, where more than 150 bison were driven to their death, then dismembered, more than 8000 years ago. Archaeologist Joe Ben Wheat showed that for several days the hunters camped by their prey as they dismembered the uppermost bison in the confused heap of dead animals before them. When they had eaten their fill and dried enough meat to last them a month or more, they simply walked away and left the rotting carcasses. Archaeologists found the articulated and butchered skeletons thousands of years later.

Interpreting butchery techniques is a complicated matter, for many variables affect the way in which the carcass is dismembered. Toughness of hide, available tools, size and portability of the animal, and potential use for skins, even horn, are a few of the variables. The only way to interpret body parts in this context is by understanding in detail the cultural system that generated them. The herders, finding a constant surplus of males beyond their breeding requirements, may castrate some of these animals and then use them for riding and dragging carts or plows. But even with some insights into the cultural system and excellent bone preservation, it is frequently hard to interpret the meaning of butchering techniques.

So many factors affect the counts of identified bones from any collection of animal remains that one must interpret the fragments in the context of artifact patterns, site-formation processes, and all other sources of data potentially bearing on the behavior of the people who killed the animals.

VEGETAL REMAINS

Gathering and agriculture are almost invariably unrepresented in most sites because the tiny seeds and other vegetable remnants that result from such activities as food storage, grinding, and harvesting are among the most fragile of all archaeological remains. Except for occasional burned seeds found in hearths or storage pits, the vegetable remains from human feces, and grain impressions in clay pot walls, almost all evidence for prehistoric gathering and agriculture comes from dry sites, where preservation conditions are almost perfect (Figure 9.5).

Recovering such fragile remains requires meticulous work with fine screens. Some archaeologists have started to use flotation methods to recover thousands of hitherto unrecoverable vegetable remains. With this technique, water or chemicals are used to free tiny seeds

Figure 9.5 A grain impression preserved on a clay pot fragment from an early farming site in eastern England (approximately 2.2 inches diameter.)

from the deposits. The freshly excavated earth is poured into a container and sinks slowly to the bottom while the light seeds float to the surface. Stuart Struever was able to recover 36,000 hickory nut fragments, 4,200 acorn shells, and 2,000 seeds from other species from ovens, hearths, and pits in the *Apple Creek* site in the lower Illinois Valley using simple flotation techniques. At the *Ali Kosh* mound in Iran, Kent Flannery and Frank Hole thought that plant remains were scarce. Then they used flotation methods and recovered 40,000 seeds from the trenches. Flotation methods have begun to revolutionize the study of plant remains, for they provide large seed samples that can be studied with statistical methods.

Most of our knowledge of such early major food crops as wheat, barley, and maize has so far come from dry caves rather than flotation. Richard MacNeish assembled a continuous sequence of human occupation for the period 10,000 years ago to the Spanish Conquest from *Tehuacán Valley* in Mexico. He dug more than a dozen open sites and caves, all so dry that they yielded 80,000 wild plant remains and 25,000 specimens of domestic corn. When the vegetable remains had been identified, MacNeish knew that the inhabitants of Tehuacán were getting 18 percent of their food from cultivation of corn and other crops in 5000 B.C., and a third of it from agriculture in 3400 B.C. Fifteen hundred years later, several hybrid varieties of maize were in use and agriculture was far more important than foraging for wild plants. He also found that the earliest maize cobs, dating to around 5000 B.C. and earlier were no more than 0.78 inch long, but later ones were far larger. Unfortunately, MacNeish was unable to identify the original wild ancestor of Tehuacán maize, probably the native grass *teosinte*.

Farmers modify the landscape around them by grazing their herds and by clearing forests. Simple, shifting cultivation techniques required new garden acreage every season. Each time cultivation required more cleared woodland drastic environmental changes were triggered. Few people have ever tried to assess how profoundly early agricultural economies affected the world environment. Danish botanist Johannes Iversen was able to spot a sharp drop in the percentages of tree pollens in layers of northern European peat bogs dating to about 3000 B.C. The forest trees declined suddenly. At the same time, the number of grass pollens increased sharply. Traces of several cultivation weeds also appeared at the same time. Iversen was able to pin down the moment when farmers first cleared natural forest to make way for their crops.

This early clearance activity dramatizes how very little we know about prehistoric agriculture and gathering, simply because the archaeological evidence is so hard to recover. Our ignorance has led to the belief that all hunter-gatherers spent their lives in a perennial state of starvation, relieved occasionally by meat-eating orgies. Nothing could be further from the truth. The !Kung San, present-day inhabitants of the Kalahari Desert in southern Africa, know of at least 85 edible seeds and roots. Most of the time they eat but 8 of these. The rest of the vegetable resource base provides a reliable cushion for this foraging population in times when key vegetable foods are scarce. Such people have a buffer against famine that many farmers with their cleared lands, much higher population densities, and crops that rely on regular rainfall rarely enjoy. Is a farming life really to be preferred? Our glimpses into prehistory raise this tantalizing possibility.

BIRDS, FISH, AND MOLLUSKS

Bird bones, although very informative, are often neglected at the expense of larger mammal remains. In 1926, Hildegarde Howard studied a large bird bone collection from an Indian midden on the eastern shores of San Francisco Bay. The inhabitants had hunted many water birds, especially ducks, geese, and cormorants. When Howard looked more closely at the bones, she found that all the geese were migrant winter visitors that frequent the bay area between January and April. Nearly all the cormorants were immature specimens, birds about five to six weeks old. Had the Indians been raiding cormorant rookeries? Howard consulted rookery records and estimated that the birds had been killed about June 28. Thus, the site had been occupied both during the winter and early summer, one of many settlements where bird bones give evidence of seasonal occupation.

Fishing, like bird hunting, became more important as people began to specialize in different lifeways and adapt to highly specific environments. Evidence for fishing comes both from artifacts and fragile fish bones, which, when they survive, can be identified with considerable accuracy.

Freshwater and ocean fish may be caught with nets or basketlike fish traps. Indians who lived on the site of modern Boston in about 2500 B.C. built a dam of vertical stakes and brush. When the Atlantic tides rose, fish were directed into gaps in the dam and trapped in huge numbers. Barbed fish spears and fish hooks are relatively common finds in some archaeological sites, but such artifacts tell us little about the weight of fishing in prehistoric subsistence. Did the people fish all year or only when salmon were running? Did they concentrate on coastal species or venture far offshore in large canoes? Such questions can be answered only by examining the fish bones themselves.

The Chumash Indians of southern California were remarkably skillful fishermen, who went far offshore in frameless plank canoes to fish with hook and line, basket, net, and harpoon. It was no surprise when the fish bones found on archaeological sites at Century Ranch, Los Angeles, included not only the bones of such shallow-water fish as the leopard shark and California halibut, but the remains of albacore,

ocean skipjack, and large rock fish, species that occur in deep water
and can be caught only there. Without the fish bones, no one would
have had any idea how effective the maritime adaptation of the Chumash and related groups was. Early Spanish accounts speak of more
than 10,000 Indians living in the Santa Barbara area of California alone,
a large population indeed. Archaeology has shown that this maritime
population was able to exploit a very broad spectrum of marine resources.

Fishing, with its relatively predictable food resources and high
protein potential, allows much more sedentary settlement than other
forms of hunting and gathering. The Northwest coast Indians enjoyed
a very rich maritime culture based on ocean fishing and salmon runs
that enabled large numbers of people to live in one area for long periods.

Shellfish from seashore, lake, or river supplied a good portion of
the prehistoric diet for many thousands of years. Freshwater mollusks
were important both to California Indians and to prehistoric people
living in the southeastern United States. Most mollusks have limited
food value and so great quantities are needed to feed even a few people. One estimate for 100 peoples' mollusk needs for a month runs as
high as three tons. In all probability, mollusks were more a supple-
mental food at set times of the year than a staple. They were simply
too much effort to collect in sufficient quantity.

Even sporadic collecting led to rapidly accumulating piles of shells
(shell middens) at strategic points on lake or ocean shores, near rocky
outcrops or tidal pools where mollusks were commonly found.

Shell midden excavations in California and elsewhere have yielded
thousands of shells, which are counted, identified, and also measured
to check for size changes. When Claude Warren sampled a shell midden near San Diego, California, he found five major species of shellfish
commonly exploited by the inhabitants. The earliest shellfish collectors concentrated on the bay mussel and oysters, both of which flourish
on rocky shores. But, by 4000 B.C., the lagoon by the shell middens
had so silted up that mud-loving scallops and Venus shells were now
collected, for the earlier species were unable to flourish in the new,
sandy environment. Soon afterward, however, the lagoon became
clogged and the shellfish collectors moved away, never to return. And
their abandoned seashells told the story of the changing environment
around the sites.

Both fresh- and saltwater shells were widely used as prehistoric
ornaments. Gulf Coast shells were bartered over enormous distances
of the southeastern and midwestern United States to peoples who had
never seen the ocean. Sometimes such ornaments could assume incredible prestige value. When nineteenth-century explorer David Liv-
ingstone visited Chief Shinte in central Africa in 1855, he found him
wearing two seashells that had come 1000 miles inland from the distant

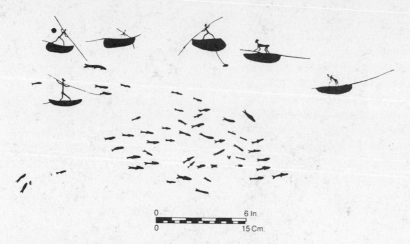

Figure 9.6 The fishing scene from Tsoelike rockshelter, Lesotho, southern Africa.

East African coast. The chief told him that two such shells would buy a slave, five a large ivory elephant tusk. Small wonder that enterprising merchants were trading china replicas of these shells in central Africa half a century later.

ROCK ART

Sometimes prehistoric rock art gives vivid insight into subsistence activities of long ago, such as hunts and fishing expeditions in the distant past. Hunter-gatherers and fishing cultures have left paintings of their daily life behind on the walls of caves and rockshelters. Careful examination of these paintings can take one back centuries and millennia to the time when the people were killing the animals whose bones lie in occupation deposits under the observer's feet. Many details of weapons, domestic equipment, and hunting and fishing methods can be discerned in these vivid scenes.

The Stone Age paintings of southern Africa have long been known for their depictions of life in prehistoric times. At Tsoelike River rockshelter in Lesotho, southern Africa, fishermen are depicted assembled in their boats (Figure 9.6). They have cornered a shoal of fish that are swimming around in confusion. Some boats have lines that seem to be anchors. The fishermen are busy spearing their quarry. Another famed scene depicts a peacefully grazing herd of ostriches. Among them lurks a hunter wearing an ostrich skin, his legs and bow protruding beneath the belly of the apparently harmless bird. One can only wonder if his hunt was successful.

The artists painted big-game hunts, honey collectors, women gathering fruit, cattle raids, even red-coated British soldiers. Scenes like these take one back to hot days when a small group of hunters pursued their wounded quarry until it weakened and collapsed. The hunters, having stalked their prey for hours, relax in the shade as they watch its death throes. Then they settle down to butcher the dead animal before carrying the meat and skin home to be shared with their group. Few artifacts survive from scenes such as these, but the objective of reconstructing ancient subsistence patterns is to re-create, from the few patterned traces that have survived in the soil, just such long days in the sun.

10

INTERACTION

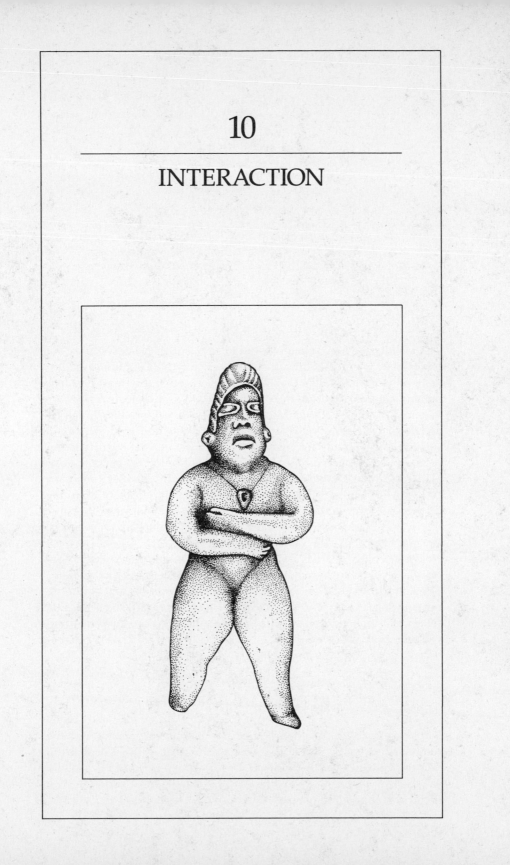

*Thus the sum of things is ever being replenished, and mortals
live one and all by give and take. Some races wax and wane,
and in a short space the tribes of living things are changed and
like runners hand on the torch of life.*

Lucretius, *De Rerum Natura*

The toolkits and food remains found in archaeological sites reflect their
inhabitants' material culture and subsistence activities. Hunter-gatherers tend to have portable toolkits, manufactured for the most part from
organic materials that do not survive well in archaeological sites (see
Figure 5.5). Many of their sites are temporary camps. Rarely can the
archaeologist look at the patterning of artifacts and food remains in
such camps, for many are gone forever. But the more sedentary farmer
settles much longer in one spot and is confronted with much more
elaborate annual tasks. The farmer has to store each year's food surplus, too, an activity that immediately adds complexity to a farming
settlement. Substantial houses, storage pits, cemeteries, threshing
floors, cattle enclosures—all these can be elements in even a small
farming village.

Archaeologists study patterning in such structures as houses and
storage pits just as thoroughly as they study artifacts and food remains.
They also study distributions in time and space of different communities and relationships between them. These activities are classified as
settlement archaeology, which reveals the many ways in which individual communities relate to one another—through trade, religious
beliefs, and social ties among others.

SETTLEMENT PATTERNS

Settlement patterns are determined by many factors, including environment, economic practices, and technological skills. The distribution of San camps in the Kalahari Desert depends on the availability
of water supplies and vegetable foods. Ancient Maya settlements in
Mexico were laid out in a pattern determined by political and religious

organization. Village layout can be determined by the need to protect cattle against lions or raiding parties. Other settlements may be strung out at intervals along a vital trade route, perhaps a river. Population growth or increases in herd size may overtax the capacity of hunting grounds or grazing areas, leading to new adaptations and alterations in the settlement pattern. Even the positions of houses are dictated by complex and various social, economic, and personal factors that may defy explanation—especially when one has only archaeological evidence to go on.

Settlement archaeology is part of the analysis of human interactions with, and adaptations to, the natural and social environment. The houses and villages of a prehistoric society, like the artifacts and food residues by their hearths, are part of the settlement pattern. This pattern involves relationships among people who decided—for practical, political, economic, ideological, and social reasons—to place their houses, settlements, and religious structures where they did. By studying settlement patterns, we have a chance to examine the intangible factors that caused culture change in prehistory.

Canadian archaeologist Bruce Trigger has recognized three distinct levels of human settlement: The first is the single building; the second, the arrangement of such buildings within a community; the third, the distribution of communities against the landscape. We will examine each of these three levels briefly.

Structures

Human structures are of infinite variety, all the way from the simple brush shelters of hunter-gatherers to the elaborate villas of Imperial Rome. The pyramids of Giza, Maya temples, even cattle pens, are all structures. Both environmental and societal factors as well as economic considerations have dictated the design of human structures. Twenty thousand years ago big-game hunters on the West Russian plains lived half-underground in houses made of skins and mammoth (arctic elephant) bones. These structures were effective in protecting their inhabitants against cold in a timberless environment. In contrast, tropical African farmers live where daytime temperatures regularly exceed 100 degrees Fahrenheit and the nights too are hot. And so they live much of their lives in the shade of their pole-and-mud huts whose thatched roofs project far beyond the walls. Grass, puddled mud, and other convenient local raw materials provide insulation for humankind—whether from summer's heat or arctic cold.

Details of house design are often determined by social and economic considerations. Many societies have had standardized house plans, for everyone had the same economic opportunities and the same amount of wealth. The householders carried out various activities at home, reflected in the patterning of artifacts in abandoned rooms. Variations in artifact content can reflect different subsistence activities, social status, wealth, and manufacturing skills.

When Kent Flannery and his students excavated farming villages in the Valley of Oaxaca, Mexico, dating to between 1350 and 850 B.C., they not only uncovered and recorded the one-room, thatched, pole-and-mud-houses, but plotted the associated artifact patterns as well. They distinguished carefully between the house with its contents and the cluster of household storage pits, graves, and garbage heaps that lay nearby. Flannery plotted household features very carefully, and he also identified areas where special activites took place from the special-ist toolkits—for bead making and the like—associated with them. Ev-ery household obtained, processed, and stored food, although the types of food consumed by each varied, and some Oaxacan households spent much time making stone tools or ornaments. These specialist activities presumably supplied the needs of the community as a whole. In this Mexican example, and in all studies of individual structures, the artifacts and activites associated with them are just as important to the archaeologist as the design and layout of the structure itself.

Communities

Every household member interacts with other members of the house-hold and also with individuals in other households within the commu-nity. And entire households interact with other households as well. Once one begins to look at a community of households, new complexi-ties enter the picture. The first is permanency of settlement, which is affected primarily by the realities of subsistence and ecology. How long San camps are occupied is determined by availability of water, game, and vegetable foods near the site; the camp moves at regular intervals. At the other extreme, early city dwellers in Mesopotamia who used irrigation in their fields never had to move their settlement.

The layout of a community is greatly determined by social and political factors, particularly by family and kinship ties. Marriage cus-toms and rules of residence and inheritance may multiply the number of houses associated with one household. A father may live with his sons in a cattle camp—their families occupy houses within his enclo-sure. Variables such as land ownership may be reflected in community layout too. The only way archaeologists can study these factors is by looking for patterns of settlement features and artifacts that may reflect kin groups and other social ties.

The largest community settlement pattern ever investigated sys-tematically is that of *Teotihuacán* where René Millon has mapped doz-ens of residential compounds, a market, and vast ceremonial structures (Figure 10.1). He even found a special quarter where foreigners from Oaxaca—revealed by their distinctive pottery—lived in an alien city

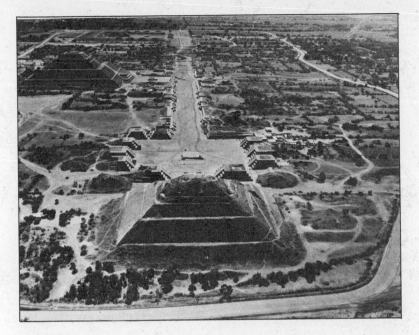

Figure 10.1 Teotihuacán, Valley of Mexico, a prehistoric city that was mapped in detail by René Millon. The Pyramid of the Moon is in the foreground; the Avenue of the Dead stretches into the distance; the giant Pyramid of the Sun is to the left of the avenue in the distance. (From *Urbanization at Teotihuacán, Mexico*, vol. 1, pt. 1, *The Teotihuacán Map: Text* by René Millon, copyright © 1973 by Rene Millon, reprinted by permission of the author.)

for centuries. Millon sought the answers to many questions. What social classes existed in the city? What specialist crafts were practiced and where? How many people lived at Teotihuacán at different periods? The only way to answer such questions was to map the entire city and make comprehensive surface collections and test excavations to give an overall picture of the total settlement pattern.

How can one measure the size of small villages, let alone huge cities like Teotihuacán? Informed guesses are sometimes useful, but the only reliable method is to calculate the population by the number of households in a village at a given moment in its history. And such calculations require large-scale excavations and complex statistical tests. In Teotihuacán, Millon counted rooms and possible sleeping spaces and came up with an intelligent guess of 125,000—a conservative estimate.

If a village is growing, there comes a time when it can grow no further. Some people then form a new settlement that flourishes alongside the original village. But sometimes, as in Oaxaca, the villagers continued to live in a steadily growing settlement. Eventually it outgrew its contemporary neighbors. Why did the villagers elect to stay together? Did the larger site survive because its location was favorable for trade or religious ceremonies? These are the sorts of questions that archaeologists can answer only by looking at the site distributions and the resources in their surrounding natural environments. A community does not exist in isolation.

Catchment Areas

A century ago, geographers studying European agriculture formed the notion of catchment areas, zones of natural resources around settlements from which they can draw. The farther the resources in an area are from a community, the less likely they are to be exploited. Anthropologist Richard Lee found that !Kung San women are unlikely to forage more than a comfortable day's walk from their camp. The camp thus has a 5-mile-radius catchment area for foraging, although, of course, the terrain will not necesarily be uniform enough for it to be circular.

Catchment areas are a useful concept in archaeology, especially in studying hunters and gatherers, people who move about over extensive areas and use a number of campsites during the year. **Site catchment analysis** has been popular in recent years as a way of making empirical statements about the sources of materials recovered in archaeological sites. The two key concepts in this type of settlement archaeology are:

The economic catchment area of a site is the territory from which the food resources consumed by the site's inhabitants are obtained. Such areas vary in size and shape according to the resources exploited, the function of the site, and the lifeway of the inhabitants. Clearly, the accuracy with which the economic catchment can be defined will depend on the precision with which one can identify food remains in the site itself.

The site exploitation territory is quite different, a theoretical statement about the area around a site. This land is *assumed* to have been used regularly for subsistence by its inhabitants. The boundary of this theoretical territory is defined by using "least-cost" principles—maximum radii of travel that people will cover on foot. Two hours' walking time is about 6.2 miles (10 km). Much depends on the type of resources and how they are exploited. Much smaller radii, say 0.6 mile (1 km), are useful when analyzing farming economies, where the land is exploited very intensively, for it is most labor- and land-intensive to use land close to the village. The boundaries of such radii are based on assumptions about normal human behavior, and on examining the economic potential of resources lying within them. Thus, this type of site catchment analysis is little more than a statement about resources that were potentially available to the site's inhabitants.

Site catchment analysis involves examining both the economic catchment and the site exploitation territory, as a way of assessing the relationship between all that was *potentially* available in the environment and that which was *actually* exploited. Typically, variations in the economic potential of a site catchment area are compared with variations on patterns of data from the site itself.

Site catchment analysis helps with a major problem in settlement archaeology: defining variations in activities at different sites and testing hypotheses about how sites were linked. The latter task is especially needed when studying prehistoric hunting and foraging territories and early trade.

One good example of site catchment analysis comes from highland Mexico. Kent Flannery examined the resources he found in excavations at San José Mogote in Oaxaca (1150–850 B.C.). By taking the many seeds found by flotation techniques, the animal bones, mineral resources such as clay and salt, and imported objects including seashells, he found that San José Mogote needed a radius of less than 1–3 miles to satisfy its basic agricultural needs. Today common minerals and seasonal wild vegetable foods are found within the 3-mile circle, game meat and construction material within the 9-mile zone. Exotic trade materials and the requirements of ceremonial life required occasional collecting trips up to 30 miles from the settlement, and some contacts over longer distances. When Flannery plotted the catchment areas of neighboring villages, he found that the 1- to 3-mile circles of each settlement did not overlap, but the wider ones, where minerals and other needs were satisfied, did (Figure 10.2). Seasonal camps were built in the outer zones, where every community shared resources.

Site Interactions and Distributions

Site catchment analysis is really a form of resource inventory, one that leads us to explore the interactions between communities. No human being has ever lived in complete isolation, for even the smallest hunter-gatherer family group has at least fleeting contacts with neighboring bands at certain times of the year. But, as human societies become more complex and settlements more lasting, intercommunity relationships become much more complicated. Different settlements depend more and more on one another for essential raw materials (salt or copper ore), and for specialist products (stone knives, religious ornaments, and the like). Growing villages might split into two settlements that, although separated in space, still maintain close ties of kinship. Human settlement patterns are not just site dots on maps. They are complex

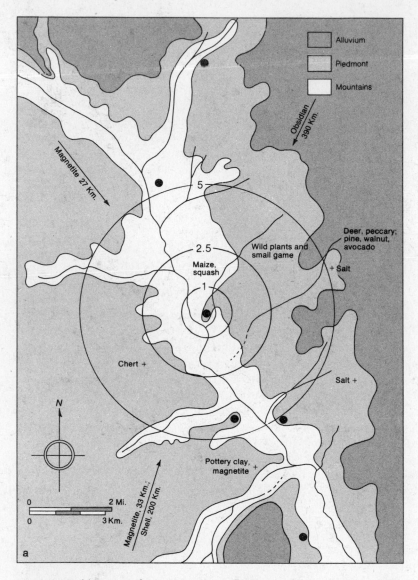

Figure 10.2 (a) Site catchment area around San José Mogote, Valley of Oaxaca. (b) The overlapping catchment zones of villages in the same area. (Radii in kilometers.)

and constantly changing networks of human interaction, of trade, religion, and social ties, of differing adaptations of local environmental challenges.

Archaeologists study settlement patterns on this scale by plotting their data on site distribution maps derived from field surveys and aerial photographs. Their ultimate goal is to reconstruct the factors that

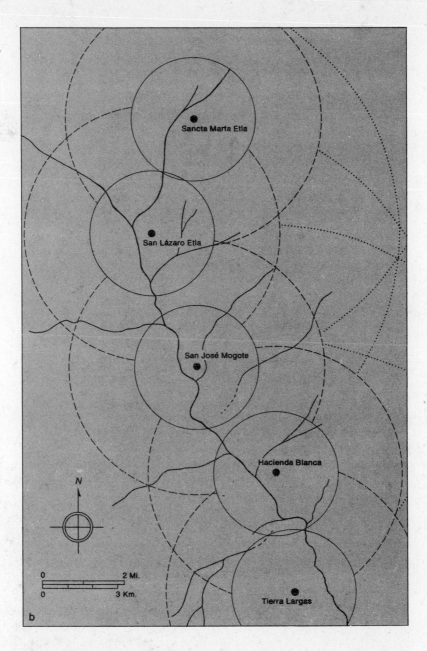

caused the settlement pattern—now a collection of site dots—in the first place. Of course, any attempt to use a distribution map involves trying to assess the reliability of the data on the map. Do the painstakingly collected data reflect human actions of the past or merely earnest guesswork by archaeologists? The analysis of distributions and settlement patterns comes under the general heading of spatial analysis.

a   Major regional center
(Complex architecture,
with over 2,000 people)

Large village (No large-
scale architecture, with
100 to 1,000 people)

Secondary regional center
(Large scale civic architecture,
with 1,000 to 2,000 people)

Hamlet
(Community of fewer
than 100 people)

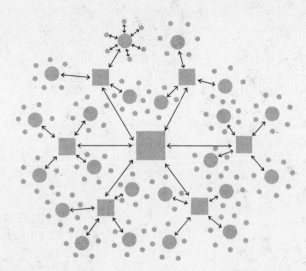

Figure 10.3 A site hierarchy in Mesoamerica. (a) Simplified hierarchy of site types. (b) Hypothetical site hierarchy on the ground,
with the major regional center serving secondary centers spaced
at regular intervals. These in turn serve larger villages and their
networks of hamlets.

Site Hierarchies

Spatial analysis in archaeology begins as we carefully draw a classification of archaeological sites in a region, such as that done by archaeologists working in the Valley of Mexico (Figure 10.3). Each of these site
types has a relationship to others, the total distribution of all site types
making up a settlement pattern. Each site type is defined by the characteristic structures, artifact patterns, and forms in it. These definitions provide us with a way to organize the sites into a hierarchy of
successive levels of settlements. We then need to look at the processes
by which the hierarchy arose in the first place.

TRADE

Human subsistence is based on exploiting the natural environment.
Many hunter-gatherer societies were self-sufficient in their dietary

needs. They used only the raw materials within their regular territory. But many societies, especially after the invention of agriculture, were no longer, self-sufficient. They needed access to a much wider range of raw materials and finished artifacts, many of which they obtained by trading with neighboring communities.

Much prehistoric trade took the form of simple exchange, often by offering an object to a trading partner on the assumption that a return gift would be given at some future date. This form of trade is common in New Guinea and the Pacific today. The bartering of day-to-day items such as foodstuffs between villagers living in different environments was obviously conducted with one set of rules, and commodities accessible in shared catchment zones, such as obsidian (volcanic glass), were subject to quite different factors. Here, of course, the distance of a community from an obsidian source and the number of people requiring it may have set the pattern of exchange. Each community could barter communally for its raw materials, which might in turn be handed over to specialist craftspeople who produced the finished artifacts for others in the group.

Trade is generally recognized in the archaeological record by exotic objects discovered in sites miles away from their point of origin. The Indians of the Lake Superior region obtained copper from natural outcrops near the lake. They traded the precious metal over thousands of miles, as far away as Ohio. Perhaps the best-known trade commodity of all is obsidian, widely prized for making knives and mirrors. Obsidian is found at a few localities in the Near East and at many more in Mesoamerica. In the Near East, it has been possible to identify the sources of the obsidian found in early farming villages by comparing the trace elements in raw obsidian from the source areas with that in traded artifacts. After dozens of sites had been examined, Colin Renfrew and other archaeologists concluded that villages spaced at regular intervals were passing about half the obsidian they received to their more distant neighbors, so that small supplies were carried over enormous distances. In Mesoamerica, obsidian was traded in regional networks through informal trading relationships that gradually became more and more organized as new local rulers began to control the valuable trade.

Trade, indeed, has been thought of as one variable that contributed to the origins of urban life and the increasing complexity of societies. Undoubtedly, trade became more complicated as social and political controls over raw materials and luxuries increased. This increased complexity may be reflected in the wider variety of exotic artifacts in individual sites.

But trade goods themselves are less important to archaeologists than the mechanisms that brought the goods to the site, and so archaeologists have followed economists and geographers in looking at trading mechanisms. All prehistoric trade involved at least two parties.

There is no such thing as trade in general. Each commodity creates specific problems of trading, particularly in transportation. The motives for trading, too, are varied. People have traded for survival, for prestige, for religious reasons, and for wealth. In more complex societies, the ruler and his or her followers generally control trade. They develop and police trade networks and employ specialist merchants and traders to keep it going.

Take the lowland Maya of Mesoamerica. They lived in a lowland rainforest environment that lacked rocks suitable for grinding maize, salt, obsidian, and many luxury materials. All these rocks could be obtained from the highlands and from the valley of Mexico, as well as from Guatemala and elsewhere. But the necessary trading networks and connections for obtaining these essentials had to be organized, not simply for individual communities but for the hundreds of lowland settlements with common assets, in an area in which communication is very difficult. The Maya built complex trade networks through the authority of the major ceremonial centers and their leaders. Imports such as grinding stones and obsidian were exchanged down through the hierarchy of Maya settlements from the larger centers to smaller ones. These state-organized trade networks made the Maya communities very dependent on one another.

These Maya trade networks are being studied in artifact patterns at hundreds of sites by tracing obsidian sources and examining the distribution of exotic tools and materials through the Maya lowlands. But these studies are merely preliminaries to considering trade as one of many elements in prehistoric settlement patterns, one that linked households, communities, and regions into trade networks controlled and regulated by chiefs, religious leaders, or specialist merchants. Many of these controls can be understood only if we examine prehistoric religious beliefs and social organization.

SOCIAL ORGANIZATION

Our old friend the old-fashioned cartoon archaeologist believed that you could never find out anything about peoples' social organization and religious beliefs from archaeological excavation. This truism is untrue. By studying artifact patterns and stylistic changes in material culture one can gain some insights in prehistoric social organization.

Many anthropologists have defined several broad levels of sociocultural evolution in prehistory. These provide a general framework for tracing human social organization from the first simple family structures of the earliest humans to the highly complex state-organized societies of the early civilizations.

All theories of cultural evolution are based on the premise that human societies have changed over long periods of time and that the general trend throughout prehistory has been toward a greater complexity of human culture and social institutions. Many archaeologists take this into account by grouping human societies in early times into two broad, arbitrary categories: Prestate societies and state-organized societies. Prestate societies are small-scale societies based on the community, band, or village. They vary greatly in their degree of political integration, and can be divided into three groupings:

Bands are autonomous and self-sufficient groups that usually consist of only a few families. They are egalitarian, with leadership coming from experience and the personal qualities of particular individuals rather than from inherited or acquired political power.

Tribes are egalitarianlike bands, but with a greater level of social and cultural complexity. They have developed kin-based social mechanisms to accommodate their more sedentary life-style, to redistribute food, and to organize some communal services. Some more complex hunter-gatherer societies, for example the Pacific Northwest coast groups, can be classified as tribes, however most were associated with village farming.

Chiefdoms are societies headed by individuals with unusual ritual, political, or entrepreneurial skills, and often hard to distinguish from tribes. Society is still kin-based, but is more hierarchical, with power concentrated in the hands of powerful kin leaders responsible for the redistribution of resources. Chiefdoms tend to have higher population densities and to display the first signs of social ranking, reflected in more elaborate material possessions for leading individuals. Chiefdoms vary greatly in their elaborateness, but reached a high level of sophistication in Hawaii, Tahiti, and among the Mississippian people of the Midwest and South after A.D. 1000.

It should be noted, however, that the general utility of the band-tribe-chiefdom classification is now seriously questioned by many archaeologists and anthropologists. One is probably better off referring to small scale, prestate societies. State-organized societies operate on a large scale, with centralized social and political organizations, class stratification, and intensive agriculture. They have complex political structures, many permanent government institutions, and are based on notions of social inequality, the assumption that privilege will reside in the hands of a few individuals.

State-organized societies are synonymous with the early urban civilizations—those of the Sumerians, Ancient Egyptians, and others—that were governed by supreme rulers with absolute powers. These preindustrial civilizations founded on social inequality and maintained by the labor of thousands, were the precursors of the industrial civilizations of later history.

The archaeological evidence for social organization comes from several sources. Burials and their associated grave goods can give information on social ranking, which can be obtained by studying the possessions and ornaments deposited with each skeleton in a site. A most spectacular example comes from the royal cemetery at *Ur-of-the-Chaldees,* Mesopotamia. British archaeologist Leonard Woolley uncovered 1850 graves, 16 of which stood out as special sepulchers because of their very rich grave furniture. The royal corpses were laid to rest in brick chambers accompanied by their personal attendants. The entire court and the royal bodyguard, complete with wagons and weapons, then lined up in order outside the burial chamber and lay down to die after taking poison. Woolley was able to describe the members of court, their order of precedence, and their distinctive costumes. All these corpses contrasted sharply with the hundreds of humbler isolated burials elsewhere in the cemetery.

RELIGIOUS BELIEFS

An anonymous archaeologist wrote cynically that "religion is the last resort of troubled archaeologists." At one time archaeologists were inclined to call any object they could not identify "ritual." Some still do. Obviously, some important sites were of religious significance. The Pyramid of the Sun at *Teotihuacán* is one, *Stonehenge* is another. Some of the earliest religious objects in the world are the so-called Venus figurines made in Europe 25,000 years ago (Figure 10.4).

Some evidence for religious rituals comes from burials. The Neanderthal peoples of western Europe may have deliberately buried their dead of 70,000 years ago with a variety of goods. Hundreds of *Adena* and *Hopewell* burial mounds dot the landscape of the Midwest, holding the graves of thousands of leaders and lesser personages, each buried with distinctive grave furniture, some with elaborate cult objects. The building of the Hopewell mounds was carried out step by step, as the dead were deposited on an earthen platform that was later covered with a large mound. The famed Great Serpent Mound in Ohio is an Adena ceremonial earthwork, whose exact religious significance still escapes us (Figure 10.5).

Many more-complex prehistoric societies enjoyed highly organized religions that were reflected in widely distributed and characteristic art styles. The *Olmec* art style of Mexico was carried over thousands of square miles of highlands and lowlands after 1000 B.C. Olmec art's snarling jaguar and human motifs coincide with distinctive religious beliefs that may have linked large and small communities all over Mexico.

Figure 10.4 A Venus figurine head from Brassempouy, France.

Most societies' religious beliefs were interpreted and maintained through regular religious rituals conducted at specific times of the year, as at harvests and plantings. These regular ceremonies were vital to the elaborate organization of newly emerging complex societies. The predictable yearly round of religious life gave society an orderly framework for redistributing food, disposing of surplus cattle, accumulating wealth, and other economic functions. The long-term effects of these new, unifying religious beliefs were startling. Between 1150 and 850 B.C., Mesoamerican society began to undergo rapid transformation. Administrative and religious authority came together in the hands of leaders of a newly ranked society, with specialists and a hierarchy of settlements. This organization contrasted with the dispersed villages of earlier times. More elaborate public buildings appeared as temples and monumental buildings began to reflect individual communities' common involvement in public works. In Mesoamerica and elsewhere, the ultimate sacred beliefs and rituals of a society are linked to the processes of social and environmental change that act upon it.

The only way in which we can hope to zero in on these types of fundamental beliefs is by looking at obvious religious artifacts and their patterning within archaeological sites. The close relationship between

Figure 10.5 The Great Serpent Mound, built by the Adena people as a
ceremonial earthwork.

the spread of Mexican religious beliefs and the trading of fine art objects, new pottery forms, conch shells, and the stingray spines used in
self-multilation rites we know of from painted murals. The distribution
of such artifacts in areas away from the Olmec lowlands, and the distribution of the same imports within individual villages, in houses and
public buildings, can give us some clues as to when the new beliefs
first took hold over a wider area. By studying burials and artifact patternings as well as the artifacts themselves we can gain insight into
how religious beliefs acted as one of the many variables affecting the
ever-changing societies of prehistoric times.

In recent years, many researchers have turned to ethnohistorical
and historical records to decipher prehistoric religious beliefs. Only
a few years after the Spanish Conquest of Mexico, missionary Fray
Bernardino de Sahagun (c. 1499–1590) laboriously recorded a mass of
information about Aztec life and civilization from Indian survivors of
the Conquest. In his great work, A General History of the Things of
New Spain, he described not only early Aztec history, but minute details of Indian religion, even Aztec philosophy and poetry. Modern
scholars are interpreting his writings and discovering that Aztec religious beliefs were at least as sophisticated and complex as the Catholic
beliefs that replaced them.

David Lewis-Williams is an expert on the prehistoric rock art in

Figure 10.6 Many Mayan stelae (carved stone monuments) record important dates in the lives of their rulers. This stela carries a date equivalent to A.D. 771.

southern Africa mentioned earlier, on an art tradition painted on the walls of caves and rockshelters for thousands of years until Europeans came. This art depicts animals, hunters during the chase, scenes of camp life, and religious ceremonies as well as complex signs and symbols. No painters survived into this century, but Lewis-Williams dug into early descriptions of the paintings by Victorian investigators, who also recorded some of the San oral traditions about the paintings. His research has enabled him to evaluate some of the paintings of eland and other animals in their ancient symbolic context. The paintings were integral to the symbolic world of the San, a world intimately tied to the animals they hunted.

One of the great triumphs of science in the past quarter century has been the decipherment of ancient Maya script (Figure 10.6) This has enabled experts to delve into the intensely symbolic world of these remarkable people, who lived in competing city states in the Mesoamerican lowlands. They have begun to translate Maya epic tales, and to unravel the history of different lowland rulers. For example, the Sky Dynasty of Tikal in Guatemala has been traced from the late fourth to late eighth centuries A.D. The first identified ruler is Jaguar Paw, who died in A.D. 376. At Palenque, also in the lowlands, a ruler named Pacal ("Shield") died on September 29 A.D. 684 at age eighty-one. He commissioned texts to record the history of the rulers that preceded him, and his successors kept up the records with wall panels until around A.D. 799. Maya art and inscriptions often concentrate on the ceremonial and ideological aspects of war—the capture and sacrifice of prisoners as a way of validating political authority.

In these and other ways, archaeologists are trying to unravel the complex and little-understood symbolic world of the ancients. We must now turn our attention to another pressing problem in archaeology—the relationship between the archaeological record and our own ever-changing world.

11

THE PRESENT
AND THE PAST

The archaeological record is contemporary; it exists with me today and any observation I make about it is a contemporary observation.

Lewis R. Binford, 1983

This chapter details a complex issue in archaeology—the relationship between the present and the past. In Chapters 3 and 6, we mentioned how site-formation processes play a vital role in determining the nature of the archaeological record that comes down to us. The archaeological record is static whereas the present is ever-changing and dynamic. How, then, does one study the relationship between the static and dynamic, between the present and the past? This issue is of critical importance to archaeology, for most of our research is based on the assumption that because an artifact is used in a specific way it was used in that way millennia before.

Such studies are based on the premise that this relationship has two parts:

The past is dead and knowable only through the present—by archaeologists studying it.

Accurate knowledge of the past is essential to understanding the present.

MIDDLE-RANGE THEORY

Archaeologists studying cultural change try to get the present to serve the past by combining three interlocking approaches:

Ethnoarchaeology—the study of living societies.

Experimental Archaeology—controlled modern experiments with ancient technologies and material culture.

Middle-Range Theory—methods, theories, and ideas that can be applied to any period and anywhere in the world to explain what we have discovered, excavated, or analyzed from the past.

The term "Middle-Range Theory" is a current "buzz-word" in archaeology, one taken from sociology. It describes a body of theory that is being formed as archaeologists try to bridge the gap between what actually happened in the past, and the archaeological record of today. This kind of activity (without the "buzz-word") has been going on since the nineteenth century. Archaeologists have used both controlled experimentation with ancient technologies and observations of living peoples to help them interpret and understand the remote past. Current thinking on the subject is a good deal more sophisticated than some of the experiments and observations of yesteryear. Today, we think of the present as dynamic, ever changing; the past is static, its dynamic elements long gone. Binford and others have been searching for "Rosetta stones" that permit one to use observations of the static past to make statements about its long-vanished dynamics. In other words, Middle-Range Theory will provide the conceptual tools for explaining artifact patternings and other material phenomena from the archaeological record.

By no means do all archaeologists agree that the archaeological record holds no direct information on human behavior. They argue that the relationship between human behavior and material culture in all times and places is what archaeology is all about. The controversy continues, but it is safe to say that ethnoarchaeology and experimental research as well as analogy have leading tasks in today's research into the past.

THE LIVING PAST

We live in a world inhabited by an astonishing diversity of human societies. A century ago, many of them were still living in much the same way as their prehistoric ancestors. But the unchanging routine of planting and harvest, of life and death, of the seasons of game and vegetable foods, has withered in the face of Western exploration and technological superiority. Today, few of these societies are still enjoying their traditional lifeways. Many are extinct. The Tasmanians vanished within 70 years of white settlement; the Indians of Tierra del Fuego disappeared in the 1950s (Figure 11.1). Ishi, the last California hunter-gatherer, managed to live in his home territory in the northern California foothills until 1911. He saw all his companions wiped out by white settlers. The surviving Indian peoples of the Amazon region are rapidly fading away in the face of large-scale commercial operations in their forest territories. Soon all traces of living prehistory will be gone forever.

Anthropology has traditionally worked with non-Western societies and with peoples who have had to make far-reaching adjustments to the twentieth century. It is no coincidence that anthropologists have

Figure 11.1 A group of Fuegan Indians walking along the shore; these and many other hunter-gatherer peoples are now virtually extinct.

followed these people as they adjusted, often becoming impoverished minorities in large industrial cities. But the archaeologist studies human culture of the past. Since the 19th century, many of the societies once studied by anthropologists have, by their death or transformation, become part of the archaeological record. No longer living groups, they have left behind them assemblages of artifacts, hierarchies of sites, a settlement pattern to be traced by surviving finds in the ground. The traditional cultures of the remaining hunter-gatherer and peasant societies are vanishing rapidly before Western technology, plastics, microwavable foods, and the personal stereo.

COMPARISONS

Early anthropologists collected vast quantities of information on traditional material culture of diverse societies all over the world. This material gave archaeologists a chance to make comparisons between still-living peoples and prehistoric peoples who lived at a similar stage of technological development. Thus, it was argued, the San, Australian aborigines, and other living hunter-gatherers who had no metals could be considered living representatives of prehistoric, stone-using hunter-gatherers. An archaeologist who dug a 20,000-year-old campsite in an arctic environment would turn to the Eskimo of today for comparative material from modern times.

But this type of reasoning was obviously simplistic if nothing else, because each human society, ancient or modern, has, or has had, its own distinctive adaptation to its environment, which helps shape all aspects of its culture in many ways. For example, the *Magdalenian* hunters of southwestern France some 18,000 years ago were expert reindeer hunters who relied heavily on the seasonal migrations of these animals for sustenance. Similarly, modern sub-arctic hunter-gatherer groups in northern Canada live off migrating caribou herds, a close relative of the reindeer. The late Ice Age environment of south-western France and that of the Canadian sub-arctic are radically differ-ent, as are the technologies each group use or used. It would be naive indeed to claim that the Magdalenians of 18,000 years ago were prehis-toric examples of modern sub-arctic caribou hunters.

Archaeologists then began to make analogies with recent societies in new ways. They worked back from known, living peoples into ear-lier times. They began by digging sites of historically documented In-dians and studying their contents, making full use of historical records to interpret their finds. Thus, photographs of Northwest coast Indian homes taken in 1890 would be compared with excavated home founda-tions from comparatively recent times, say 1500. If the features of both were the same, then it was reasonable to interpret the design of prehis-toric houses from this model. The house would then be traced back-ward into prehistoric times in sites many centuries earlier than the historic settlements.

This method, very simply stated, is the basis upon which archaeol-ogists use ethnographic records to interpret prehistoric artifacts and sites. Considerable controversy surrounds such interpretations, for so-phisticated research methods are needed if comparisons are to be made between modern artifact patternings and those found in prehis-toric sites. For this reason many archaeologists are strongly interested in "living archaeology (or "ethnoarchaeology")."

LIVING ARCHAEOLOGY

Much of the ethnographic material available to archaeologists was col-lected when anthropology was much less sophisticated than it is today. Very often ethnographers collected object after object or information on customs without recording detailed information on settlement lay-out or artifact patternings, the types of information that archaeologists now need so badly. One can hardly blame the pioneers, for they were out to record as much information about vanishing cultures as they could before it was too late. And subtle settlement details hardly seemed a high priority.

Today, many of the settlements the anthropologists studied have themselves become archaeological sites. They are now virtually indis-tinguishable from prehistoric sites with their middens and crumbled hut foundations. They offer a unique opportunity to study the pro-cesses by which abandoned settlements turn into archaeological sites.

Figure 11.2 Living archaeology. A !Kung San brush shelter and windbreak, recorded by archaeologist F. Van Noten shortly after it was abandoned.

Understanding these processes makes archaeological interpretation in general much easier, and so some archaeologists have gone out in the field to study "living archaeology" for themselves. Anthropologist Richard Lee, who has spent many years studying the !Kung San of southern Africa, took archaeologist John Yellen with him on one of his expeditions. Yellen spent many months studying the ways in which the San butchered animals and also the fragmentary bones that resulted from butchery, cooking, and eating. (Figure 11.2). He drew plans of recently abandoned sites of known age, recorded the positions of houses, hearths, and occupation debris, and talked to people who had lived there as a way of establishing precise population estimates and the social relationships of the inhabitants.

Yellen found that the San camps developed their layouts through conscious acts, such as building a shelter or a hearth as well as through such casual deeds as discarding animal bones and debris from toolmaking. There were communal areas that everyone used and private family areas gathered around hearths. Some activity areas, such as places where women cracked nuts in the heat of the day, were simply located under a convenient, shady tree. Yellen recorded that most food preparation took place in family areas. Most activities in San camps were related to individual families. Theoretically, therefore, one should be able to study the development of the family through time by studying changing artifact patternings. To do so in practice, of course, requires very comprehensive data and carefully formulated research designs.

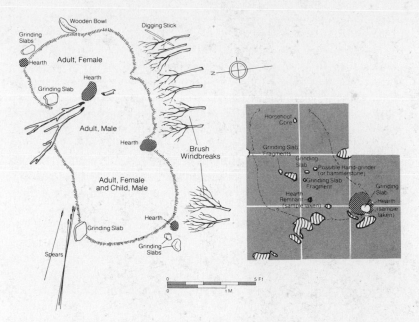

Figure 11.3 Comparison of a prehistoric campsite at Puntutjarpa rock-shelter, Australia, at right, with a modern Australian aborigine campsite.

Ethnography and archaeology can complement each other beautifully. When Richard Gould was looking for archaeological sites in the western Australian desert, he came across a few bands of nomadic aborigines. These local people not only guided him to archaeological sites but also told him who had lived here, giving details of the sacred traditions associated with the settlements and describing the activities that had taken place at each (Figure 11.3). At Puntutjarpa rockshelter, Gould excavated stone tools dating back from modern times to about 6800 years ago. Many of them were indistinguishable from tools still used by the locals. The aborigines identified the tools for Gould, gave him their terminology, and explained how each was used. Gould then studied ancient and modern tools, looked at the wear on the working surfaces, and was even able to say that some 5000-year-old stone tools had been hafted with wooden handles. He could make this statement with certainty because identical modern examples were so hafted. Gould's research was successful because he combined archaeology and ethnography to study not only individual artifacts but also patternings of artifacts in ancient and modern sites. He even used his modern data to estimate a prehistoric population density for the area based on an average of 3.55 persons per camp.

It is of interest to note that San camps are fairly compact, with dwellings erected close to one another. In contrast, Australian settlements tend to be more scattered, more open. Gould and Yellen believe this is because the San must worry about nocturnal predators and the protection of women and children left in camp, while there are no predators in Australia.

Lewis Binford's study of the Nunamiut caribou hunters of Alaska was designed to learn as much as possible about an Eskimo group's hunting practices. The Nunamiut depended heavily on meat, supplementing their flesh diet with the partially digested contents of caribou stomachs and about a cupful of vegetable foods a year. They relied extensively on stored food for eight-and-a-half months a year, fresh meat being freely available for only about two. Binford soon found that Nunamiut food-procurement strategy was based on complicated decisions that involved not only the distribution of food at different seasons, but the storage potential of different animals, and parts of them as well as the logistics of procurement, carrying, and storing meat. Was it easier to move people to the herds or to carry meat back to base? His researches convinced him that the linkages between the facts of animal anatomy and the realities of lifeway strategies held the key to meaningful analysis of animal bones.

Binford studied the annual round of the Nunamiut, and also their butchery and storage strategies, developing indexes to measure utilization of different body parts. He also compared observations from modern kill sites to 42 archaeologically known locations that dated to earlier times. The Nunamiut research is valuable not only for the large body of empirical data it generated but also because it showed just how locally confined any cultural adaptation is. The restriction can, in turn, lead to major variations in archaeological sites, as well as in artifacts and other archaeological remains *even if the adaptive strategies and other factors affecting people's decisions remain constant*. Thus, one can never assume that all variability in the archaeological record is directly related to cultural similarity and difference.

EXPERIMENTAL ARCHAEOLOGY

Archaeologists love experimenting with the past and have done so ever since the eighteenth century. One ardent early experimenter, Dr. Robert Ball of Dublin, Ireland, blew a prehistoric horn so hard that he produced a sound like a bellowing bull. Unfortunately, his heroic effort caused him to burst a blood vessel and die. Not all experimental archaeology is so risky, however. Archaeologists have been making stone implements, floating over oceans on rafts, and trying to recreate the past ever since. Some of their achievements are remarkable.

Louis Leakey not only dug prehistoric campsites, but also spent many years perfecting his skills as a stone toolmaker. He could shape a perfect prehistoric handaxe and skin an antelope with it in a few minutes—a favorite demonstration at conferences. One of the most remarkable experiments of all was Norwegian Thor Heyerdahl's *Kon-*

Tiki expedition, on which he attempted to prove that Polynesia had been settled by adventurous Peruvians who had sailed balsa rafts across thousands of miles of ocean. Heyerdahl did succeed in reaching Polynesia. His expedition merely proved, however, that long ocean voyages in *Kon-Tiki* rafts were possible. He did not prove that the Peruvians settled Polynesia.

People have cleared thick Danish woodland with stone axes and grown prehistoric crops in the American Southwest under conditions identical to those of centuries ago. The latter experiments lasted 17 years. Good crop yields were obtained in all but 2 years, when drought killed the young crops. Experiments in living the prehistoric life-style have proved popular, especially in Britain and Denmark, where television networks have financed long-term experiments involving volunteer "prehistoric peoples." Controlled burnings of some faithful reconstructions of ancient houses have been undertaken, too, to show what the structures would look like when reduced to ashes—as structures are in many actual sites. British archaeologists have even built an entire experimental earthwork that they are digging up at regular intervals over 128 years. The resulting information on soil decay and artifact preservation will be invaluable for interpreting equivalent prehistoric sites.

Many recent experimenters have concentrated on replicating such phenomena as wear on the working edges of prehistoric stone tools. Lawrence Keeley and other researchers have examined stone artifacts such as Paleo-Indian points under high- and low-power microscopes. They are now able to distinguish between wear polishes associated with materials including wood, bone, and hide. This approach is now reliable enough to allow one to state whether a tool was used to slice wood, cut up vegetables, or strip meat from bones.

Sometimes, edge-wear studies can yield remarkable results, especially when combined with **refitting,** reassembling flakes with the parent core from which they were struck. David Cahen and Lawrence Keeley collaborated in a study of a 9000-year-old Stone Age campsite at Meer in northern Belgium. By reassembling some of the stone flakes and cores, studying the wear patterns on tool working edges, and examining distribution of stone fragments throughout the site, they were able to show that two people, one of them left-handed, had made some tools then used to bore and shape fragments of bone.

COMBINING APPROACHES

The most powerful examples of living and experimental archaeology are those that combine many different approaches to acquire data as a basis for constructing Middle-Range Theory. Such an approach yielded rich dividends on the Maya highlands near the Mexico/Guatemala border, where Brian Hayden and a research team studied traditional stoneworking, especially the manufacture of *metates* (grinding stones) and *manos* (pestles). They combined descriptive research with new theoretical, highly exploratory approaches, focusing on everything from the properties of the stone used to make artifacts to the efficiency of the manufacturing process and patterns of waste disposal. They worked closely with a stoneworking specialist, doing time-and-motion studies, analyzing the toolmaking process, even carrying out edge-wear studies on the stone tools he used to peck the *metates* into final shape. The result was an invaluable body of data not only on traditional manufacturing techniques, but information of use for interpreting enigmatic tools, like blunt axes found in ancient sites. Edge-wear experiments showed they were used for freshening up the surface of grinding stones and pestles once they were no longer serviceable for woodworking. This fascinating study also threw light on site-formation processes. The stoneworkers were careful to throw debris away, to avoid injury from sharp flakes, and worked well away from living areas of their houses, so the archaeological record of a specialist's house might well show no signs of specialist stoneworking activity at all.

In this, and many other innovative projects, archaeologists are using the present to better understand the past, bringing a new rigor to archaeological interpretation. This rigor is having an important effect on studies of culture change, as discussed in the following chapter.

12

EXPLAINING THE PAST

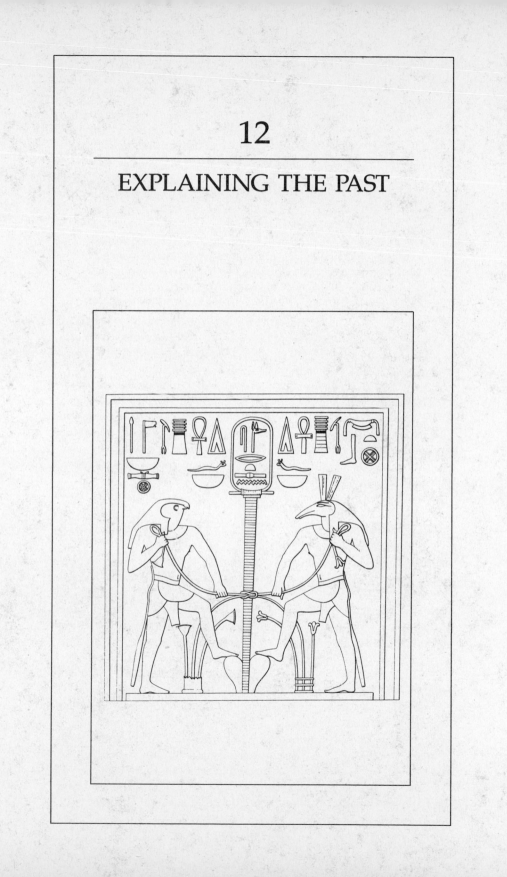

Academics in universities are often theorists, intoxicated by theory or haunted by it. To the field-worker, their theories compete and multiply like insects in a hot-house, the dominant species being variously social, processual, analytical, behavioural, cognitive, structural, symbolic, or contextual, each with its own plumage and coterie.

M. O. H. Carver, 1989

We have now described many of the ways in which archaeologists reconstruct the past—the planning of research, the acquisition and analysis of archaeological data, the construction of culture histories, and the reconstruction of ancient lifeways. There remains one objective of archaeology—the explanation of culture change. This chapter examines some of the ways in which archaeologists approach the study of cultural process.

CULTURE HISTORICAL INTERPRETATION

The ordering of archaeological data is a descriptive process. It highlights the patterning and regularities in archaeological data. The concepts and units of culture historical studies are devices used to organize data as a preliminary to studying culture change. These classificatory units put artifacts and other culture traits into a context of time and space developed by using distribution maps, stratigraphy, seriation and cross-dating, and chronometric dating methods.

Culture history is a sound way of describing the past, but it is of minimal use for explaining variability in the archaeological record. It is based on inductive research methods, the development of generalizations about a research problem that are based on numerous specific observations, and on a normative view of culture. This assumes that abstract rules govern what culture considers normal behavior. The normative view of culture is a descriptive one, one that can be used to describe culture during one particular time period or throughout time. Archaeologists base it on the assumption that surviving artifacts, such as potsherds, display stylistic and other changes that represent the changing norms of human behavior through time.

So far we have dealt with components, phases, and other units as phenomena in isolation. We have assumed that the artifacts they contain reflect gradual, evolutionary change in human society. But the archaeological record does not invariably reflect an orderly and smooth chronicle of culture change. A radical new artifact inventory may suddenly appear in components at several sites, while earlier toolkits suddenly vanish. The economy of sites in a local sequence may change completely within a century as the plow revolutionizes agricultural methods. Such changes are readily observed in thousands of local sequences all over the world. But how did these changes come about? What processes of cultural change were at work to cause major and minor alterations in the archaeological record? A number of descriptive models have been formulated to characterize culture change—some cultural, others noncultural. Several involve internal change, others external influence. These descriptive models include inevitable variation, cultural selection, invention, diffusion, and migration.

Inevitable Variation and Cultural Selection

Inevitable variation is rather similar to the well-known phenomenon of genetic drift in biology. As people learn the behavior patterns of their society, inevitably some differences in learned behavior will appear from generation to generation, which, although minor in themselves, accumulate over a long time, especially in isolated populations. The snowball effect of inevitable variation and slow-moving cultural evolution can be detected in dozens of prehistoric societies. The great variation in *Acheulian* handaxe technology throughout Europe and Africa between a million and 150,000 years ago can be explained in part by the effects of inevitable variation.

Inevitable variation often results from isolation, a very low density of humans per square mile. It should not be confused with broad trends in human prehistory that grew over long periods. For example, the more and more complex burial rituals in the *Adena* and *Hopewell* cultures of the American Midwest between 500 B.C. and A.D. 300 probably resulted from trends toward greater complexity in religious beliefs and rituals as well as from political and economic organization over a long time, and not from isolation.

Inevitable variation is also quite different from what happens when a society recognizes that certain culture changes or inventions may be advantageous. Perhaps, many hunter-gatherer societies deliberately took up cultivating the soil once they saw the advantages it gave neighboring peoples, who had already adopted the new economies (see discussion of diffusion on page 196).

Invention

Invention is the creation or evolution of a new idea. Many inventions, such as new social institutions or religious beliefs, leave no trace in the archaeological record. But some innovations are reflected in new types of surviving artifacts, such as the plow, or the iron axe. If an invention such as plowing is sufficiently useful to be attractive to more than a few people, the new idea or a product of the idea will spread widely, and often rapidly.

Archaeologists have studied ways in which inventions spread by tracing the distribution of such distinctive artifacts as plowshares from their place of origin. The earliest occurrence of ironmaking was in northern Turkey about 1500 B.C. Iron tools first appear in the archaeological record of Europe and Egypt very much later. Because the earliest presently known and dated iron artifacts occurred in Turkey, we can say that ironmaking may have been invented there.

In the early days of archaeology, people assumed that metallurgy and other major inventions were invented in only one place—in many cases, the Near East. These innovations then spread all over the world as other societies realized how important the new ideas were. But as the importance of environment and adaptation in the development of human culture have become better understood, this simple view of invention has been rejected. Agriculture is now known to have developed quite independently in the Near East, Southeast Asia, Mesoamerica, and Peru. Complex adaptive processes occurred in all these areas. Scholars now try to identify the many interacting factors that caused people to modify their life-styles to adopt food production. The genius of humanity was that it recognized opportunities when they came along and adapted to new circumstances. The issue is not to discover who first cultivated corn but rather to study the dozens of major and minor alterations in human culture that were the result of adaptive changes over time.

Diffusion

The spread of ideas, over short or long distances, is termed **diffusion**. Ideas can be transmitted in many ways other than by the movements of entire societies or communities. Regular trade between neighboring villages or more distant peoples results in the exchange not only of goods, but of ideas as well, especially when much of this trade is conducted reciprocally. Reciprocity implies a two-sided relationship, in which both parties exchange goods, services, and of course, ideas. Ideas such as a new religious belief are transmitted from individual to individual and ultimately from group to group. But neither the exchange of ideas nor that of technological innovations necessarily involve actual movements of people. Even the spread of material objects

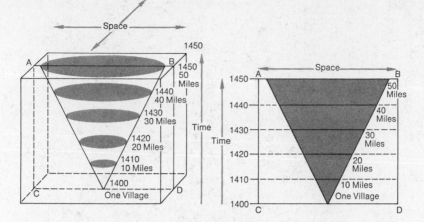

Figure 12.1 The spread of a culture trait in time and space: the cone effect.

and abstract ideas can have a quite different effect in a new area. The classic example is that of the Hopi Indians of the Southwest. They received American trade goods but still retained their own culture, trading objects but rejecting the ideas of an alien culture.

Let us say that a new type of painted pot is invented in one village in A.D. 1400. The advantages of this new vessel are such that villagers 10 miles away learn about it at a beer party a year later. Within ten years, their potters are making similar receptacles. In a short time the pot form is found commonly in villages 10 miles farther away. Half a century later, communities in a 50-mile radius are making the now well-established vessel design. If we put this stirring tale on paper, we end up with the cone effect shown in Figure 12.1. The cone effect is the type of distribution we study when identifying diffusion in the archaeological record.

Archaeologically, diffusion is difficult to identify unless one can use very distinctive artifacts obviously of common origin to demonstrate that the artifacts were invented in only one place, and trace the distribution of the artifact in space and time from its origin point to neighboring areas. To do so means establishing that the tool was first made in one place and other sites nearby later (Figure 12.1). Instances of diffusion in prehistory are common. A classic example is the Chavín art style of Peru, which diffused widely over the lowlands from a homeland in the highlands, where it appeared about 900 B.C.

Migration

Migration involves movements of entire societies that deliberately decide to expand their sphere of influence. English settlers moved to North America, taking their own culture with them. Spanish conquistadors occupied Mexico. Migration involves not only the movement of ideas but a mass shift of people that results in social and cultural changes on a large scale. A classic prehistoric migration was that of the Polynesians, who deliberately voyaged from island to island. In each case, new land masses were found by purposeful exploration, then colonized by small numbers of people who moved to an uninhabited island.

These types of mass migration are rare in prehistoric times. They would be reflected in the archaeological record by totally new components and phases or by skeletons of a totally new physical type. To be proved, the migration would have to show up as new complexes in the cultural sequence at many neighboring sites.

A second type of migration is on a smaller scale, when a group of foreigners move into another region and settle there as an organized group. A group of Oaxacans did just that at *Teotihuacán* in the Valley of Mexico. When René Millon mapped the whole of this remarkable city, he found a concentration of distinctive Oaxacan artifacts in one residential area. This Oaxacan colony flourished for centuries in an alien city. In this and many other cases, the immigrants adopted some features of the host culture but retained their own cultural identity.

There are other types of migration, too. Slaves and artisans are often unorganized migrants, sometimes taking new technological devices with them. Great warrior migrations, like those of Zulu regiments in South Africa in the early nineteenth century, can cause widespread disruption and population shifts. Such migrations leave few traces in archaeological sites. Within a few generations, the warriors settle down and adopt the sedentary life of the conquered. Only a few new weapon forms reveal the presence of strangers.

NONCULTURAL MODELS

Culture change triggered by alterations in the natural environment is an integral part of culture history. Earlier noncultural models tended to be simple, stating for example that agriculture began in the Near East when population pressure caused game and plant food shortages, causing people to turn to farming instead. However, the most recent research in archaeology has focused heavily on specific details of the relationship between environment and prehistoric cultures. The complex models that are emerging from this research show that earlier explanations were far too general to explain these ever-changing environment-culture relationships.

As is obvious, great amounts of data are needed to identify invention, diffusion, or migration in the archaeological record. The *identification* of these classic cultural processes is largely a mechanical, descriptive activity because the artifacts used, be they stone axes, pots, or swords, are considered in isolation and not as an element of the cultural system of which they are part. The *explanation* of culture change requires more sophisticated research models, based on the notion that human cultural systems are made up not only of many complex interacting elements—religious beliefs, technology, subsistence, and so on—but that these cultural systems also interact with the natural environment and other complex systems.

PROCESSUAL ARCHAEOLOGY

Processual archaeology is based on deductive research methodology that employs research design, formulation of explicit research hypotheses, and testing of these against basic data. Its methods are cumulative; that is, initial hypotheses are designed that propose a working model to explain culture change. These hypotheses are tested against basic data and some are discarded, while others are refined again and again until the factors that affect cultural change are isolated in highly specific form.

The processual approach is firmly based on culture history and data obtained from inductive research. It must be, for the chronological and spatial frameworks for prehistory come from such investigations. The difference between the processual and systems-ecological approaches lies in the orientation of the research. Processual archaeologists rely on deductive strategies, formulate testable hypotheses, and then gather data to test them. Very often, however, the initial hypotheses are based on data derived from inductive culture history.

THE SYSTEMS-ECOLOGICAL APPROACH

Deductive research is extremely valuable for the study of the past, provided that realistic account is taken of the uniqueness of archaeological data. In many respects, archaeologists are grappling with many theoretical problems also encountered by biologists working on change in living organisms. It is for this reason that evolutionary theory is playing an increasingly important part in archaeology.

The most common processual approach deals with the ways in which cultural systems function, both internally and in relation to external factors such as the natural environment. The systems-ecological approach involves three basic models of cultural change: systems models, which are based on general systems theory; cultural ecology, which provides complicated models of the interaction between human cultures and their environment; and multilinear evolution, which combines both systems approaches and cultural ecology in a theory of the cumulative evolution of culture over long periods through complex adaptations to the environment. It is, as archaeologist Kent Flannery once put it: "The search for the ways human populations (in their own way) do the things that other systems do."

General systems theory came to archaeology from the sciences, and has caused archaeologists to think of human cultures as "open" systems, regulated in part by external stimuli. This general concept is most applicable to human cultures that interact intimately with the natural environment. Systems theory is little more than a general concept in archaeology, with the advantage that it frees one from having to look at only one agent of culture change, such as migration or diffusion. It allows one to focus instead on relationships between different components of a cultural system, and between a cultural system and its environment.

Cultural ecology is a means of studying human culture that gives a picture of the way in which human populations adapt to, and transform, their environments. Human cultural systems have to adapt to other cultures and also to the natural environment. Indeed, so many factors influence cultural systems that the processes by which cultural similarities and differences are generated are not easy to understand. Cultural ecologists see human cultures as subsystems interacting with other major subsystems, among them the biotic community and the physical environment. Thus, the key to understanding cultural process lies in the interactions between these various subsystems.

The adaptation of any population is achieved primarily by effective subsistence strategies and technological artifices, but social organization and religious beliefs are important in ensuring cooperative exploitation of the environment as well as technological cooperation. For instance, religious life provided an integrating force in many societies, not least among them the Maya of Mexico and the Sumerians of Mesopotamia. There are obvious difficulties in studying the interactions between people and their environment, especially when preservation conditions limit the artifacts and other data available for study. Fortunately, however, artifacts and other elements of the technological subsystem often survive. Because technology is a primary way in which different cultures adapt to their environment, detailed models of technological subsystems allow archaeologists to obtain a relatively comprehensive picture of the cultural system as a whole.

Multilinear cultural evolution is a branching, cumulative process which results from cultural adaptations over long periods. Multilinear evolution recognizes that there are many evolutionary tracks, from simple to complex, the differences resulting from individual adaptive solutions. Thus, cultural adaptations are complex processes that are fine-tuned to local conditions, with long-term cumulative effects. These adaptations can be studied on a large- and small-scale by a systems-ecological approach. Multilinear cultural evolution, then, is the vital integrative force that brings systems theory and cultural ecology together into a closely knit, highly flexible way of studying and explaining cultural process.

The systems-ecological approach produces very complex interpretations of major developments in prehistory, for example, the origins of literate civilization in the Near East. Early theories invoked single causes, such as population pressure, the invention of irrigation agriculture, even warfare or trade, as the ultimate single causes, prime movers if you will, of civilization. Systems-ecological models argue that there was a whole series of important variables with complex interrelationships and variations that caused the emergence of civilization. Under this rubric, the rise of civilization should be thought of as a series of interacting and cumulative processes that were triggered by favorable cultural and ecological conditions, which continued to develop cumulatively as a result of continuous positive feedback. For example, farming communities were established in the low-lying Mesopotamian delta between the Tigris and Euphrates about 7300 years ago. These settlements triggered three processes that set up critical feedback relationships: slow but steady population growth within the delta, increased specialization in food production by different groups within society, and a demand for and acquisition of raw materials from outside the delta region. In time, each of these processes set off feedback reactions that became more and more complex as time went on. A need for more fields to feed more people, more centralized planning and administration, larger and more densely populated settlements that took up a minimum of agricultural land, irrigation farming, and finally an administrative elite that controlled people's access to resources— all were complex reactions to long-term processes of cultural change (Figure 3.2).

POSTPROCESSUAL ARCHAEOLOGY

Processual archaeology tries to identify relationships between variables in cultural systems, such as those that contributed to the beginnings of urban civilization. It assumes that prehistoric societies were rational in dealing with their environments, one of the reasons why ethnoarchaeology and experimental archaeology are of use in interpreting the past. No question, this view is productive of important insights, but recent theoretical argument has focused on an alternative view. It stresses the mental "structure" of prehistoric societies, on sets of rules, or codes, that might be thought of as being equivalent to those operating in chess, which are followed as people go about living and adapting to their environment. This, and other postprocessual approaches are an attempt to go beyond technological and materialist interpretations of the past, to look at objects not only in terms of how they were used, but how their original owners viewed them. Structural archaeology is thought of as a way of finding out how people bring order into their world by using central, powerful, and flexible symbols, expressed in belief and religion.

The concept of structural archaeology is all very well in theory, but few if any, archaeological studies have yet provided convincing accounts of the relationships between the "codes" and social and ecological organization. A fierce theoretical debate surrounds the validity of this and other postprocessual approaches (Chapter 2), and about the validity of evolutionary approaches to archaeology.

RECONSIDERING EVOLUTIONARY ARCHAEOLOGY

Postprocessual archaeologists have criticized the use of evolutionary theory in archaeology, for they tend to believe that human culture is independent of biology. It is, however, both more useful and more convincing to assume that natural selection produced culture by conferring some reproductive advantage on its early human bearers. So thought and action were channeled by natural selection in directions that were adaptive for an evolving humanity. The legacy of this is a tendency for humans to think and act in certain ways and not in others. The result is that very diverse human societies with very different institutions and beliefs tend to think and act in the same general ways. Archaeologists of this persuasion believe that natural selection has constrained human thought and action, that one can understand the ways in which people behave by comprehending the constraints placed on the human mind by its long evolutionary heritage. It should be remembered, however, that the environment in which the human mind evolved is very different from that in which we live today, and have lived for many thousands of years.

Following this argument, the reality that *Homo sapiens sapiens* is a product of biological evolution, probably dominated by natural selection, underlies the ways in which we think and act. From the archaeological point of view, the existence of what Mithen calls "universal psychological propensities" means that we have a link that connects modern humans with prehistoric, anatomically modern people—our common behavioral characteristics. On these grounds alone, the validity of evolutionary approaches to archaeology is probably established beyond a reasonable doubt.

Intimately linked with the evolutionary approach is the notion of adaptation, the morphological, behavioral, and cognitive traits of any organism that increase its chance of survival and reproduction and that of its biological kin. By no means all behavioral traits are adaptive all the time, or in all environments. One must demonstrate how they allow the survival and reproduction of individuals in the past, a demonstration that requires considerable reasoning, for it is one thing to discover evidence of, say, more sea-mammal hunting and quite another to show that this resulted in a variety of social consequences such as increased prestige. One must carry out research "armed with humility in the face of the complexity of human cognitive functioning and social systems."

The evolutionary approach to archaeology considers adaptation as a process, with flexible behavior and creative thought on the part of individuals as the driving forces behind decisions to change social and physical environments. Nowhere can this be more clearly seen than in the case of the Khoi Khoi cattle herders who lived at the Cape of Good Hope, the southernmost tip of Africa, in the fifteenth century. Like all human societies, the Khoi Khoi were a society of individuals, each of whom pursued individual goals within the broad compass of a herder society. Their society disintegrated in the face of European colonization in the seventeenth and eighteenth centuries, largely because *individuals* made short-term decisions about selling off their breeding cows for immediate advantage. Within a generation or so, the long-term consequences were apparent—the loss of the ability to breed stock, and loss of wealth in a society where cattle were the primary source of prestige and adaptation. The centuries-old lifeway of the Khoi Khoi was no longer adaptive as a result of individual decision-making some generations earlier.

Until now, most evolutionary studies in archaeology have been more concerned with prehistoric subsistence and interaction with the natural environment, and less focused on adaptations to the social environment. In the future, they may be directed more toward identifying the extent to which individual choices and the patterns in the archaeological record resulting from them can be explained in adaptive terms.

This form of evolutionary archaeology is very different from the type espoused by cultural ecology, which tends to focus on static group adaptation. It will involve developing new methodologies that integrate evolutionary ecology and human psychology and ways of relating short-term individual behavior to the inevitably generalized data from the archaeological record.

13

ARCHAEOLOGY
TOMORROW

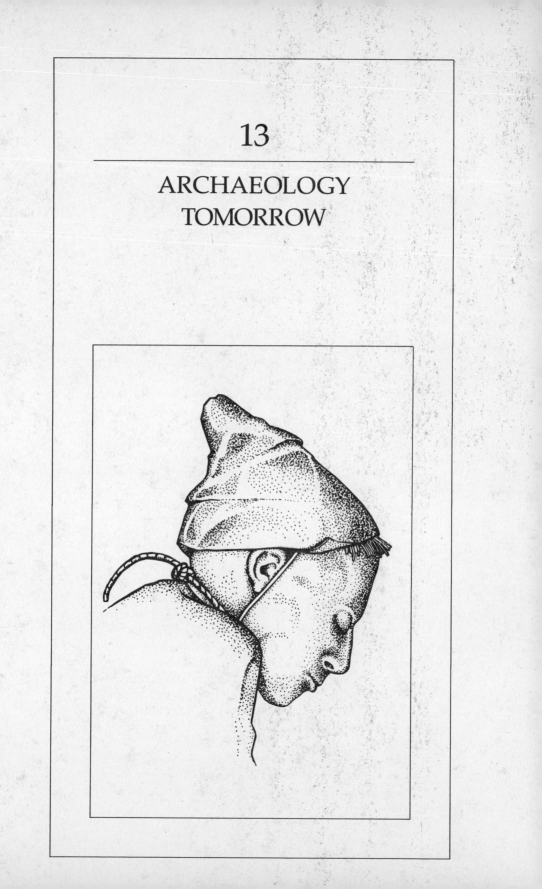

Of late years great encroachments have been made . . . by the plough which threatens the ruin of this fine champain, and of all the monuments of antiquity thereabouts.

William Stukeley, 1740

Archaeology tells us the remarkable story of human prehistory, from its very beginnings on the East African grasslands right up to the time, some 5000 years ago, when state-organized societies emerged in Egypt and Mesopotamia, and far beyond. This sophisticated science is, in a real sense, an integral part of twentieth-century life, for it gives us unrivaled perspectives on evolving humanity over more than 2.5 million years, and proves that all of us humans are part of a single, if diverse, family. The lessons it teaches us about ourselves are of vital importance to everyone in an ever-more complex and diverse world. Yet archaeology is in crisis, threatened by a tidal wave of destruction and looting of the finite archives of the past, a past that offers a unique cultural identity to much of humankind.

THE FUTURE OF THE PAST

Anthropology tells a story of human biological and cultural evolution that climaxes in urban civilization and the extraordinary diversity of the modern world. But the very emergence of civilization has hastened the evolution of new, much larger, global societies. Scores of societies are now linked by religious beliefs, political ideologies, or remarkable heights of technological achievement. Our own Western society, with its ability for instant communication and its capacity to feed more people than ever before, has reached out to the farthest corners of the world in search of new economic and spiritual domains to conquer. The results for many societies have been traumatic.

The Polynesians encountered the Western world in the eighteenth century. A hundred years later, they were a shadow of their previous selves, exploited and missionized almost to death. Millions of American Indians perished from exotic diseases brought by Europeans that spread in advance of actual white settlement. Few bands of Australian aborigines retain even a part of their millennia-old culture. The alternatives for the members of these societies were extinction or assimilation into a culture where they were, at best, second-rate citizens. Only in the 1960s and 1970s have some of them been able to stand on their own feet again, as newly independent groups or nations trying to reestablish their identity in a much-changed world.

Nationalism can be seen as one of the major historical trends of recent decades. It is manifested in new nations and in ethnic minorities that have begun an ardent search for their own historical identity. Alex Haley's *Roots* rightly caused a sensation when it recounted how Haley found his ancestry in West Africa. For many people, such oral traditions were lost in the enormous adjustment their nonliterate societies have made in the past century. Thus, archaeology remains the primary source of historical data about the Australian aborigines, the Tahitians, the American Indians, and hundreds of other non-Western societies. If asked whether archaeology has any use, one need only to point to the huge gaps in world history that still await archaeologists' attention—if any sites are left to excavate.

The breathtaking pace of agricultural and industrial development in recent years has taken a massive toll on the past. Thousands of American Indian sites have been destroyed by flooding behind hydro-electric dams, by deep plowing and strip mining, and by thousands of acres of urban development and freeway construction. Pothunters, too, have taken their toll. We may be the last generation of Americans to see many undisturbed archaeological sites. Charles McGimsey of the University of Arkansas has estimated that few untouched sites remain in his state. Probably fewer than 5 percent undisturbed sites of all prehistoric periods that originally existed are left in Los Angeles County. Despite many newly passed laws regarding antiquities in recent years, which mainly protect sites on federal land, there is a real danger that archaeology in North America is doomed. The finite resource base of sites is being eroded with little thought for the history these priceless archives contain. It is genocide, not of the living, but of the dead.

The popular interest in archaeology still revels in ancient mysteries, the excitement of discovery, and buried treasure. Many people regard archaeology as a luxury with no relevance to the cultural history of humankind. It is a means for gratifying their urge to possess things. Projectile points, Maya pots, and bronze swords look good on a mantle shelf or in a museum display case. So great is the demand for such treasures that a flourishing antiquities market has grown up to satisfy our greed. Archaeological sites have been destroyed for commercial ends ever since the eighteenth century. The early collections of the Metropolitan Museum of Art in New York and many other major museums were very often accumulated by purchase of looted objects handled by large-scale dealers in the past. Today's prices are astronomical.

So much damage has been done that more and more museums and wealthy collectors are competing for fewer and fewer finds. Entire Inca cemeteries and Maya ceremonial centers have been decimated in search of salable objects. Many sites in the American Southwest had been ravaged beyond repair by the early years of this century.

Almost nothing can be, or has been, done about the illegal trade in antiquities. Unscrupulous collectors and museums do not care, the

Figure 13.1 Two possibilities for the future of the past. Top: removal of the Abu Simbel temples was an international effort at rescue archaeology. Here, the face of Ramses II is lifted to the new location of the Great Temple. Bottom: pothunters at work do irreparable damage to a site. Compare this scene of devastation with the excavations illustrated in Chapter 7.

dealers do not care, and the treasure hunting supports whole villages of poor farmers in many countries. Worst of all, the public as a whole does not care. Despite highly sophisticated conservation movements in the United States, archaeology still lies outside the mainstream of environmental activism in this country and elsewhere. This is surprising, for archaeological sites are an integral part of the modern environment that we seek to conserve. In the case of North America, this may be because most Americans do not feel a direct cultural and emotional link to the sites and artifacts of the American Indian. Unfortunately, the future of arhaeology lies in everyone's hands, and many people destroy archaeological sites without realizing it or because they consider them useless (Figure 13.1).

ARCHAEOLOGY AND YOU

How can you become involved in archaeology? Are there career prospects as an archaeologist? What can a lay person do to help save the past? There are many ways to become involved.

Hundreds of archaeologists work in the United States. Many teach in universities and colleges, some in high schools. Others head up archaeological departments of national, city, state, or local museums all over the country or direct state archaeological surveys. Archaeologists work for the National Park Service and other federal agencies. Others support themselves by part-time teaching or undertake contracts on federal projects or for companies seeking cultural resource management services.

The research interests of these archaeologists range from early Indian settlements on the plains to historical sites in New England, from theoretical models of early agriculture to computer simulation. One can find almost more specialties than archeologists. And many of America's archaeologists work overseas—in Africa, Europe, Mesoamerica, Peru, and even farther afield. You can find someone who will teach you almost any type of archaeology you want, above or below ground, under the water, even in the air. Unfortunately, however, job opportunities are in short supply.

Most archaeological jobs, whether in a college, museum, or university, require a minimum of a master's degree, most often a doctorate as well. The doctorate is a research degree requiring comprehensive seminar, course, and field training in graduate school and then a period of intensive fieldwork that, when written up, forms the dissertation, which is submitted to a committee of examiners. The average doctoral program takes between four and seven years to complete. Once you have the degree, you still have to find a job as a faculty member or museum officer somewhere. And that, in these days of great numbers of Ph.D.'s, is not easy.

The M.A. degree normally takes one or two years of graduate work and gives you broad, general training in the basic methods and theory of archaeology as well as world prehistory, with some specialization in a local area or in cultural resource management. The degree is satisfied by courses and seminars. You may have to write a library thesis as well and obtain some digging experience. The M.A. does not give you as much access to research funds and opportunities as a Ph.D. You can, however, do invaluable work in cultural resource management or local archaeology. Various universities and colleges do offer certification programs for people interested in contract, conservation archaeology, work for which no Ph.D. is required. Consult your professors about such opportunities.

Anyone who considers becoming a professional archaeologist must have a superior academic record with in-depth coverage of anthropology and archaeology. A course average of "A" is a minimal requirement for entrance to good graduate schools. Some field experience on a dig or survey is also necessary, as is strong and meaningful support from at least two qualified archaeologists willing to write letters of recommendation. As for attitude, strong motivation to become an archaeologist is a must, and, for the Ph.D., a specific research interest. An archaeologist who thrives on hard work and who can tolerate some discomfort, a mass of detail, and long hours of routine laboratory work, will be a happy one. An interest in teaching and a moral commitment not to collect artifacts for profit or personal gain are the remaining prerequisites on this formidable list. If the list sounds rigorous, remember that archaeologists of the next generation have the future of the past in their hands.

Let us say you do want to become an archaeologist. Which graduate school should you apply to? You should choose your school according to your specific interests. It is wise to apply to more than one department and to make sure first that your faculty advisers really support your application.

Many people want to gain digging experience whether they intend to go to graduate school or not. The best way to learn is to take a course in field methods, then volunteer to dig for a period on a summer excavation. Details of digs are normally posted on anthropology department bulletin boards or at local museums. Alternatively, take a general introductory course in archaeology, then go to a field school. Many university-sponsored field schools offer academic credit for your participation. Such summer programs are well worth the time, for they combine lectures and seminars with actual digging and laboratory experience. And the camaraderie of such digs can be a memorable experience.

Some people venture farther afield and join an excavation overseas for some weeks. Cheap charter flights have made Europe readily accessible. By contacting such organizations as the Council for British

Archaeology in London, it is possible to obtain details of excavations in progress where volunteers are needed. Bear in mind that very few digs in this country or overseas pay you to be an excavator. At the costly end of the spectrum are package travel tours that take students to such faraway places as Israel to dig and learn archaeology under close supervision. These tend to be expensive experiences, often of variable academic quality. But whatever type of dig you choose, an excavation experience is a good way of testing your commitment.

An undergraduate degree in archaeology is insufficient qualification for a job in the field. But good undergraduate training can give you a perspective on archaeology that will be with you for the rest of your life. There are many ways to enjoy archaeology as a lay person. You can join a local archaeological society, participate in excavations and volunteer museum programs, keep an eye on endangered sites in your community. The background in archaeology you take with you into later life will enable you to see famous sites all over the world as an informed visitor, to enjoy the achievements of prehistoric peoples to the full. Above all, you can influence the ways in which other people think about, and behave toward, archaeological sites and accidental discoveries. And your contacts with former instructors and other professional archaeologists may help you prevent damage to important, undisturbed sites.

This book may be the only experience you have of archaeology. We hope it has given you some insight into how archaeologists reconstruct the prehistoric past. But how can you help save the past for future generations? How should responsible people live with the finite resources of prehistory? Here are some guidelines:

> *Treat every archaeological site and artifact as a finite resource that can never be replaced once destroyed.*

> *Report all archaeological discoveries to responsible archaeological authorities* (archaeological surveys, museums, university or college departments, government agencies).

> *Obey all laws relating to archaeological sites.*

> *Never dig a site without proper training or supervision.*

> *Never collect archaeological finds from any country for your private collection or for profit.* If you must collect, collect reproductions.

> *Respect modern and prehistoric Indian burial grounds and sacred sites.* They have deep spiritual significance.

Is there a future for the past? Yes, if we want one. It is up to all of us.

SITES AND CULTURES
MENTIONED IN THE TEXT

These brief descriptions give some background on prehistoric cultures and sites mentioned in the text, they are not meant to be precise definitions. Ask your instructor for more information and references if you need them.

Acheulian.   A widespread early Stone Age culture named after the town of St. Acheul in northern France. The Acheulian flourished in Africa, western Europe, and southern Asia from before a million years ago until less than 100,000. The Acheulians made many types of stone artifacts, including multipurpose butchering hand axes and cleaving tools.

Adena.   A distinctive burial cult and village culture in the Ohio Valley of the Midwest. It flourished between about 700 B.C. and A.D. 200 and was remarkable for its long-distance trading and distinctive burial cults expressed in large earthworks and mounds.

Ain Ghazal.   An early farming village in the Jordan Valley, occupied some 8000 years ago. It is remarkable for its clay female figurines, perhaps evidence for an early fertility cult.

Ali Kosh.   Early farming site on the Deh Luran plain in Iran, where evidence for cereal cultivation was found by flotation techniques. The site dates to as early as 7500 B.C.

Apple Creek, Illinois.   An Archaic site, where people engaged in intensive collecting of wild vegetable foods after 3000 B.C. They concentrated on hickory nuts, acorns, and other common species.

Clovis.   Paleo-Indian culture that flourished in North America, and perhaps further afield, between 9500 and 9000 B.C. and perhaps a little earlier.

Colonial Williamsburg.   Reconstruction of Virginia's first capital city, carried out partly with the aid of archaeological research.

Folsom.   Paleo-Indian culture that flourished on the North American Plains after 9000 B.C.

Giza.   The Pyramids at Giza were built in the desert near Cairo during Egypt's Old Kingdom, around 2600 B.C. The Great Pyramid
is 481 feet high and covers 13.1 acres.

Hadar.   A region of Ethiopia where early hominid fossils dating to as
early as four million years ago have been found.

Hohokam.   A southwestern cultural tradition that originated as early
as 300 B.C. and lasted until A.D. 1500. The Hohokam people were
farmers who occupied much of what is now Arizona. Their cultural
heirs are the Pima and Papago Indians of today.

Hopewell.   Between 200 B.C. and A.D. 600, the "Hopewell Interaction Sphere" flourished in the Midwest. Hopewell religious cults
and distinctive burial customs were associated with an art tradition
that spread far and wide through long-distance trading connections.

Ipiutak.   A sea-mammal hunting tradition that was a variant of the
Norton tradition of Alaska in the first millennium A.D. Ipiutak sites
are remarkable for their decorated harpoon heads and other art
objects, especially in the permanent settlements near Point Hope.

Koobi Fora.   A location on the eastern shores of Lake Turkana in
northern Kenya, where the earliest traces of human culture have
been found, dating to more than two million years ago.

Koster.   From before 7000 B.C. until less than 1000 years ago, hunter-
gatherers and later farmers settled at this location on the Illinois
River to exploit the fertile river bottom. The site is unusual for its
long stratigraphic sequence of Archaic and Woodland settlements
and abundant food remains.

Kourion.   A small Roman port in southwestern Cyprus in the eastern
Mediterranean overwhelmed by a great earthquake early on the
morning of July 21, 365. Excavations at the village have revealed
many details of a long-forgotten disaster.

Laetoli.   This site in Tanzania yielded the earliest hominid footprints,
potassium–argon dated to more than three-and-a-half million years
ago.

Lovelock Cave, Nevada.   A desert site in the far West occupied as
early as 7000 B.C. Located near a desert marsh, it has yielded minute details of prehistoric desert adaptations over a long period.

Magdalenian.   Late Ice Age culture that flourished in central and
western Europe between about 18,000 and 12,000 years ago. Expert artists and reindeer hunters.

Oldowan.   Technological tradition associated with *Homo habilis* and the earliest humans, which flourished in Africa from about 2.4 million years ago until approximately 1.6 million years ago.

Olmec.   One of the earliest lowland Mexican state-organized societies, Olmec culture flourished from around 1500 to 500 B.C. Olmec people traded widely, had a distinctive art tradition that depicted humanlike jaguars and both natural and supernatural beings, and developed many of the religious traditions that were to sustain the Maya and other Mesoamerican civilizations such as Teotihuacán.

Olsen-Chubbuck, Colorado.   An 8000-year-old bison kill site on the North American plains that revealed many details of Paleo-Indian hunting and butchering techniques.

Ozette, Washington.   A coastal settlement in Washington state occupied for at least 1000 years by ancestors of the present-day Makah Indians. Ozette suffered disaster two centuries ago when houses were buried by mud slides and preserved in perfect condition for archaeologists to investigate in the 1970s.

Pazyryk.   Siberian burial mounds of prehistoric horsemen, where refrigerated soil conditions have preserved every detail of the dead, including skin tattoos. The Pazyryk mounds date to about 2300 years ago.

Pecos, New Mexico.   An Anasazi pueblo in the Southwest that was occupied for much of the past 2000 years, and provided the first stratigraphic sequence for Southwestern prehistory as a result of A. V. Kidder's excavations.

Shang Civilization.   Early Chinese civilization that flourished from as early as 2700 B.C., when the Xia dynasty arose in the north. The Shang dynasty rose to power around 1766 B.C. and ruled until 1122 B.C. Its rulers occupied a series of capitals near the Yellow River, the most famous being Anyang, occupied around 1400 B.C.

Snaketown.   A Hohokam pueblo in Arizona, occupied about 850 to 500 years ago, and famous for its ball court and platform mounds. The Snaketown people probably maintained trading contacts with Mexican communities to the south.

Star Carr.   A postglacial hunting stand in northeast England dating to about 8200 B.C., remarkable for the bone and wooden artifacts recovered from a small birchbark platform at the edge of a small lake.

Stonehenge.   Stone circles in southern Britain that formed a sacred precinct as early as 2700 B.C. and remained in use until the second millennium B.C. Some authorities believe Stonehenge was an astronomical observatory, but this viewpoint is controversial.

Sumerians.   Creators of the civilization that flourished in southern Iraq between about 2900 and 2000 B.C., Sumerians lived in small city-states that perennially quarreled with one another. Depended on irrigation agriculture.

Tehuacán Valley, Mexico.   A valley in which evidence for a gradual shift from hunting and gathering to deliberate cultivation of squashes and other minor crops, then maize, has been documented. Tehuacán was occupied as early as 10,000 B.C., with maize agriculture appearing about 5000 B.C.

Teotihuacán.   A vast pre-Columbian city in highland Mexico that flourished from as early as 200 B.C. until it declined in around A.D. 750. Teotihuacán maintained extensive political and trade contacts with lowland Mexico, and is famed for its enormous public buildings and pyramids.

Tikal.   Classic Maya city in the Guatemalan lowlands, which reached its height in about A.D. 600.

Ur-of-the-Chaldees.   Biblical city in southern Iraq that grew from a tiny farming hamlet founded as early as 4700 B.C. Known for its Early Dynastic Sumerian burials, where a ruler's entire retinue committed institutionalized suicide.

FURTHER READING

The technical literature of archaeology is immense; we can guide you to no more than a few key references on each of the major topics covered in this book. For more detailed information, consult one of the major summaries listed here or ask your instructor.

General Summaries

Two major college texts provide a comprehensive background on the method and theory of prehistoric archaeology. This text is a much shortened version of my own *In the Beginning*, 7th ed. (New York: Harper Collins, 1991). R. J. Sharer and Wendy Ashmore, *Archaeology: Discovering the Past* (Palo Alto: Mayfield, 1987) is an equivalent volume.

The major developments of world prehistory are described in my *People of the Earth*, 6th ed. (Boston: Little, Brown, 1989). Another excellent account is Robert Wenke, *Patterns in Prehistory*, 2nd ed. (New York: Oxford University Press, 1984). J. Gowlett, *Ascent to Civilization* (New York: Random House, 1985) is excellent for the Stone Age. *The Adventure of Archaeology* (Washington, D.C.: National Geographic Society, 1985) is a beautifully illustrated description of how archaeology began.

Special Fields of Archaeology

Historical Archaeology: Ivor Nöel Hume, *Historical Archaeology* (New York: Alfred Knopf, 1968). Classical archaeology is summarized by Paul L. McKendrick, *The Greek Stones Speak* and *The Mute Stones Speak* (both New York: St. Martin's Press, 1962 and 1961, respectively). Underwater archaeology is covered by George Bass, *Archaeology Underwater* (New York: Praeger, 1966) and by the same author's magnificent *A History of Seafaring Based on Underwater Archaeology* (London: Thames and Hudson, 1972) and *Ships and Shipwrecks of the Americas* (London: Thames and Hudson, 1988).

Atlases and Dictionaries of Archaeology

The best atlas for the general reader is Chris Scarre (ed.), *Past Worlds: The Times Atlas of Archaeology* (London: Times Books, 1988). A good dictionary. Warwick Bray and David Trump, *A Dictionary of Archaeology* (London: Penguin Press, 1970).

Major Archaeological Journals

The dozens of international, national, and local archaeological journals are designed mainly for specialists. Among those carrying popular articles on archaeology are *National Geographic, Natural History, Smithsonian,* and *Scientific American. Archaeology is* a superb magazine for enthusiasts, whereas *Antiquity,* the *Journal of World Prehistory,* and *World Archaeology* carry articles of wide interest to serious archaeologists. American archaeologists rely heavily on *American Antiquity,* the journal of the Society for American Archaeology. *American Anthropologist* sometimes carries archaeological pieces, and Old World archaeologists publish in *Man, Nature,* and the *Proceedings of the Prehistoric Society.* The *Journal of Field Archaeology* is of high technical value.

Chapter 1: Archaeologists Learn to Study Past Cultures

This history of archaeology is easily accessible. Glyn Daniel's *A Short History of Archaeology* (London: Thames and Hudson, 1981) is a brief factual summary. *The Adventure of Archaeology,* already mentioned, is a more popular account. Gordon Willey and Jeremy Sabloff, *A History of American Archaeology,* 2nd ed. (New York: W. H. Freeman) is widely quoted. Bruce Trigger's *A History of Archaeological Interpretation* (Cambridge: Cambridge University Press, 1989) is the definitive work on the subject.

Chapter 2: Archaeology as Anthropology

James Deetz, *Invitation to Archaeology* (Garden City, NY: Natural History Press, 1967), covers many of the points in this chapter. So too does Grahame Clark, *Archaeology and Society* (New York: Barnes & Noble, 1965)—an old account that has never been bettered. Rose Macaulay, *The Pleasure of Ruins* (London: Thames and Hudson, 1959) is a delight for tourists. Massimo Pallotino, *The Meaning of Archaeology* (New York: Abrams, 1968) is a thoughtful account of the issues raised in this chapter.

Chapter 3: Culture

Few archaeologists have dared to write a summary of the controversial issues covered in this chapter. Gordon Willey and Philip Phillips,

Method and Theory in American Archaeology (Chicago: University of Chicago Press, 1958) is fundamental. So also is V. Gordon Childe's insightful *Piecing Together the Past* (London: Routledge and Kegan Paul, 1956). Later developments in archaeology can be surveyed in Lewis Binford's somewhat biassed *In Pursuit of the Past* (London: Thames and Hudson, 1983). See also P. J. Watson, Steven Le Blanc, and Charles Redman, *Archaeological Explanation* (New York: Columbia University Press, 1984). A magnificent assessment of contemporary American archaeology appears in David Meltzer, Don Fowler, and Jeremy Sabloff, eds., *American Archaeology Past and Future* (Washington, DC: Smithsonian Institution Press, 1986).

Chapter 4: Time

No one has yet rivaled Sir Mortimer Wheeler's classic description of stratigraphy in his *Archaeology from the Earth* (Oxford: Clarendon Press, 1954). Dating techniques are mainly described in journal articles, but Stuart Fleming, *Dating in Archaeology* (London: St. Martin's Press, 1977) is informative. So too is R. E. Taylor and C. W. Ceram, eds., *Chronologies in New World Archaeology* (New York: Academic Press, 1978).

Karl Butzer, *Archaeology as Human Ecology* (Cambridge: Cambridge University Press, 1982) and Dov Nir, *Man: A Geomorphological Agent* (Boston: Reidel Publishing, 1983) are of fundamental importance; so also is Butzer's *Environment and Archaeology*, 2nd ed. (Chicago: Aldine, 1971).

Chapter 5: Space

Once again, V. Gordon Childe, *Piecing Together the Past* (London: Routledge and Kegan Paul, 1956) is one of the few accounts. Kent V. Flannery, ed., *The Early Mesoamerican Village* (New York: Academic Press, 1976) covers some key concepts, but is better read in the context of Chapter 10. For the law of association, read John Rowe's paper: "Worsaae's Law and the Use of Grave Lots for Archaeological Dating," *American Antiquity* (1962), 28:2, 129–137. Much of the literature for this chapter is scattered in periodicals: consult an expert.

Chapter 6: Preservation and Survey

The study of site-formation processes is fundamental to this chapter. Michael Schiffer, *Site Formation Processes of the Archaeological Record* (New York: Academic Press, 1987) is a good starting point. Here are some examples of outstanding sites: Owen Beattie and John Geiger, *Frozen in Time: The Fate of the Franklin Expedition* (London: Bloomsbury Publications, 1986) recounts the story of the Franklin graves. John Romer, *The Valley of Kings* (New York: William Morrow,

1981) is fascinating on Ancient Egyptian tombs, including Tutankhamun. The Koster site in Illinois: Stuart Streuver and Gail Houart, *Koster* (New York: Anchor Doubleday, 1980). P. V. Glob, *The Bog People* (London: Faber and Faber, 1969) describes a number of well-preserved prehistoric corpses from waterlogged Danish bogs; even the skin and intestines survive. Sergei I. Rudenko, *Frozen Tombs of Siberia: The Pazyryk Burials of Iron Age Horsemen* (Berkeley: University of California Press, 1970), as translated by M. W. Thompson, examines spectacular prehistoric graves where the permafrost soil has literally refrigerated such organic materials as rugs. The remarkable Ozette site is described by Ruth Kirk, with Richard Daugherty, in *Hunters of the Whale* (New York: Morrow, 1975).

Archaeological survey is a hotly debated subject at the moment, but mainly in specialist journals. You can get some useful leads by consulting either of the major textbooks referred to above. Cultural Resource Management is another difficult subject, remarkable for the complexity of its jargon. Charles McGimsey, *Public Archaeology* (New York: Seminar Press, 1972) is a pioneer work. George Gumerman's *A View from Black Mesa: The Changing Face of Archaeology* (Tucson: University of Arizona Press, 1984) gives the general reader a good impression of rapid changes in CRM approaches. Michael Schiffer and George Gumerman, eds., *Conservation Archaeology* (New York: Academic Press, 1977) has useful material.

Chapter 7: Excavation

We lack a comprehensive, up-to-date excavation manual for American archaeology, except for H. S. Dancey, *Archaeological Field Methods: An Introduction* (Minneapolis: Burgess, 1981). Mortimer Wheeler, *Archaeology from the Earth* (Oxford: Clarendon Press, 1954) is a timeless account of basic principles, based on larger sites. Quite apart from its other merits, it is readable! Phillip Barker, *Understanding Archaeological Excavation* (London: Batsford, 1986) has a strong European orientation, but is very perceptive. The same author's *The Techniques of Archaeological Excavation* (London: Batsford, 1983) and Martha Joukowsky, *A Complete Manual of Field Archaeology* (Englewood Cliffs, NJ: Prentice-Hall, 1981) are basic sources for the serious student. For sampling: John A. Mueller, ed., *Sampling in Archaeology* (Tucson: University of Arizona Press, 1974). Two exemplary case studies of archaeological excavation in historical settings are Ivor Nöel Hume, *Martin's Hundred* (New York: Alfred Knopf, 1983) and Kathleen Deagan, *Spanish St. Augustine: The Archaeology of a Colonial Creole Community* (New York: Academic Press, 1983).

Chapter 8: Ordering the Past

V. Gordon Childe, *Piecing Together the Past* (London: Routledge and Kegan Paul, 1956) is still one of the best accounts of the problems of ordering. So too is Gordon Willey and Philip Phillips, *Method and Theory in American Archaeology* (Chicago: University of Chicago Press, 1958), which describes some of the archaeological units used in the New World. Robert Dunnell's *Systematics in Prehistory* (New York: Free Press, 1970) is a technical but fascinating account of classification problems. The concept of type is covered in this book, and the article by Albert Spaulding referred to by the director is "Statistical Techniques for the Study of Artifact Types," *American Antiquity* 18:4 (1953), 305–313. Robert Whallon and James A. Brown, eds., *Essays on Archaeological Typology* (Kampsville, Ill.: Center for American Archaeology, 1982) updates the earlier literature and is a fundamental source.

For quantitative methods in archaeology, try Stephen Shennan, *Quantifying Archaeology* (San Diego: Academic Press, 1988), which is intelligible to a beginner.

Chapter 9: Subsistence

Zooarchaeology is well served by S. J. M. Davis, *The Archaeology of Animals* (London: Batsford, 1987). Richard Klein and Kathryn Cruz-Uribe, *The Analysis of Animal Bones from Archaeological Sites* (Chicago: University of Chicago Press, 1984) and Donald Grayson, *Quantitative Zooarchaeology* (New York: Academic Press, 1984) are more advanced essays. Lewis Binford's widely read and controversial *Bones* (New York: Academic Press 1981) is an essay about the basic problems of animal bones in archaeological sites. For plants: Jane Renfrew, *Palaeoethnobotany* (London: Methuen, 1973). Deborah Pearsall, *Paleoethnobotany: A Handbook of Procedures* (New York: Academic Press, 1989) is an excellent starting point. The Tehuacán discoveries are summarized by Richard MacNeish, *The Prehistory of the Tehuacán Valley*, vol. 1 (Austin: University of Texas Press, 1967), whereas Frank Hole, Kent V. Flannery, and A. J. Neely, *Prehistory and Human Ecology of the Deh Luran Plain* (Ann Arbor: Museum of Anthropology, University of Michigan, 1969) describe the Deh Luran finds. Richard Ford (ed.), *Early Food Production in North America* (Ann Arbor: Museum of Anthropology, University of Michigan, 1985) contains essays on early crops in the New World, and can be amplified with Bruce Smith's "The Archaeology of the Southeastern United States," *Advances in World Archaeology* (1986) 5: 1–92, in which Smith discusses some of the results gained from subsistence studies in an area of North America.

Chapter 10: Interaction

K. C. Chang, *Settlement Archaeology* (Palo Alto: National Press, 1968) is a basic source, and Kent V. Flannery, ed., *The Early Mesoamerican Village* (New York: Academic Press, 1976) is essential reading for everyone interested in this subject, if only for the fascinating and hypothetical dialogues that communicate different viewpoints about contemporary archaeology. Teotihuacán: René Millon and others, *Urbanization at Teotihuacán, Mexico,* vol. 1 (Austin: University of Texas Press, 1973). A superb monograph on settlement archaeology: W. T. Sanders, Jeffrey R. Parsons, and Robert S. Santley, *The Basin of Mexico: Ecological Processes in the Evolution of a Civilization* (New York: Academic Press, 1979).

For Social ranking, try Robert Chapman et al., (eds.), *The Archaeology of Death* (Cambridge: Cambridge University Press, 1981). Jeremy A. Sabloff and Karl Lamberg-Karlovsky (eds.), *Ancient Civilizations and Trade* (Albuquerque: University of New Mexico Press, 1975), and E. Brumfield and T. K. Earle (eds.) *Specialization, Exchange, and Complex Societies* (Cambridge: Cambridge University Press, 1987) discuss long-distance exchange, while Robin Torrence, *Production and Exchange of Stone Tools* (Cambridge: Cambridge University Press, 1986), is an admirable study of the obsidian trade of the Aegean Sea.

Chapter 11: The Present and the Past

Middle-range theory is best summarized by Lewis Binford, *In Pursuit of the Past* (London: Thames and Hudson, 1983). His *Nunamiut Eskimo Ethnoarchaeology* (New York: Academic Press, 1977) is a detailed account of his own attempts to grapple with issues of Middle-Range Theory and ethnoarchaeology. For living archaeology, see Richard Gould, *Living Archaeology* (Cambridge: Cambridge University Press, 1980). The !Kung San: Richard B. Lee, *The !Kung San* (Cambridge: Cambridge University Press, 1979). This book provides background on all aspects of !Kung life-style referred to in these pages. John Coles, *Archaeology by Experiment* (London: Hutchinson University Press, 1973) is the best summary of this subject. For a project combining both approaches: Brian Hayden (ed.), *Lithic Studies Among the Contemporary Highland Maya.* (Tucson: University of Arizona Press, 1987).

Chapter 12: Explaining the Past

The literature is enormous and sometimes acrimonious. A good starting point is Lewis Binford's *In Pursuit of the Past* (London: Thames and Hudson, 1983). Also, P. J. Watson, Steven A. LeBlanc, and C. L. Redman, *Archaeological Explanation* (New York: Columbia University Press, 1984) and Guy Gibbon's *Anthropological Archaeology* (New York: Columbia University Press, 1984). Postprocessual archaeology has generated a profuse literature, well summarized in two books by M. Shanks and C. Tilley: *Reconstructing Archaeology: Theory and*

Practice (Cambridge: Cambridge University Press, 1987) and *Social Theory and Archaeology* (Albuquerque: University of New Mexico Press, 1987). Anyone navigating these shark-infested academic waters should read Steven Mithen, "Evolutionary theory and post-processual archaeology," *Antiquity* 63(1989):483–494. This admirable paper identifies future directions of debate with great clarity.

Chapter 13: Archaeology Tomorrow

There is surprisingly little literature on archaeology in the modern world. More's the pity, for it is a major issue in contemporary archaeological scholarship. Karl Meyer, *The Plundered Past* (New York: Athenaeum Press, 1973) is required reading for everyone. Charles McGimsey, *Public Archaeology* (New York: Seminar Press, 1972) highlights the crisis in archaeology. Last, Ernestine Green, ed., *Ethics and Values in Archaeology* (New York: Free Press, 1984) assembles essays on these vital topics.

GLOSSARY

This glossary gives informal definitions of key words and ideas in the text. It is not a comprehensive dictionary of archaeology. Jargon is kept to a minimum, but a few technical expressions are inevitable. Terms such as *adaptation* and *mutation,* which are common in contexts other than archaeology, are not listed. A good dictionary will clarify these and other such terms.

absolute dating Dating in calendar years before the present; chronometric dating.

activity area A patterning of artifacts in a site indicating that a specific activity, such as stone toolmaking, took place.

activity set A set of artifacts that reveals the activities of an individual.

analogy A process of reasoning whereby two entities that share some similarities are assumed to share many others.

analysis A stage of archaeological research that involves describing and classifying artifactual and nonartifactual data.

analytical type Arbitrary groupings that an archaeologist defines for classifying human-manufactured artifacts. Analytical types consist of groups of attributes that define convenient types of artifacts for comparing sites in space and time. They do not necessarily coincide with actual tool types used by prehistoric people.

anthropology The study of humanity in the widest possible sense. Anthropology studies humanity from the earliest times up to the present, and it includes cultural and physical anthropology and archaeology.

antiquarian Someone interested in the past who collects and digs up antiquities unscientifically, in contrast to the scientific archaeologist.

archaeological context See **context.**

archaeological culture A group of assemblages representing the surviving remains of an extinct culture.

archaeological data Material recognized as significant as evidence by the archaeologist and collected and recorded as part of the research. The four main classes of archaeological data are artifacts, features, structures, and food remains.

archaeological reconnaissance Systematic attempts to locate, identify, and record the distribution of archaeological sites on the ground and against the natural geographic and environmental background.

archaeological theory A body of theoretical concepts providing both a framework and a means for archaeologists to look beyond the facts and material objects for explanations of events that took place in prehistory.

225

archaeological unit Arbitrary unit of classification set up by archaeologists to separate conveniently one grouping of artifacts in time and space from another.

archaeologist Someone who studies the past using scientific methods, with the motive of recording and interpreting ancient cultures rather than collecting artifacts for profit or display.

archaeology A special form of anthropology studying extinct human societies using material remains. The objectives of archaeology are to construct culture history, reconstruct past lifeways, and study cultural process.

archaeomagnetic dating Chronometric dating using magnetic alignments from buried features, such as pottery kilns, which can be compared to known fluctuations in the earth's magnetic field and produce a date in years.

Archaic In the New World, a period when hunter-gatherers were exploiting a broad spectrum of resources and may have been experimenting with agriculture.

area excavation Excavation of a large, horizontal area, usually used to uncover houses and prehistoric settlement patterns.

artifact Any object manufactured or modified by human beings.

assemblage All the artifacts found at a site, including the sum of all subassemblages at the site.

association The relationship between an artifact and other archaeological finds and a site level, or other artifact, structure, or feature in the site.

attribute A well-defined feature of an artifact that cannot be further subdivided. Archaeologists identify types of attributes, including form, style, and technology, in order to classify and interpret artifacts.

attribute analysis Analyzing artifacts using many of their features. Usually these attributes are studied statistically to produce clusters of attributes that can be used to identify statistical classes of artifacts.

attritional age profile The distribution of ages in an animal population that results from selective hunting or predation.

Australopithecus Primates whose fossil remains have been found mainly in eastern and southern Africa. They are thought to be closely related to the first human beings, who may, indeed, have evolved among them.

band The simple form of human social organization that flourished for most of prehistory. Bands consist of a family or a series of families, usually ranging from 20 to 50 people.

battleship curve Shape on a seriation graph formed by plotted points representing, for instance, the rise in popularity of an artifact, its period of maximum popularity, and its eventual decline.

biome Major biotic landscapes in which distinctive plant and animal communities live together in harmony.

biosphere All the earth's living organisms interacting with the physical environment.

blades Parallel-sided stone flakes, usually removed from a carefully prepared core, often by means of a punch.

burin Blade tool, flaked on either or both ends to form a small chisel or grooving tool.

cambium A viscid substance under the bark of trees, in which the annual growth of wood and bark takes place.

carrying capacity The number and density of people per square mile that a specified area of land can support, given a particular subsistence level.

catastrophic age profile Distribution of ages in an animal population as a result of death by natural causes.

causes In archaeology, events that force people to make decisions about how to deal with new situations.

central-place theory A geographical theory applied to archaeology, stating that human settlements will space themselves evenly across a landscape depending on availability of natural resources and other factors. Eventually these will evolve into a hierarchy of settlements of different size that depend on one another.

ceramics Objects of fired clay.

chiefdom A form of social organization more complex than a tribal society, which has evolved some form of leadership structure and some mechanisms for distributing goods and services throughout the society. The chief who heads such a society and the specialists who work for the chief are supported by the voluntary contributions of the people.

chronological types Types defined by form that are time markers.

chronometric dating Dating in years before the present; absolute dating.

clan Group of people from many lineages who live in one place and have a common line of descent—a kin grouping.

class A general group of artifacts, like "hand axes," which will be broken down into specific types, like "ovates," and so on.

Classic In both Mesoamerica and Peru, the period of vigorous civilization characterized by numerous ceremonial centers and small states.

Classical archaeologist A student of the Classical civilizations of Greece and Rome.

classification The ordering of archaeological data into groups and classes, using various ordering systems.

closed system A system that is internally self-regulating and receives no feedback from external sources (a good example is a household heating and cooling system).

cluster analysis The process of analyzing clusters of sites in space.

cognitive archaeology See **structural archaeology.**

community In archaeology, the tangible remains of the activities of the maximum number of people who together occupy a settlement at any one period.

complex In archaeology, a chronological subdivision of different artifact types such as stone tools, pottery, etc.

component An association of all the artifacts from one occupation level at a site.

conservation archaeology Another name for cultural resource management.

context The position of an archaeological find in time and space, established by measuring and assessing its associations, matrix, and provenience. The assessment includes study of what has happened to the find since it was buried in the ground.

coprolite Excrement preserved by desiccation or fossilization.

core In archaeology, a lump of stone from which human-struck flakes have been removed.

core borer A hollow tubelike instrument used to collect samples of soils, pollens, and other materials from below the surface.

cranial Of or pertaining to the skull (cranium).

crop marks Differential growth in crops and vegetational cover that reveals the outlines of archaeological sites from the air.

cross-dating Dating of sites by objects of known age, or artifact association of known age.

cultural anthropology The aspect of anthropology focusing on cultural facets of human societies (a term widely used in the United States).

cultural ecology Study of the dynamic interactions between human societies and their environments. Under this approach, culture is the primary adaptive mechanism used by human societies.

cultural evolution A theory similar to that of biological evolution, which argues that human cultures change gradually throughout time, as a result of a number of cultural processes.

cultural process A deductive approach to archaeological research that is designed to study the changes and interactions in cultural systems and the processes by which human cultures change throughout time. Processual archaeologists use both descriptive and explanatory models.

cultural resource management The conservation and management of archaeological sites and artifacts as a means of protecting the past.

cultural selection The process that leads to the acceptance of some cultural traits and innovations that make a culture more adaptive to its environment; somewhat akin to natural selection in biological evolution.

cultural system A perspective on culture that thinks of culture and its environment as a number of linked systems in which change occurs through a series of minor, linked variations in one or more of these systems.

cultural tradition In archaeology, a distinctive toolkit or technology that lasts a long time, longer than the duration of one culture, at one locality or several localities.

cultural transformations Changes in the archaeological record resulting from later human behavior, such as digging a rubbish pit into earlier levels.

culture Human culture is a set of designs for living that help mold our responses to different situations. It is our primary means of adapting to our environment. A "culture" in archaeology is an arbitrary unit meaning similar assemblages of artifacts found at several sites, defined in a precise context of time and space.

culture area An arbitrary geographic or research area in which general cultural homogeneity is to be found.

culture history An approach to archaeology assuming that artifacts can be used to build up a generalized picture of human culture and descriptive models in time and space and that these can be interpreted.

cuneiform From the Greek word *cuneus,* meaning a wedge. The earliest known, wedgelike script from Mesopotamia.

curation Deliberate attempts by prehistoric peoples to preserve key artifacts and structures for posterity.

cybernetics General systems theory.

cylinder hammer technique Stone-flaking technique using a bone hammer that removes small, flat flakes from a core.

datum point A location from which all measurements on a site are made. The datum point is tied into local survey maps.

deduction A process of reasoning that involves testing generalizations by generating hypotheses and testing them with data. Deductive research is cumulative and involves constant refining of hypotheses. Contrasts with inductive approaches where one proceeds from specific observations to general conclusions.

deductive-nomological reasoning A way of explaining observable phenomena by means of formal scientific methods, testing hypotheses generated from general laws governing human behavior. Some archaeologists believe this is the appropriate way to explain cultural process.

demography The study of population.

dendrochronology Tree-ring chronology.

descriptive types Types based on the physical or external properties of an artifact.

detritus Debris or droppings.

diffusion The spread of a culture trait from one area to another by means of contact between people.

direct historical analogy Analogy using historical records or historical ethnographic data.

direct historical approach Archaeological technique of working backward in time from historic sites of known age into earlier times.

ecofact Archaeological finds which are of cultural significance but which were not manufactured by humans, such as bones and vegetal remains. Not a commonly used term.

ecosystem An environmental system maintained by the regulation of trophic levels (vertical food chains) and by patterns of energy flow.

ecotone A transition zone between habitats.

epiphysis The articular end of a long bone, which fuses at adulthood.

ethnoarchaeology Living archaeology, a form of ethnography that deals mainly with material remains. Archaeologists carry out living archaeology to document the relationships between human behavior and the patterns of artifacts and food remains in the archaeological record.

ethnography A descriptive study, normally an in-depth examination of a culture.

ethnohistory Study of the past using non-Western, indigenous historical records, and especially oral traditions.

ethnology A cross-cultural study of aspects of various cultures, usually based on theory.

evolutionary archaeology An explanatory framework for the past that accounts for the structure and change in the archaeological record.

excavation The digging of archaeological sites, removal of the matrix and observance of the provenience and context of the finds therein, and the recording of them in a three-dimensional way.

exchange system A system for exchanging goods and services between individuals and communities.

exogamy A rule requiring marriage outside a social or cultural unit (opposite of *endogamy*).

experimental archaeology The use of carefully controlled modern experiments to provide data to aid in interpretation of the archaeological record.

extrasomatic Outside the body.

feature An artifact such as a house or storage pit, which cannot be removed from a site; normally, it is recorded only.

feces Excrement.

feedback A concept in archaeological applications of systems theory reflecting the continually changing relationship between cultural variables and their environment.

fire setting Quarrying stone by using fire to shatter the outcrops of rock.

fission-track dating The observance of accumulations of radioactivity in glass and volcanic rocks to produce absolute dates.

flake tools Stone tools made of flakes removed from cores.

flotation In archaeology, recovering plant remains by using water to separate seeds from their surrounding deposit.

focus Approximately equivalent to a phase.

form The physical characteristics—size and shape or composition—of any archaeological find. Form is an essential part of attribute analysis.

form analysis Analysis of artifacts based on the assumption that the shape of a pot or other tool directly reflects its function.

formation processes Humanly caused or natural processes by which an archaeological site is modified during or after occupation and abandonment.

Formative In Mesoamerica, the period when more complex societies and settlement patterns were coming into being; these led to the complex states of later times (contemporary with the rise of agriculture).

form types Artifact types based on the shape of an artifact.

formulation In archaeology, the process of making decisions about a research project as a preliminary to formal research design.

foot survey Archaeological reconnaissance on foot, often with a set interval between members of the survey team.

function In an evolutionary context, the forms that directly affect the Darwinian fitness of the populations in which they occur.

functionalism The notion that a social institution within a society has a function in fulfilling all the needs of a social organism.

functional type Type based on cultural use or function rather than on outward form or chronological position.

general systems theory The notion that any organism or organization can be studied as a system broken down into many interacting subsystems, or parts; sometimes called cybernetics.

geoarchaeology Archaeological research using the methods and concepts of the earth sciences.

geochronology Geological dating.

glacial eustacy The adjustments in sea levels and the earth's crust resulting from expansion and contraction of Pleistocene ice sheets.

habitat An area in the biome where different communities and populations flourish, each with specific locales.

half-life The time required for one half of a radioactive isotope to decay into a stable element. Used as a basis for radiocarbon and other dating methods.

hieroglyphs Ancient writing form with pictographic or ideographic symbols; used in Egypt, Mesoamerica, and elsewhere.

historical archaeology The study of archaeological sites in conjunction with historical records. It is sometimes called historic sites archaeology.

history Study of the past through written records.

hominid A member of the family *Hominidae*, represented today by one species, *Homo sapiens*.

Homo erectus Human beings who evolved from Lower Pleistocene hominids. They possessed larger brains and made more elaborate stone tools than their predecessors and settled in much more extreme environments, as far apart as western Europe, Asia, and tropical Africa.

horizon A widely distributed set of culture traits and artifact assemblages whose distribution and chronology allow one to assume that they spread rapidly. Often, horizons are formed of artifacts that were associated with widespread, distinctive religious beliefs.

horizontal (area) excavation Archaeological excavation designed to uncover large areas of a site, especially settlement layouts.

household unit An arbitrary archaeological unit defining artifact patterns reflecting the activities that take place around a house and assumed to belong to one household.

ideology The knowledge or beliefs developed by human societies as part of their cultural adaptation.

induction Reasoning by which one proceeds from specific observations to general conclusions.

industrial archaeology The study of sites of the Industrial Revolution and later.

industry The industry at a site is all the particular artifacts (bone, stone, wood) found at that site and made at the same time by the same population.

inevitable variation The notion that cultures change and vary with time, cumulatively. The reasons for these changes are little understood.

inorganic materials Material objects that are not part of the animal or vegetable kingdom.

interpretation The stage in research at which the results of archaeological analyses are synthesized and we attempt to explain their meaning.

kinship In anthropology, relationships between people that are based on real or imagined descent or, sometimes, on marriage. Kinship ties impose mutual obligations on all members of a kin group; these ties were at the core of most prehistoric societies.

knapper Someone who manufactures stone artifacts.

leaching Water seeping through the soil and removing from it the soluble materials.

limited-area reconnaissance Comprehensive door-to-door inquiries, supported by actual substantiation of claims that sites exist by checking on the ground. This method fails to give information on proportions of different sites in an area.

lineage A kinship that traces descent through either the male or female members.

lithic Of or pertaining to stone, as in lithic technology.

lithic experimentation Experimenting with the manufacture of stone tools. A useful analytical approach to the interpretation of prehistoric artifacts.

loess Windblown glacial soil.

lower-level theory A means of identifying site-formation processes.

magnetometer A subsurface detection device that measures minor variations in the earth's magnetic field and locates archaeological features before excavation.

material culture Normally refers to technology and artifacts.

matriarchal Family authority resting with the woman's family.

matrilineal Descent reckoned through the female line only.

matrilocal Married couples living with or near the wife's mother.

matrix The surrounding deposit in which archaeological finds are situated.

Mesolithic Rather dated name sometimes applied by Old World Archaeologists to the period of transition between the Paleolithic and Neolithic eras. No precise economic or technological definition has ever been formulated.

mica A mineral that occurs in a glittering, scaly form, widely prized for ornament.

midden A deposit of occupation debris, rubbish, or other by-products of human activity.

middle-range theory A way of seeking accurate means for identifying and measuring specified properties of past cultural systems.

midwestern taxonomic system System of archaeological units developed before World War II to organize artifacts and sites in North America; still in widespread use in modified form.

mitigation In archaeology, measures taken to minimize destruction on archaeological sites.

model A theoretical reconstruction of a set of phenomena, devised to understand them better. Archaeological models can be descriptive or explanatory.

modified diffusionism Form of diffusionist theory, espoused by Gordon Childe and others, which allowed for some local cultural evolution.

monotheistic Religion recognizing one god.

multilinear cultural evolution A theory of cultural evolution that sees each human culture evolving in its own way by adaptation to diverse environments. Sometimes divided into four broad stages of evolving of social organization (band, tribe, chiefdom, and stage-organized society).

natural transformations Changes in the archaeological record resulting from natural phenomena that occur after the artifacts are deposited in the ground.

natural type An archaeological type coinciding with an actual category recognized by the original toolmaker.

negative feedback A response to a system that lessens the chance of change.

Neolithic A dated Old World term referring to that period of the Stone Age when people were cultivating without metals.

niche The physical space occupied by an organism, its functional role in the community, and how it is constrained by other species and external forces.

normative view A view of human culture arguing that one can identify the abstract rules regulating a particular culture; a commonly used basis for studying archaeological cultures throughout time.

object-clustering An approach to typology based on clusters of human artifacts that are seen as specific classificatory types.

obsidian Volcanic glass.

open system In archaeology, cultural systems that interchange both energy and information with their environment.

oral tradition Historical traditions, often genealogies, passed down from generation to generation by word of mouth.

ordering In archaeology, the arranging of artifacts in logical classes and in chronological order.

organic materials Materials such as bone, wood, horn, or hide that were once living organisms.

ossification Fusion of a limb bone with its articular end. Implies the stagnation or calcification of soft tissue into bonelike material.

osteologist One who studies bones.

paleoanthropologist An archaeologist who studies the archaeology of the earliest human beings.

paleobotanist One who studies prehistoric botany.

paleoecology The modern study of past ecology.

Paleolithic The Old Stone Age.

paleontology The study of fossil (or ancient) bones.

palynology Pollen analysis.

patrilineal Descent reckoned through the male line only.

patrilocal Married couples living with or near the husband's father.

patterns of discard Remains left for investigation after natural destructive forces have affected artifacts and food remains abandoned by their original users.

pedology Scientific study of soil.

periglacial Surrounding a glacial area.

period An archaeological unit defining a major unit of prehistoric time; it contains several phases and pertains to a wide area.

permafrost Permanently frozen subsoil.

petrological analysis Examining thin sections of stone artifacts to determine provenience of the rock used to make them.

petrology The study of rocks; in archaeology, usually refers to analysis of trace elements and other characteristics of rocks used to make such artifacts as axe blades, which were traded over long distances.

phase An archaeological unit defined by characteristic groupings of culture traits that can be identified precisely in time and space. It lasts for a relatively short time and is found at one or more sites in a locality or region. Its culture traits are clear enough to distinguish it from other phases.

physical anthropology Basically, biological anthropology, which includes the study of fossil human beings, genetics, primates, and blood groups.

Pleistocene the last major geological epoch, extending from about two million years ago until about 11,500 B.C. It is sometimes called the Quaternary, or the Great Ice Age.

population In sampling methods, the sum of sampling units selected within a data universe.

positive feedback A system's response to external stimuli that leads to further change and reinforces it.

Postclassic A stage in Mesoamerican and Andean prehistory during which militarism arose, such as that of the Aztec and the Inca.

potassium–argon dating An absolute dating technique based on the decay rate of potassium ^{40}K, which becomes ^{40}Ar.

potsherd A fragment of a clay vessel.

Preclassic See **Formative**.

prehistory The millennia of human history preceding written records. Prehistorians study prehistoric archaeology.

pressure flaking A stoneworking technique in which thin flakes are removed from a core or artifact by applying hand or chest pressure.

primary context An undisturbed association, matrix, and provenience.

process In archaeology, the process of cultural change that takes place as a result of interactions between a cultural system's elements and the system and its environment.

provenience The position of an archaeological find in time and space, recorded three-dimensionally.

proximal Opposite to distal: the end of a bone nearest to the skeleton's center line.

pulse radar Use of a pulse-induction meter that applies pulses of magnetic field to the soil; this method can be used to find graves, metals, and pottery.

Quaternary Geological time since the beginning of the Pleistocene up to recent times. The exact date of its commencement is uncertain, but it is more than two million years old.

radiocarbon dating An absolute dating method based on measuring the decay rate of the carbon isotope, carbon 14, to stable nitrogen. The resulting dates are calibrated with tree-ring chronologies, from radiocarbon ages into dates in calendar years.

reciprocity In archaeology, the exchange of goods between two parties.

redistribution The dispersal of trade goods from a central place throughout a society, a complex process that was a critical part of the evolution of civilization.

refitting The reassembling of stone debitage and cores to reconstruct ancient lithic technologies.

region A geographically defined erea in which ecological adaptations are basically similar.

relative chronology Time scale developed by the law of superposition or artifact ordering.

remote sensing Reconnaissance and site survey methods using such devices as aerial photography to detect subsurface features and sites.

research design A carefully formulated and systematic plan for executing archaeological research.

resistivity survey Measurement of differences in electrical conductivity in soils, used to detect buried features such as walls and ditches.

scanner imagery A method of recording sites from the air using infrared radiation that is beyond the practical spectral response of photographic film. Useful for tracing prehistoric agricultural systems that have disturbed the topsoil over wide areas.

science A way of acquiring knowledge and understanding about the parts of the natural world that can be observed. A disciplined and highly ordered search for knowledge carried out systematically.

seasonality Seasonal occupation.

secondary context A context of an archaeological find that has been disturbed by subsequent human activity or natural phenomena.

selective excavation Archaeological excavation of parts of a site using sampling methods or carefully placed trenches that do not uncover the entire site.

seriation techniques Methods used to place artifacts in chronological order; artifacts closely similar in form or style are placed close to one another.

settlement pattern: Distribution of human settlement on the landscape and within archaeological communities.

site Any place where objects, features, or ecofacts manufactured or modified by human beings are found. A site can range from a living site to a quarry site, and it can be defined in functional and other ways.

site catchment analysis Inventorying natural resources within a given distance of a site.

site plans Specially prepared maps for recording the horizontal provenience of artifacts, food remains, and features. They are keyed to topographic maps.

site survey Collection of surface data and evaluation of each site's archaeological significance.

slip Fine, wet clay finish applied to the surface of a clay vessel prior to its firing and decoration.

social anthropology The British equivalent of cultural anthropology, with emphasis on sociological factors.

sociocultural Combining social and cultural factors.

spectrographic analysis Chemical analysis that involves passing the light from a number of trace elements through a prism or diffraction grating that spreads out the wavelengths in a spectrum. This enables one to separate the emissions and identify different trace elements. A useful approach for studying metal objects and obsidian artifacts.

stage A technological subdivision of prehistoric time that has little chronological meaning but denotes the level of technological achievement of societies within it, such as the Stone Age.

stela (or stele) A column or stone slab, often with inscribed or sculptured surface.

stratified sampling A probabilistic sampling technique used to cluster and isolate sample units when regular spacing is inappropriate for cultural reasons.

stratigraphy Observation of the superimposed layers in an archaeological site.

stratum A single-deposited or cultural level.

structural archaeology Theoretical approach to archaeology based on the assumption that codes and rules produce observed systems of relations in human culture.

style In an evolutionary context, a means of describing forms that do not have detectable selective values.

stylistic analysis Artifact analysis that concentrates not only on form and function, but on the decorative styles used by the makers—a much-used approach to ceramic analysis.

stylistic attributes and types Such phenomena based on stylistic features.

stylistic type Type based on stylistic distinctions.

subarea Subdivision of an archaeological area, usually defined by geographic or cultural considerations.

sub-assemblage Association of artifacts denoting a particular form of prehistoric activity practiced by a group of people.

surface survey The collection of archaeological finds from sites, with the objective of gathering representative samples of artifacts from the surface. Surface survey also establishes the types of activity on the site, locates major structures, and gathers information on the most densely occupied areas of the site that could be most productive for total or sample excavation.

synthesis The assemblage and analysis of data preparatory to interpretation.

systematics In archaeology, procedures for creating sets of archaeological units derived from a logical system for a particular purpose.

systematic sampling A refinement of random sampling in which one unit is chosen, then others at regular intervals from the first. Useful for studying artifact patterning.

taphonomy Study of the processes by which animal bones and other fossil remains are transformed after deposition.

taxonomy An ordered set of operations that results in the subdividing of objects into ordered classifications.

technological analysis Study of technological methods used to make an artifact.

technological attributes (technological types) Attributes based on technological features of an object.

tectonic A term referring to the earth's crust; a tectonic movement is an earthquake.

tell A mound; a term referring to archaeological sites of this type in the Near East.

temper Coarse material such as sand or shell added to fine pot clay to make it bond during firing.

tempering A process for hardening iron blades, involving heating and rapid cooling. Also, material added to potters' clay.

test pit An excavation unit used to sample or probe a site before large-scale excavation or to check surface surveys.

thermoluminescence A chronometric dating method that measures the amount of light energy released by a baked clay object when heated rapidly. Gives an indication of the time elapsed since the object was last heated.

three-age system A technological subdivision of the prehistoric past developed for Old World prehistory in 1806.

topographic maps Maps that can be used to relate archaeological sites to basic features of the natural landscape.

total excavation Complete excavation of an archaeological site. Usually confined to smaller sites such as burial mounds or campsites.

trace elements Minute elements found in rocks that emit characteristic wavelengths of light when heated to incandescence. Trace-element analysis is used to study the sources of obsidian and other materials traded over long distances.

tradition Persistent technological or cultural patterns identified by characteristic artifact forms. These persistent forms outlast a single phase and can occur over a wide area.

transformational processes Processes that transform an abandoned prehistoric settlement into an archaeological site through the passage of time. These processes can be initiated by natural phenomena or human activity.

tribe A larger group of bands unified by sodalities and governed by a council of representatives from the bands, kin groups, or sodalities within it.

type In archaeology, a grouping of artifacts created for comparison with other groups. This grouping may or may not coincide with the actual tool types designed by the original manufacturers.

type fossil A tool characteristic of a particular "archaeological era," a dated concept borrowed from geology.

typology The classification of types.

underwater archaeology Study of archaeological sites and shipwrecks beneath the surface of the water.

uniformitarianism Doctrine that states the earth was formed by the same natural geological processes that are operating today.

unilinear cultural evolution A late-nineteenth-century evolutionary theory envisaging all human societies as evolving along one track of cultural evolution, from simple hunting and gathering to literate civilization.

unit In archaeology, an artificial grouping used for describing artifacts.

use-wear analysis Microscopic analysis of artifacts to detect signs of wear through use on their working edges.

vertical excavation Excavation undertaken to establish a chronological sequence, normally covering a limited area.

votive Intended as an offering as a result of a vow.

zooarchaeology A study of animal remains in archaeology.

ILLUSTRATION CREDITS

Chapter 1: *Opening illustration*, From M. C. Bishop, *Antiquity* 63, 241, 1989, p. 698. Reprinted by permission; *Fig. 1.3*, Courtesy of Museum of New Mexico (Neg. No. 58337).

Chapter 2: *Fig. 2.1*, Hirmer Fotoarchiv München; *Fig. 2.3*, Courtesy of the Colonial Williamsburg Foundation.

Chapter 3: *Fig. 3.1*, Courtesy of the National Park Service; *Fig. 3.2*, From *The Rise of Civilization* by Charles L. Redman. Copyright © 1978 W. H. Freeman and Company. Reprinted with permission; *Fig. 3.3*, Adapted from Stuart Piggott, *Ancient Europe*. Copyright © 1965 by Stuart Piggott. Used by permission of Aldine de Gruyter (A Division of Walter de Gruyter, Inc.) and Edinburgh University Press; *Fig. 3.4*, Carl Frank/Photo Researchers, Inc.

Chapter 4: *Fig. 4.2*, From James Deetz, *Invitation to Archaeology*, illustrated by Eric G. Engstrom. Copyright © 1967 by James Deetz. Reproduced by permission of Doubleday & Company, Inc.; *Fig. 4.3*, Adapted from R. S. MacNeish, *The Prehistory of the Tehuacán Valley*, Vol. 3. Copyright © 1970 by The University of Texas Press, Austin; *Fig. 4.6*, Adapted from D. R. Brotherwell and Eric Higgs, *Science in Archaeology*, London: Thames & Hudson Ltd.

Chapter 5: *Fig. 5.3*, Courtesy of the Society of Antiquaries, London; *Fig. 5.5*, Irven DeVore/Anthro-Photo.

Chapter 6: *Fig. 6.1*, Griffith Institute, Ashmolean Museum, Oxford; *Fig. 6.2*, Redrawn from "The Swanscombe Skull: A Survey of Research on a Pleistocene Site" (Occasional Paper no. 20, fig. 26.3) with the permission of the Royal Anthropological Institute of Great Britain and Ireland; *Fig. 6.3*, Danish Information Office; *Fig. 6.4*, Ruth Kirk and Richard D. Daugherty, *Hunters of the Whale* (New York: William Morrow & Company, 1974). Photo by Harvey Rice; *Fig. 6.5*, Dr. Owen Beattie, University of Alberta, Edmonton; *Fig. 6.6*, University of Alaska Museum; *Fig. 6.7*, Copyright reserved by Dr. J. K. St. Joseph.

Chapter 7: *Fig. 7.1*, Redrawn from Stuart Streuver and James A. Brown, "The Organization of Archaeological Research: An Illinois Example," Fig. 1, p. 278 in Charles L. Redman, *Research and Theory in Current Archaeology* (New York: John Wiley & Sons, 1973). Also courtesy of the Center for American Archaeology, 1911 Ridge Avenue, P.O. Box 1499, Chicago, IL 60204; *Fig. 7.3*, Richard S. MacNeish and the Robert S. Peabody Foundation for Archaeology, Andover, Massachusetts; *Fig. 7.4*, Courtesy of J. A. Tuck, Memorial University of Newfoundland; *Fig. 7.6*, From M. D. Leakey, *Olduvai Gorge*, vol. III, "Excavations in Beds I and II," London: Cambridge University Press, 1971. Copyright © 1971. Reprinted by permission; *Fig. 7.7*, Courtesy of the Peabody Museum, Harvard University; *Fig. 7.8*, Courtesy of the Society of Antiquaries, London; *Fig. 7.9*, Wilfred Shawcross; *Fig. 7.10*, Photograph by Ledyard Smith. Courtesy of the Peabody Museum, Harvard University.

Chapter 8: *Fig. 8.2*, Courtesy of Lowie Museum of Anthropology, University of California at Berkeley; *Fig. 8.3*, From James Deetz, *Invitation to Archaeology*, illustrated by Eric G. Engstrom. Copyright © 1967 by James Deetz. Reproduced by permission of Doubleday & Company, Inc.; *Fig. 8.5*, "Nine-thousand-year-old Mesolithic artifacts," Fig. 35, from J. C. D. Clark, *Excavations at Star Carr*, London: Cambridge University Press, 1954. Copyright © 1954. Reprinted by permission.

Chapter 9: *Fig. 9.1*, After Sonia Cole, *The Neolithic Revolution*, 1959. Reproduced by permission of the Trustees of the British Museum (Natural History); *Fig. 9.2*, From S. J. M. Davis, *The Archaeology of Animals*, Batsford, London, 1987, Figure 1.1. Reprinted by permission; *Fig. 9.3 (lower)*, Redrawn from M. L. Ryder, *Animal Bones in Archaeology*. Blackwell Scientific Publications Ltd., Oxford, 1969; *Fig. 9.4*, From Richard G. Klein, *The Analysis of Animal Bones from Archaeological Sites*. Chicago: The University of Chicago Press, 1984, Fig. 5.4; *Fig. 9.5*, Cambridge University Museum of Archaeology and Anthropology; *Fig. 9.6*, Patricia Vinnecombe, "A Fishing Scene from the Tsoelike River, South-Eastern Basutoland," *South African Archaeological Bulletin*, 15:57, March 1960, p. 15, Fig. 1.

Chapter 10: *Fig. 10.1*, From *Urbanization at Teotihuacán, Mexico*, Vol. 1, Part 1. Copyright © 1973 by René Millon. Reproduced by permission of the author; *Fig. 10.2a*, Redrawn from *The Early Mesoamerican Village*, edited by Kent V. Flannery, New York: Academic Press, 1976; *Fig. 10.4*, Courtesy of the Musée de l'Homme, Paris; *Fig. 10.5*, Courtesy of the Museum of the American Indian, Heye Foundation, New York; *Fig. 10.6*, Courtesy of the University Museum, University of Pennsylvania.

Chapter 11: *Opening illustration*, Bodleian Library, University of Oxford (MS ARCH BELDEN A.1 fol. 60); *Fig. 11.1*, Colonel Charles Wellington Furlong; *Fig. 11.2*, Dr. F. L. Van Noten, Musée Royal de l'Afrique Centrale; *Fig. 11.3*, Richard A. Gould, "The Archaeologist as Ethnographer," *World Archaeology*, 1971, pp. 143–177, Fig. 18.

Chapter 12: *Opening illustration*, From Barry Kemp, *Ancient Egypt*, London: Routledge, 1989, Fig. 6, p. 28. Reprinted by permission; *Fig. 12.1*, From James Deetz, *Invitation to Archaeology*, illustrated by Eric G. Engstrom. Copyright © 1967 by James Deetz. Reproduced by permission of Doubleday & Company, Inc.

INDEX

Abri Pataud rockshelter, France, 121
Absolute dating, 63–72
Abu Simbel temples, 208
Accidental discovery, 97–98
Acheulian culture, 145
Acheulian stone axes, 91, 195
Acosta, José de, 10–11
Activity areas, 80–81
Adaptation, 202–203
Adena culture, 124, 178, 180, 195
Aerial survey
   photography, 101–103
   remote sensing, 103–104
   sensor imagery, 104–106
Age of animal bones, 157–158
Age of Humanity, 57
Agriculture
   analysis of remains of, 159–161
   Mayan, 103–104
   origins, 31–32, 196
Ain Ghazal, Jordan, 119
Alcubierre, Rocque Joaquin de, 3
American Indian culture, 10–11, 37, 126, 207
Analogy, 186–187
Analysis, 109, 111
   classification of data, 128–145
   subsistence, 148–164
Animal bones, 150–159, 161–162
Anthropology, 13–14, 36–37
Antiquities market, 207–209
Antiquity of humankind, 4–6
Apple Creek, Illinois Valley, 160
Archaeological record, 86–91. See
   also Artifacts; Sites
Archaeological sites. See Sites
Archaeological survey, 98–106
Archaeology
   anthropology and, 13–14, 36–37
   career in, 209–211
   defined, 25
   goals, 43–45
   historical development, 3–18

romance, 20–21
theory, 4–6, 14–16, 18, 45
types, 25–28
Area excavation, 115–117
Arnold, J. R., 67, 69
Arrowheads, 78, 79
Art
   Chavín style, 136, 137, 145, 197
   Mayan, 181–182
   Olmec style, 178
   rock, 163–164, 180–181
Artifacts, 87
   assemblages, 78–80, 130, 139, 141–142
   associations of, 75–78
   attributes, 47–49, 130–133
   chronometric dating, 63–72
   classification, 47, 128–145
   context in space, 74–83
   context in time, 49–50, 52–72
   defined, 46
   deterioration of, 89–90
   discard behavior and, 88
   fishing, 161
   heirloom, 88
   of known origin, 63–64
   patterning, 38–39, 42, 75, 80, 124, 139, 141–142
   preservation, 91–96
   processing, 109, 128, 130
   relative chronology, 55–58
   religious, 178–182
   replication, 191, 192
   reuse of, 88
   of social organization, 178
   subassemblages, 78–80
   subsistence analysis and, 148, 149
   of trade, 175
Art sites, 46
Assemblages, 78–80, 130, 139, 141–142
Association, law of, 75–78
Assyrian culture, 7–9

240